SURVIVING THE ISLAND

OF GRACE

ALSO BY LESLIE LEYLAND FIELDS

Out on the Deep Blue

The Entangling Net

The Water Under Fish

LESLIE LEYLAND FIELDS

Surviving the Island of Grace

A MEMOIR OF ALASKA

THOMAS DUNNE BOOKS
ST. MARTIN'S PRESS ☙ NEW YORK

THOMAS DUNNE BOOKS.
An imprint of St. Martin's Press.

Grateful acknowledgment is made for permission to quote from the following:
"The Leg," *New and Selected Poems 1940–1986*, by Karl Shapiro. © 1987 The University of Chicago Press. By permission of Wieser & Wieser, Inc.

www.stmartins.com

Book design by Kate Nichols

Library of Congress Cataloging-in-Publication Data

Fields, Leslie Leyland, 1957–
    Surviving the island of grace : a memoir of Alaska / Leslie Leyland Fields.
        p. cm.
    ISBN 0-312-29140-X
    1. Fields, Leslie Leyland, 1957– 2. Women fishers—Alaska—Biography.
3. Salmon fisheries—Alaska.   I. Title.

SH20.F54 A3   2002
331.4'8392'092—dc21   2002069273
[B]

First Edition: October 2002

10   9   8   7   6   5   4   3   2   1

For all of my children,
the story of our beginnings.
You write the ending.

Contents

1. Finding the Island   *1*

2. Stocking and Settling   *19*

3. First Pick   *37*

4. Hurled to the Shark   *53*

5. Houses, Houses   *68*

6. Falling Off the Face   *79*

7. Killing and Eating   *102*

8. Winter Travels   *113*

9. Boundaries   *129*

10. Escapes from Immobility   *141*

CONTENTS

11. Living in the Kingdom of Clean-Enough *158*

12. Gaining Ground and Losing *174*

13. Looking for Language *188*

14. An Island of Our Own *207*

15. A House from Africa *217*

16. Building *226*

17. Migration *246*

18. More than a Place of Labor *254*

19. Oil Spill *271*

20. Staying Ashore *284*

21. Nursing Babies, Killing Fish *298*

22. Between Land and Water *313*

Preface

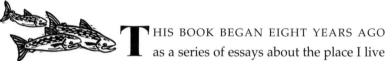THIS BOOK BEGAN EIGHT YEARS AGO as a series of essays about the place I live in: a tiny island off Kodiak Island in the Gulf of Alaska where I have spent each summer since 1978. There is much to tell about this place on the far edge of America, where there are no roads or cars, telephone poles or electricity lines, where bears rule the wilderness mountains, where whales, otters, seals, and dolphins are nearly daily sights, where the wind and rain never seem to stop, where every fish camp must, literally, build itself from the ground up. But there is more to tell than this. I am here with my husband and children for commercial salmon fishing—a laborious three- to four-month harvest of one of the most abundant resources in the world. We catch fish the way it has been done for centuries: working out on the ocean, in open skiffs, with nets, by hand. There is more here than I can tell in all of the

danger, the exhaustion, the exhilaration of working out on this wild blue piece of an ocean.

While these essays found homes in books and magazines, my editors and agents were not satisfied. "Where is *your* story, Leslie? Tell us the story of this place *through your own life.*" Though my life has been anything but usual, I resisted this, feeling no particular compulsion for self-revelation. In my Writing Life Stories class, I tell my students what Annie Dillard wrote in *An American Childhood,* that memoir, contrary to its first two letters, should not be about "me." It should dare to range much further than the limited landscape of a single self. And how, I wondered, in the middle of my own middle-aged life, could I assemble its ongoing dramas into a single narrative with a mappable plot and a satisfying denouement? There were other objections. Some in my family of origin did not want to be returned to our growing-up years, no matter how much discretion I exercised. And, not least, once the book came out, how would I go about my life in a small town on a nearly roadless island where most of us know each other without feeling as though my buttons and zippers were forever undone?

All of these were convincing reasons to forego my own story, but somewhere along the way I discovered again some lines that lured me through the forbidding door of memoir. The words are Frederick Buechner's, a writer of essays, memoirs, and novels who often soothes my ache for the spiritual in a world so persistently material. He writes,

> Listen to your life. See it for the fathomless mystery that it is. In the boredom and pain of it no less than in the excitement and gladness: touch, taste, smell your way to the holy and hidden heart of it because in the last analysis all moments are key moments and life itself is grace.

I FELT COMPELLED to test his claim: to listen to every part of my life, to record the parts of it that I could, and to find. . . .

The title of the book tells part of what I found. Yes, he is right—life itself is grace. That of all the acres in the world I should end up here on this windswept speck of an island in Alaska with Duncan and my children is lavish grace. But Buechner's words did not tell it all—it is fierce grace too, that terrifies and isolates, that sometimes threatens my very life and the lives of those I love. Both kinds reside on that island and are here in these pages.

There is one more thing the reader needs to know. The book ends in 1991, but the story and the plot keep twisting. Now, in 2002, as I write this, we may be facing the loss of our cannery, the shutdown of the next salmon season, and perhaps more. Last Sunday's front-page headlines of the *Anchorage Daily News* said it all: ON THE ROCKS: ALASKA'S HISTORIC SALMON INDUSTRY FACES UNPRECEDENTED THREAT. The threat is not too few fish, but too many. Over the last ten years, worldwide salmon farms have stolen the market from Alaska's natural wild salmon. Wild pink salmon, the most abundant species, are selling for 5 cents a pound, if a cannery even wants them.

Suddenly, what I have chafed against for twenty-five years, the strictures that geography and the fishing season string around my neck, may suddenly be gone. But I don't feel freed. What will I and my husband and five children do without fishing? It is as though a brightly beaded necklace has broken. My hands instinctively reach to my throat to catch the beads, to clasp the broken strands. As you read the pages of this story, know that this is how I am standing now—hand at my throat, beads falling through my fingers, mouth open, wondering if this is grace, too, and if so, which kind of grace might it be?

ALASKA

N

ALASKA PENINSULA

Larsen Bay
Bear Harvester

KODIAK
ISLAND

TOWN OF
KODIAK

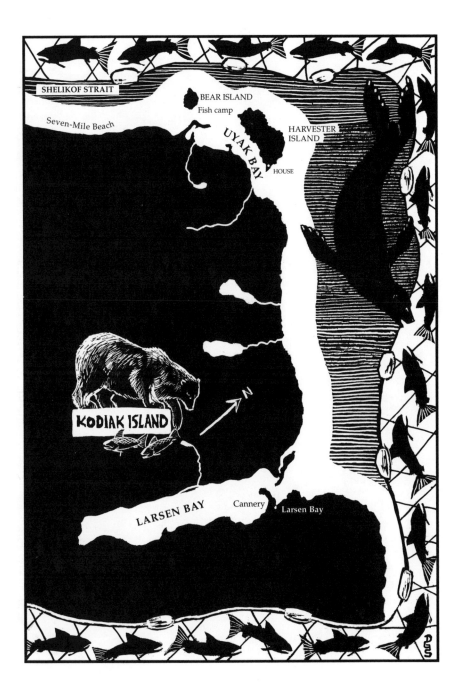

SHELIKOF STRAIT

BEAR ISLAND
Fish camp

Seven-Mile Beach

UYAK BAY

HARVESTER
ISLAND

HOUSE

KODIAK ISLAND

N

LARSEN BAY   Cannery   Larsen Bay

SURVIVING THE ISLAND

OF GRACE

1

Finding the Island

AS I RISE FROM CHOPPING THE HEAD of a bull kelp, I see more over my shoulder. I signal with my machete, pointing starboard so Duncan can see the raft of kelp just one hundred feet from us, drifting straight for the net. They look remarkably human with their bulbous heads that float them above the water, the "hair" sprouting from the top, broadening to flat, slick fronds. They are an improbable enemy, yet enemy they are: Once uprooted by high tides or stormy weather, they gang up and drift en masse into our nets, floating them as effectively as buoys. As long as our nets are skimming the top of the water, we won't catch any salmon. And catching salmon is the point of our existence right now. With a twist of his wrist, Duncan blurts the outboard, and I assume the position again: belly over the wooden skiff railing,

my upper body hanging out over the water, my right arm and knife poised overhead.

As we approach the tangled brown mass—a mass so dense and buoyant it would likely float me—I begin chopping, my arm hacking the brown tubes into slices, each strike making a satisfying thwack, followed by a series of watery glubs as the once watertight plants are swallowed by the ocean. Duncan circles me around and around the brown island, my arm and knife as a single entity, mechanical now, rhythmically decapitating the heads of kelp again, again, until a final pass minutes later sees the last of the tangle sinking from sight. I stand up and wearily adjust my back.

"I think that's about got it." Duncan scans the gray waters for more.

"Yeah, for now. But the nets'll be floating again by this afternoon," I proclaim pessimistically. There's nothing we can do about it—we are in the highest tides of the month for the Shelikof Strait: twenty-one footers, which means all the kelp washed up on the beaches will be water-borne once more. All it will take is the shift of the tide and the same work begins again.

"Okay, let's get back to the net." The moment of rest is over. Duncan smartly wheels the skiff around; within two minutes we are back to business.

By the time we finish with this net and move to the next—the Outside, we call it, because it sits straight into the Shelikof Strait and is unprotected, the wind has picked up—a northeast, blowing now maybe 20. The forecast is for NE 35. It has happened in minutes, which means the 35 could stew over us in minutes as well. I never knew weather anywhere could change as fast as it does here. "Please let us finish and go in before it blows harder," I offer silently as a wish-prayer. The wind hits my face under the brim of my hat, spray lashes us now from both sides. "Get ready to grab the net!" Duncan yells to me above the wind. He is running hard up to the net against the wind. He'll slow and aim the bow at the net and just before it hits he'll go into neutral, then reverse to swing the stern around so we are parallel to the net. My job is to lean over the side, grab the net in the water as soon as I can and then hold on no matter what happens. In calm weather, and if the tide is not running too strong, this is not a difficult maneuver, but now. . . .

I pull my cap tighter and lower over my head, lean out poised for the net as we approach, the water white around us and just a roar and howling in my ears. I am in knots, knowing I have to get the net. I can't miss. All of me is focused on that cork, there. We speed toward it, my hand is out, I'm leaning almost over the side—now! My arm pounces, makes a swipe—missed! Again, lean a little farther, arm into the water now past my elbow—can't get it! The net is too tight, like a steel bar. It won't pull to me at all. I straighten, look apologetically at Duncan, who doesn't change his expression, a frown of utter concentration. He wheels the skiff around in the wind, readies for another approach, and I know I've broken a rule, the rule that you get it the first time, not the second or third, especially when it's blowing. I will do it this time. I have to. "Got it!" I yell with relief. The line is in my hands but so tight I can't pull it up over the sides. I hang out of the skiff, both arms anchored to the running line of the net, which wants to pull me over, and wait, without seeing—I can't turn or move until Duncan brings the stern around parallel. The wind is stronger now, I think. Duncan is gunning the kicker and trying to reverse into place, but the wind won't allow it. The waves slap and douse us as he tries to move sideways with the lesser force of reverse gear, but I can't hang on any longer against the wind. My arms give out. I let go and the wind propels us away from the net instantly. I feel help-less and weak.

Duncan turns the skiff again for yet another try. I want to scream at him, "Why is this so important? Can't we just leave it until the weather calms?" But I know the answer. I glance back. He stands darkly resolute, as if there were no storm blasting around us, the only upright and seemingly untouched object in my entire vista. I can find no island of calm within me, just storm inside and out.

This time, I vow, I will hang on until my arms pull out of their sockets, if need be. It seems a small sacrifice. Once again, the head-down approach straight into the wind, my arm out, my stomach hard on the skiff edge as my fulcrum. A breaking wave catches me on the face and shoulder; an icy stream finds my neck and trails down my back as I hang like a tortured fig-urehead, and then "Got it!" I yell behind me, then the second arm joins the first, and two-armed, ready to hang on till death, I wait for the maneuver, and it works. Duncan angles the stern over to the net, he leans in a flash and has the net, and together with one mighty pull we lift it over the side and into our skiff. I am exhausted, immensely relieved, and the pick for this net begins.

I'm not good at this yet, balancing with my legs in a rolling skiff while holding, pulling the net against the wind and still picking fish. It's blowing about 35 now—this is war. All the usual tasks of fishing and picking fish are blown up to twice their usual proportion. "Keep an eye on the waves!" Duncan cautions over the wind as he is bent over a badly tangled fish. The waves come at us relentlessly, speaking as they move to-ward us, a sshhhing sound as the tops break and pull the waves forward to either lift us or to break against us. They are eight-foot waves, I guess. In the sixteen-foot open skiff, I feel lost in a mountain range, their rolling peaks and valleys a volcanic, violent terrain.

We keep pulling the net, inching our painful way down its length, pulling out the few pathetic fish and trying to keep our balance, still watching each wave as it approaches to see what it will say, how the skiff will handle it. We are almost to the hook, the last third of the net, when a wave we didn't see hits us sideways, knocks me to the floor of the skiff, filling the bottom. We've had several of these already when we put out the nets, but this is the worst. The blow is keening higher by the minute.

"Unhook the net! Let's get outta here!" Duncan shouts.

I am hoping that means we will go in, but we don't. We move back to the more protected nets, where the winds have to bend around the island. They come at us now with some of the squall lost and I relax a bit as we begin this net. It will be easier. We work the inside three nets until near dark. I am so tired I can hardly stand.

After we deliver our fish to the tender, we head home across blustery black waters. My eyes are closed as I begin to slide away from the day and night's work. Then something in the water behind us moves. A jumper, probably. On reflex, I turn to look. A few seconds later, the unmistakable spume of a whale whooshes noisily into the air, then another beside it. Their black metal bodies slide slow motion behind the spray, sinking like great ships into the deep. They are less than a quarter mile from us. I almost didn't see them.

ON MY FIRST VISIT to this island in 1976 I saw everything. I was in New Hampshire finishing a summer of waitressing, while Duncan was at the tail end of his commercial fishing season in Alaska. We were engaged at that point. I was working at The

Hawaiian Isle in Concord, New Hampshire, a new restaurant that had just opened that summer. It was the first Chinese-Polynesian restaurant in the all-white capital city, and it defined exotic. The massive double doors opened into a cool dark interior that led the customer down a walkway, across a bridge over a fish pond stocked with giant goldfish and carp. Chinese lanterns hung from the ceiling, and the tables were dressed in fine yellow linens.

The year before, I had followed the progress of the new building with great interest from my vantage point across the street. There, under the turquoise roof of Howard Johnson's, and dressed in a gaudy orange plaid polyester uniform whose aesthetics I could only redeem by hemming it as short as possible, I contemplated mutiny. I had waitressed at HoJo's for four years, long enough to have worked all the shifts and to have gained several reputations. To the smart-mouthed broads on the breakfast crew who loudly discussed their current methods of birth control with one another behind their customer's tables, I was Pollyanna, good for some laughs when I dumped the pancakes on the floor or blushed furiously under the cook's proposition-ings. To the lunch gang, I could be counted on to hold my station down without needing help. After the lunch rush, they expected an array of regulars who seemed always to know my schedule, old men, who came in and sat in my booths for toast and tea. The dinner roster of waitresses thought me snobbish and aloof because I didn't join them in their amusements, most of which centered around their unsuspecting customers. To the cooks, I was a piece of meat, like the Salisbury steaks they threw on the grill—but good for more entertainment than that. They made bets on who could make me blush the most, the longest; on who could actually get me to go out with him. One cook casually suggested on our mutual break that we go and make out in the walk-in freezer. Another pinned me to the wall in the storage closet.

The food was even more unsavory, most of it prepackaged and frozen or canned, thrown in a microwave and tossed on a plate. Sometimes it was heated through, other times not. Often I was ashamed of the meals I delivered on my metal tray, and if the manager wasn't there, I would meekly apologize as I served my customers, my face burning. It seemed the restaurant was built on an impossible concept—down-home cookin' at a fast food pace. We could deliver neither one.

Across the street, linen tablecloths, the other waitresses reported, some as interested in defection as I was. *An eight-page menu. People come to relax and linger over their meal. Dinners that you light on fire with a match, and everyone cheers you like you've just performed a circus act. You don't have to wear a dress—just a tunic and white pants.*

But it wasn't that easy for me to leave. The manager, Ed Finnegan, a florid-faced man who could be found in the bar most any time, had unofficially crowned me "Miss Howard Johnson's" earlier this summer. That night, I was having dinner in the break room, a yellow graffiti-covered cell in the basement. I was writing a letter to a guy I had met last spring in college—a fisherman from Alaska. I had forgotten to bring the pad of paper I usually kept with me, so I used the back of a paper placemat. Sitting in this room, a light bulb hanging from the ceiling, three moths beating at the bulb, one of the cooks blowing smoke over my head and the other eating from an enormous tray of fried chicken stolen from the kitchen, I tried to wrap my words around it all to send it to him the long, many miles to Kodiak, that place on the map where he was. I didn't know much about the island he lived on, or much about his fishing. I couldn't call any image to my mind except the few photos he had shown me, but I knew it had to be as different from this as anything could be. Somehow this placemat would span the two worlds.

Halfway through the letter, Mr. Finnegan suddenly appeared in the door. He clapped his hands and rubbed them together eagerly.

"Let's go, everyone. We're having a meeting in the banquet room. Right now!"

The three of us looked at each other blankly, blinking in surprise.

"What's this? A meeting? We've never had no goddamn meeting before," the cook named Steve complained.

"Maybe he's gonna give us all a raise," the other suggested with a sneer as he got up from the table.

I folded my letter and stuck it in a locker on the way out, as curious as they were. I had never been in the banquet room before, which attested to the popularity of HoJo's as a banquet site.

There were fifteen of us gathered, waitresses, busboys, and cooks—a fleet of orange. There were usually plenty of waitresses on the floor, since we worked for only a dollar an hour. Whatever else we made came from tips, which also supported the busboys. Mr. Finnegan stood in the center of the room, clearly charged up about something, with all of us bunched loosely against a table near the wall. He was dressed neatly, as always, in expensive slacks that hung without a wrinkle, a pressed yellow shirt.

"I just received word that we are going to host the Small Business Association banquet in two weeks! Now, you know we haven't done a banquet for a little while." He looked at us admonishingly, as if this were our fault. "If we all do a good job, there will be more. And I can assure you, you're going to make good money! We'll charge the tip right in there so you'll all be paid well."

He looked around at our faces for any trace of excitement. The Concord restaurant was the bad boy of the chain, known as a low revenue producer with a high level of employee theft and nonexistent morale. We all knew it, too. We kept hearing rumors that it was going to close.

As he scanned the circle, his eyes lit on me. I knew he liked me in some way because occasionally when he ate dinner in the restaurant, he would call me over to his table and ask me to sit down with him. He didn't flirt, which was a great relief. It seemed more that he was curious. He would ask my views about church—why were there so many different denominations? Why did I go to church? And questions about God—wouldn't God be satisfied if he lived a basically good life? The question I wanted to ask him was, "Why me? Why are you asking a seventeen-year-old waitress?" Now he called my name.

"Leslie! Come here!"

I froze. I had no idea what this was about. I hesitantly stepped out a few feet.

"No, come on out here!" He signaled to a spot next to him.

I stood there uncomfortably, waiting for further humiliation.

"Now, everyone look here at Leslie. Look at her shoes. See how white they are?"

I glanced down at my shoes, incredulous. They were clean? Oh yeah, I had finally wiped them off yesterday because the splotches of multicolored ice creams and condiments had finally gotten to me. One time a customer had chided me for my dirty shoes.

"And look at her uniform. See how clean it is, how neat she looks?"

This was unbelievable. I hated this uniform more than I had hated any article of clothing, more even than the brown Girl Scout shoes I had to wear for six years. I didn't bother trying to tone down the despicable orange with accessories, and I wasn't particularly concerned about its cleanliness.

"Now, I want you all to look like Leslie—professional! At this banquet, I want to see you all there neat and clean and professional."

I was waiting for the tiara and sash to appear—orange and turquoise plaid, of course, but thankfully, he was done. Everyone broke up with as much enthusiasm as they had gathered, but now snickering at me. I was snickering myself at this honor—that I was chosen poster child for a morally and financially bankrupt restaurant also guilty of repeated crimes against good taste.

Somehow, though, that silly charade, plus the tableside chats with Mr. Finnegan, fueled a loyalty to him and to the place that made leaving difficult. But linen tablecloths, food you could serve without apology . . . I crossed the street, finally, next summer, the summer Duncan and I were engaged. But I couldn't leave without saying something to Mr. Finnegan.

He was in his office, a drink on his desk beside him as he worked, looking freshly laundered.

I knocked on the open doorway.

"Come in, Leslie!" He didn't smile—he seldom did—but he waved me in vigorously.

I had come in my real clothes, as my real self. We all did this, showing up at the restaurant at odd hours in our regular clothes, just to let the others see who we really were. After hours in the uniform, we surprised even ourselves at our transformations. "Ah, Mr. Finnegan, I just wanted to come and say good-bye. I gave notice last month."

"Oh. Well, I'm sorry to lose you, Leslie. My god, how long have you worked here now?

"Four years." He was being kind, and I appreciated it.

"Where are you going?"

"Well, actually, I've got another job. But after that I'm getting married."

"You're getting married? How old are you?"

"I'm almost twenty."

"That's too young, too young. Who are you marrying?"

"A man from Alaska that I met at college."

"Alaska! You're too young to be making a decision like this. You'll both change!"

I was flattered at this display of concern, but, I thought, what did he know? He was an alcoholic; he was stuck with the restaurant, and I sensed things weren't good between him and his wife. I liked him and I felt sorry for him, but I knew I would do better with my life.

"No, I know this is right, Mr. Finnegan. I'm older than you think."

He looked at me almost pityingly. "Believe me, when you get to my age, you have a little more wisdom and experience. I think you're making a mistake." Then, seeing I was not going to reply, he added, now conciliatory, "I'm sure he's a good man. Does he believe what you believe?"

"Yes."

"Well, maybe you have a chance then. Good luck," he said, and held out his hand.

We shook and I left, walking one last time through the kitchen and the greasy tiled floor, Steve at the grill ogling at me out of blind habit, the dishwasher numbly loading plates into the machine, looking right through me as I passed, then on out

the swinging door, past the morning lineup of waitresses, and I was gone.

THE HAWAIIAN ISLE kept all its promises to me that summer, but it hardly mattered. I wasn't as bodily present as I had been at the other restaurant, too aware that this was my last summer of waitressing, my last summer in New Hampshire, my last summer single. And even this last summer was cut short, since in August I was flying up to Alaska, out to Duncan's island to see him.

One day at the end of July, my mother found me reading in my room.

"I think Duncan's on the phone," she said tersely, as though this were an everyday event. It wasn't. He had never called because, unbelievable to me at the time, the island he lived on was so remote it had no phone.

I ran downstairs, breathless. At the other end of the line I could hear only a snarl of static. Somewhere from its center came Duncan's voice, pitched to nearly a shout.

"Leslie! Can you hear me? How do you copy?"

"Duncan! How are you? I can't believe you're calling!" I gushed. "I thought you didn't have a phone!"

"Do you have your ticket? Over." Then a long beep and a strange whining sound.

"Yes, I've got it. How has your season gone?"

Three seconds of static, then, "We'll talk about that later. Do you have a pen there? Over." His voice was crisp and business-like.

"Yeah, go ahead." By this time it was clear to me that this was not a love call. Was this from the same person who wrote all those romantic letters, letters so mushy even I was embarrassed?

"When you get to Larsen Bay, if I'm not there, walk down from the airstrip to the cannery. You copy so far?"

"Yeah, I got it. Walk to the cannery. How will I know how to get there?"

And on we went, me writing it all down, Duncan delivering information in a shout with liberal doses of "Affirmative," "Negative," "Roger that," what I considered cheap CB talk. I chalked it up to the 3,000 air miles between us and the unknowns of the wilderness, from which he clearly was speaking. Just as we were closing off this strange conversation, a woman's nasal, staticky voice interrupted, as if she had been there all along, which she had: "This is the Kodiak marine operator signing off. . . ."

" 'Bye, Duncan!" I fairly yelled, trying to get in one last lick. "I love you and it will be so good to see you!" I said in an outburst of affection, not knowing then that the entire phone conversation was broadcast on everyone's radio in the bay. And had I known, I wouldn't have cared.

THE FLIGHT UP, my first time in an airplane, from New Hampshire to Chicago to Anchorage, I sat by the window stunned by the sea of mountains with glaciers and snow so deep no one could know the end of it. I heard Duncan's voice reciting Robert Service: "It's the land, have you seen it? It's the cussedest land that I know, from the deep dizzying mountains that screen it, to the deep, death-like valleys below. . . ." I loved it when Duncan spoke long passages of Service's corny singsong poetry on our dates. He was right, I knew, as I looked out the plane window. Duncan was right to love this land. I took out my journal and tried to compress all of this into language, but I gave up finally and began to write instead of what weighed on me—the finality and extremity of this choice. I was glad to leave home and its blank future: an affectionless family; a father who could not keep a job and who was absent virtually all of the time, either in mind or in body; a mother overwhelmed and emotionally and physically depleted with the work of rebuilding houses so we could pay bills and buy food. My two sisters had fled as soon as they were able, one at sixteen, the other at eighteen. My brothers were locked in, not knowing where to go, what to do. I had left at seventeen for college, and soon, at twenty, I would be leaving for good. Could I do this, though? I planned to work in the boats with the men. Though the other two women in the family—his mother and his sister-in-law, Beverly—did not, Duncan and I were determined to share the work, to share our lives, not compartmentalizing into male and female. It wasn't much of a leap for me since I had grown up with a mother who did whatever our neglected houses required. Gender was entirely irrelevant to the work, both for her and for the six of us, three girls and three boys, who did whatever was assigned to us: laundry, cooking, cleaning, scraping and repainting the house, sanding wood floors, chopping wood, putting up Sheetrock. It was simply work that had to be done. Duncan was from a more traditional home: His father was a rancher, fisherman, and a longshoreman, his mother a teacher and musician. All the in-house duties were hers alone; the out-of-house duties were his. Our arrangement would be harder for him, I guessed. Yet I cried there in my seat while over the Canadian Rockies, with my face turned into the window so my seatmate couldn't see. "A fisherman I will become," I wrote. I knew nothing about fishing, hated the taste and smell of fish, as my mother reminded me when I told her of our engagement, but what else was possible? I loved Duncan and I was ready for another life.

From Anchorage I boarded a smaller plane to Kodiak, and then a smaller plane again, this one amphibious that loaded on the beach and then, to my great surprise, spun around gustily and took off into the water—a World War II Widgeon. I landed on a gravel beach in Larsen Bay beside weathered warehouses of an old cannery, and Duncan was there with a ruddy beard and black rubber hip boots, but he still had his smile, the smile that made him look like a little boy. He came over and put his arm around me in a crushing one-armed hug, smelling of salt air. Wanda and DeWitt, Duncan's parents, were also there, with smiles and awkward laughs and back pats all around. Then we clambered into a small skiff, all of us sitting shoulder to shoulder on the seat, and the final leg of the journey began, to Bear Island.

It was sunny that day, the bay as wide as an ocean, the hills and mountains green above us cresting into cliff. I felt so small in that skiff and loved it, that this world could billow around me like a sail! That it was moving, going places—everything alive, the water, trees, wind, us skating across the surface, leaving just a small mark that faded back into blue, puffins plowing the tops of the waves as they tried to raise their bellies into the air, a reclining sea otter that Duncan pointed to crushing clams on his chest, unsurprised at our passing. Then around the last corner, an island, no, two islands, the farther one at the end of Duncan's finger. "There, Leslie, that's Bear Island. See how the cliff profiles a bear's face?" A small circle of an island rising gracefully from the water, sweeping up to a rounded crest, settled like a Maine fishing village, six tidy buildings painted red, trimmed in white. No trees, bare, but grass green around the cabins, thick and bushing on the hill. A rough black-graveled beach, then the tour: a two-holer outhouse at the end of a snaky path, sitting on the edge of a grassed bank; water from a rusty bucket down a rope into a shallow well, then carried in two buckets to the house; a wringer washer like my mother used when I was little; clothes out to dry on the line; a banya where they took steam baths; a single sideband radio for occasional communication with the outside world; the back porch sagging with cans of peas, beans, fruit cocktail, Bisquick, oatmeal, flour; piles of nets, corks, buoys around the buildings; overturned skiffs; fuel drums clustered near the beach. A simple economy—everything open, the necessities of living and livelihood acknowledged and set where needed. Then over there, by the laundry lines, DeWitt hanging something bulging yellow from the wire line—a halibut stomach, stretching and curing it to carry water, like the Alutiiqs used to do. His smoked salmon hanging in the smokehouse, 130 pairs hanging stiff in a thick, smoky-brined air. Wanda, the next day, stopping me as I dashed her drying laundry into the house as it started to rain, leaving six lines of laundry out while it rained, not bothering to scamper them into the cabin, they were just getting a second rinse! Cleaning the top of her oil stove with a block of pumice floated over from an eruption . . . How else to live on an island in the bush of Alaska? And the colors! A shade of green that goes so deep it hums; the ocean a sizzling blue, the breathless white of the snowed mountains across the Strait. These were fourth-dimensional and, together with the air, always new, brushing over a set of volcanic mountain ranges on the west and south, from richly greened mountains on the east—the air went deeper into my lungs than any other air I had breathed. I wore the same clothes for three and four days, and never had I felt so clean and alive.

THE WORK BEGAN in earnest the next day, the work of putting away a fishcamp for the season: scraping skiffs to paint next year, cleaning the nets of kelp for winter storage, painting buildings, boarding up windows, pulling and storing anchors, buoys, and lines. Fourteen-hour workdays. One day, we painted the old warehouse at the other island, Harvester Island, leaning against

ladders, until the heat simmered on our backs. "Leslie," Duncan
turned to me on a ladder next to mine. "Let's jump in the water!
Off the dock!" his eyes flashed. My eyes lit up as bright as his.
I knew how cold the water was. But minutes later there I was,
standing on the dock's edge in T-shirt and shorts, trying not to
look at the water. I took a side glance at Duncan beside me, who
was himself preparing for the jump, then legs out, one arm up,
the other holding my nose, the war cry and then the slam into
water like an ice explosion, and the water closing over my head
too deep but don't scream or suck in until up, kick, and then a
high-pitched "AAAAHHHH!" as I broke through the surface,
knowing now with all of my body why people didn't swim in
these Alaskan waters unless they were trying to prove something, or in love, or both. Duncan's turn now, the bare skin of
his chest and legs so naked-white below his burnished face, like
two men's bodies put together. He screamed too on the way
down, and the slapping landing, and we were climbing back up
for another run, laughing, ouching and oohing on the sharp
rocks, shivering, Duncan's parents still painting the warehouse,
but watching and laughing with us, amazed. I stood on the dock
and jumped again and again. This was my future. Duncan flew
me up for this very reason, so that I could survey it all, so that
I would see and know about this place before I said yes. Duncan
should have given me the ring right then, it was as good as done,
that baptism into those waters of grace—so undeserved—every
leap and icy plunge a resounding yes, yes.

2

Stocking and Settling

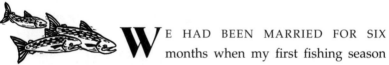WE HAD BEEN MARRIED FOR SIX
months when my first fishing season
began; all of those months, from December 1977 to June 1978,
had been spent at Cedarville College, a small Christian liberal
arts school plunked in the cornfields of southeastern Ohio. I had
just finished my junior year, Duncan his senior, though he would
return for a fifth year with me the next year. We took our finals
the last week, spilling our cups of hastily gained knowledge that
last quarter back into little blue books, filling one, sometimes two
of the twenty-page booklets with our theories, surmises, as-
sumptions, and elaborately conceived guesses to the questions
about ethics, nineteenth-century American literature, the history
of Christianity, in the five to six classes we had each squeezed
into our schedules. At nearly the moment of the closing of the
last book, Duncan and I grabbed our duffel bags stuffed with

books and a few clothes and headed to the airport. We felt like eight-year-olds on the last day of school, running home, free from blackboards, chalk dust, from squirming in seats while the crickets sawed their songs into the open summer windows. . . .

I KNEW THE TRAVELING DRILL, having done it the summer before, but it felt new with Duncan now beside me the whole way, the flight from Cincinnati to Chicago, then the red-eye from Chicago to Anchorage. A five-hour layover in Anchorage, me collapsed on the floor behind the glass casing of a stuffed brown bear, then the flight across the northern Gulf waters to Kodiak Island. With each plane, as we flew farther and farther west and north, I felt Duncan's excitement coiling in him like a spring in his chest, tighter and tighter. His eyes were brighter, his hands itched, his feet jiggled. When the plane landed Duncan fairly leaped down the entire stairway onto the runway; he did not walk, he bounced. Energy came pouring through his smile, his greeting for his parents, the friends he saw at the airport. It appeared he had missed Kodiak with his whole body. I watched him secretly, wondering how and why Kodiak meant so much to him, wondering what it felt like to be returning to a place you loved.

THE NEXT DAY, though sloe-eyed with the loss of three nights of sleep, I stood on the city dock of Kodiak waiting to do my part in a roundup as wild as any I had seen—it was the day of loading the tender, the boat hired by the cannery to, literally, tend to the fishermen. Duncan told me this was the same boat that would later take all our fish from our skiffs and deliver them to the cannery. Now, the tender's job was to ferry everything we needed for the fishing season the twelve hours out to Bear Island.

I was both bemused and amazed by the volume and variety of what appeared throughout the day as the dock became the platform and stage, advertising four months' worth of my new family's needs and desires. Every family member was dispatched to every corner of the road system, gathering the year's accumulation of goods, hauling them down to the city dock. There were the usual items that showed up in every other camp's stash as the people waited to load: drums of gasoline and stove oil, pallets of food, a new skiff, new nets, a new outboard, a cart for the ATV three-wheeler, but our pile was always bigger—more than sixty drums of fuel, twenty-five tanks of propane, dock timbers salvaged from an old cannery, the makings of an entire building, from foundation to roofing and everything in between. There were other notables: a black bull caged in a crate, a sagging couch destined for DeWitt and Wanda's cabin, a wringer washing machine, bales of hay for the cows on Harvester Island, a plastic rocking horse, old wooden Blazo boxes now holding dozens of laying chickens, two stainless steel sinks DeWitt had retrieved from a dump . . . all of it lifted by crane, swung over the dock, into the deep hold of the seventy-five-foot tender, or, for the live cargo, deposited carefully on deck. The sheer mass of the goods jolted me. I was almost embarrassed at what seemed like excess as it formed its own pyramid, but I remembered that we also fished two, three, four times the gear of other fish sites.

It took until midnight to finish, all of us cramming sandwiches down our throats while driving or unloading through the day, stopping for nothing but strategies and directions. "I got a bathtub out there at the ranch by the Quonset hut I want you to git," DeWitt instructed, ignoring our barely concealed frustration. "It's right by the pile of winders next to that little warehouse. And while you're out there, why don'cha bring some of those winders in," and we were off for another hour-plus trip through a mountain pass and back.

The tender was leaving as soon as everything was secured, sometime between one and two in the morning. I would fly out to the island on the morning mail plane, ready to help unload, while Duncan and his younger brother, Wallace, eighteen, would ride out all night on the boat, crawling into whatever bunk or space was available.

Around noon that next day we saw the large blue hull approach Bear Island and heard the radio suddenly cough to life.

"Bear Island, Bear Island, Van Elliot."

DeWitt got up to answer. "Van Elliot, Bear Island. How was your trip, Toby? Over."

"Yeah, smooth sailing this time. We made pretty good time. High tide's not till six, though. How 'bout we get going around then?"

"Yeah, that's a roger. We'll be ready for ya then."

Good. Time for a rest before what looked to be a mini-Normandy invasion.

Six o'clock came and brought with it the full waters that swallowed up our deep rocky beach, transforming it into a shallow beach, less distance to lug everything. The tractor came out, the three-wheeler, and all of the island's residents—DeWitt and Wanda, Duncan's oldest brother, Weston, and his wife, Beverly, Wallace, Duncan, me, and a young man from town hired just for this. Then it began. Skiffs running back and forth; the careful lift from the deck or hold over the side to the waiting skiff; the perilous balance of lumber, aluminum sheeting for the roof, 2 by 4's; here comes the tub, the couch, the chickens, pallets of cases and cases of food, more than any army could eat in a lifetime, I think. . . . Everything met at the beach by waiting hands, arms, then piece by piece labored up the beach, all of us leaning heavier in our hip boots, on up to the house, the yard, the chicken house, wherever it belonged. We worked for hours, the sun still out though nearing 11:00 P.M., and then on into the early morning, the floodlights lighting the dusk, and now we have come to the fuel drums. DeWitt drives the tractor down to the water's edge, where the drums are rolled from the skiffs. He hitches a chain, and one by one, slowly, they are pulled to the grass, until about halfway through, thirty drums left to go, the tractor breaks down, and now we are rolling them by hand up the slow-sanded beach, each one a Sisyphean boulder.

As I have worked, I've figured out that everything that lands on this beach, from toothpick to foundation beam, has been handled seven times. By now, I am thoroughly fatigued, running on determination only, like everyone else, but the night and the lights that shine off the water create a powerful sense of disassociation. My body was wholly grounded, stuck, even in the heavy sand as I carried up box after box, yet the whole night felt magical, as though nothing existed until we brought it into the circle of yellow lights, as though we were assembling and constructing an entire island by ourselves. As indeed we were.

ON THAT, my first tender run, I saw that what we brought out to fishcamp—and what we did not bring—had everything to do with how we would live once there. I would not have known how to think about Bear Island and the life there without the trip around the bay we had made the summer before, when I was visiting. During those ten days on the island, DeWitt suddenly declared a day off from work. Duncan's parents, Duncan, Wallace, and I all packed into a Boston Whaler with a sense of celebration and went traveling in Uyak Bay, visiting as many fishcamps as we could squeeze into the day.

The bay looked immense to me, but Duncan had shown me a yellowed topographical map the night before and outlined with his finger the route we would take. We would begin on the outside of the bay, traveling down the Shelikof Strait, then back to Bear Island, crossing next over to the other side of the bay and then following a circular pattern, visiting the camps along the edges, till we returned, full circle, back to Bear Island. All told, we would log somewhere between 40 and 45 miles. Without that visual orientation, my body and eyes would have guessed a journey much longer, much farther.

We began at Bill and Kay Wood's camp, down on Seven-Mile Beach, four miles away from Bear Island, and visible from our own shore. As we approached their beach, I stared incredulously at their place. They lived in a shack built out of driftwood that was staked into a crumbling bank that was obviously on the slide. The cabin's deposit into the Shelikof Strait was only a matter of time. Unbelievably, I learned it had been built in 1929, by Chris Helgeson, Kay's father-in-law. To get up to the entrance, we balanced on a narrow catwalk up to the door, which was hinged with a piece of inner tube. Kay opened the door with an enthusiastic "Come in! Come in! Don't mind the mess," as she waved her hand dismissively to the tiny room. Would we all fit in here? There were five of us, clearly more than this little shack was designed for. "Gee, if I'da knowed you was coming, I woulda made somethin' good. But I got some squaw candy, and I always got coffee on." Her voice was growly but warm. She looked in her early sixties, her face lined horizontally, her hair still a deep chestnut. She was shorter than I was, just a little over five feet, and heavyset, her walk a forward-leaning shuffle. Without asking, she handed us all thick white coffee mugs, the same navy surplus we used at Bear Island, as we sat on the edge of a built-in bunk bed against the wall. Immediately, without asking, she began filling them all with a thick charcoal brew. Then she sent around an oily plastic bag filled with strips of pungent smoked salmon—squaw candy. "Bill's out working on one of the leads. Got all rolled up last openin'. He'll come soon's he looks up and sees your skiff."

As I chawed on the salmon, and acted as though drinking the coffee, I looked around surreptitiously, without moving my head. The cabin, both inside and out, felt like something that had washed ashore. There were no colors—everything was a driftwood gray, as indeed, nearly everything had been made out of the hundreds of logs that steadily floated in to land on their beach. The door was slanted, leaning back on the right corner, the walls crooked. There were no cupboards, just a few open shelves, one over our head as we sat on the couch, that held flour, Krusteaz pancake mix. The sink was the smallest I had ever seen. Her only stove was a little wood-fueled pot-belly. That and a two-person table, handmade out of drift-wood, it appeared, composed the room. There was just one other room—the bedroom, all in the same grayed tones, in a rectangular room seemingly designed just to fit a double bed and a dresser and nothing more. Then the outhouse, another precarious boardwalk through the noxious, chest-high weeds known as pushki, over the steep, boggy bank to a one-holer with a roof and just three walls, the back open to the bank. Even so, the wind was such that the roll of toilet paper sat in a coffee can to keep it from blowing away. All of this made Bear Island a veritable estate, and Wanda and DeWitt's hum-ble six-hundred-square-foot cabin with linoleum, the kitchen a bright blue and white, framed pictures on the wall—seem citi-fied and luxurious.

While we nursed our coffee and salmon, we heard heavy steps. The door flung open and Bill—it had to be Bill, strode in, his face in a welcoming smile as DeWitt and Duncan stood up to shake his hand, everyone calling a greeting. It appeared these friends didn't see each other often enough. I knew Bill, an Alaskan native, was in his late fifties, but he looked a lot younger, his face a warm brown, his jet-black hair neatly oiled and combed straight back. He was wearing a flannel shirt with the sleeves cut off; either that or they had burst their seams, which looked entirely possible—his arms were as muscled as thighs. I had heard Duncan and his brothers talk of his strength in tones reserved for telling tall tales, but they swore this was true. Bill was so strong, he didn't need a tractor to get his fuel drums up to his cabin. He simply picked them up—full—and walked them up his beach.

I had heard about Bill and Kay before I met them: two characters in a whole panoply of legends and tales Duncan told on our study dates and road trips in college that made up my vicarious knowledge of Alaska and Uyak Bay. The stories were true, I saw, even on that first visit. Bill fished mostly by himself in a beautiful blue sixteen-foot dory, a double-ender, narrow, so that he could turn from one side of the boat to the other without a step. Kay was no pansy either. When coming ashore one night after picking the net, the breakers—always a force to contend with—flipped their dory, sending it crashing down on her arm. They limped ashore, Kay with a broken arm. She set it herself, and soon after continued the construction project she was working on—rebuilding the walls of the outhouse. "It came out kinda crooked, though, with my arm stove up like that, but I got 'er done," she told me later.

We stayed for an hour, long enough for Kay to break out the pancake mix and canned bacon for a proper meal, and after that we were off.

WES AND DEBBIE WILEY WERE NEXT, down past the Woods' place, near the end of Seven-Mile Beach. They were appropriately known as "Driftwood Haven," since their end of the beach collected an enormous and unending supply of derelict logs of every size and shape imaginable. They were heaped up, like stacks of bones, all bleached white with sun and age, a magnificent, chaotic tangle as wondrous as anything I had seen. I realized, seeing it, that people did not treat wood that way, ever. Wood was used for planing into measured planks, for stacking, for arranging into houses, for curving into tight, perfect skiffs— all order, structure, alignment. But here, this wood—cedar, oak, spruce, alder, beechwood—from forests anywhere in the world, was arranged by a higher power, tossed together by tides and winds with absolute abandon and excess. And once landed here, each piece was locked in place by the same forces that landed it, so the whole shoreline appeared to me as a gauge of time, the passage of minutes and years ticked off by the steady stacking of debris.

Wes and Debbie's cabin was nearly invisible, sheltered behind the berm of wood, and built out of its excess. Still unpainted, the walls constructed in vertical planks and logs, it appeared much like the other cabins I had seen by then. They lived in Kodiak during the year. Both had grown up there, Wes a classmate of Weston's through school. Debbie was young, my age, just starting out in her fishing life. I was glad to know there was one other woman in the bay my age. She, like me, was full of questions when we got alone: Did she fish? Was I going to fish? Did she do all the cooking and cleaning? How well would Duncan and I work together in the skiff? How about her and Wes? We didn't have many answers for each other then, mostly questions, fears, doubts, and excitement, too, for whatever lay ahead.

We went back to Bear Island then, and across the bay, a twenty-minute ride, to Danny and Sandy Earle, whose site was known as "Bird Rock." Their cabin was straight out of a Maine fishing village, hand-froed cedar shakes, eight-pane windows, some with the old wavy glass. The cabin had the original hardwood floor, hand-painted now teal and fuchsia; batik coverings on a futon; candles everywhere; on the wall, the side off an old salmon crate with a salmon swimming diagonally.

Danny and Sandy were in their thirties, both strikingly goodlooking, dressed casually in jeans, Sandy with a scarf and earrings, looking like she had just stepped out of an art studio. They were from Baltimore originally. Sandy still spoke with an accent, though they had come up here years before, in the sixties, dropping out of college and lives they no longer wanted. They were known as hippies then to everyone in Larsen Bay, Danny with his long hair and beard, Sandy with her hooped earrings and offbeat taste in clothes. Their first year here they fished for Dora Aga; then later they fished with Dora's brother, Eddie Paakkannen. Despite a generation between them and the radically different cultures they came from, Danny, Sandy, and Eddie lived and commercial-fished together on his thirty-eight-foot seiner, the *Victory*, all of one summer. It was the beginning of a colorful string of adventures and sojourns in Alaska. Some winters they spent as watchmen at Parks cannery, a remote salmon canning plant five miles from Larsen Bay. Another few winters they spent in the village of Larsen Bay; another year they were watchmen at Munsey's Bear Camp, and just five years before they had bought this camp and begun fishing their own setnet sites, setting down roots.

I was intrigued by their lifestyle as well as their history. They

chose not to have a generator, which meant no refrigerator and no freezer. (This did not feel utterly anachronistic—the presence of these two appliances at Bear Island hardly made us thoroughly modern, since they were only on when the light plant was on, which was just three hours in the evening. This meant that the frozen goods constantly shifted between states of freezing and thawing, and the food in the refrigerator was seldom cooler than the outside air.) For light they used Coleman lanterns and candles; they cooked on an Olympia oil stove and a wood stove, no gas. Although they had water to the kitchen sink, they used an outhouse and banya. But far from being primitive, everything about their place was pleasing. Every way that I turned, I saw something artful: bottles of vinegar and oil arranged with shells and beach glass, canning labels framed in the kitchen, a stone wall lining the pathway, old Spanish corks hanging on the weathered wood of the storehouse. Everything they touched, it seemed, turned beautiful.

Then on down the east side of the bay to Tom Keck's place, known as "Greenbanks." Like Kay's, it was set in the middle of a bank slowly eroding into the waters it faced. Tom was a retired high school math teacher, a bachelor, who had acquired six setnetting permits. To run an operation this size, he hired what seemed a horde of young men, as many as ten. They all shared a cabin not much bigger than Bill's and Kay's and in the same condition, with the same level of amenities, the boys sleeping on bunk beds crammed into the back room. Tom, tall, lean, and handsome, in his late forties, offered us what I was beginning to think was the staple of all fishermen in Alaska and Uyak Bay in particular: Krusteaz pancakes on paper plates.

After Greenbanks, we rode back across the bay, which seemed to me like its own ocean, and, twenty-five minutes later, got to Eddie Paakkannen's place, a little blue cabin built just above the high-tide mark near Larsen Bay. Eddie greeted us at the door with great enthusiasm. "Ya! How ya doin'!" his grin almost swallowing up the rest of his face.

"How you doin', Eddie?" DeWitt, Duncan, and Wallace all offered back, grinning just as fiercely, slaps on his back, everyone full of bonhomie and cheer as we entered his cabin. I was grinning along with the rest—how could I resist such contagion? I watched Eddie's face the whole time, struck by his features, but more by his manner, which was charmingly childlike, despite his age. He was in his fifties, stocky, with gray hair buzzed so low you couldn't see it. Beneath his short forehead, he had high Slavic cheekbones, a ski-jump nose and a mouth nearly empty of teeth that was seldom closed or straight—he was either talking or laughing. I had heard about Eddie long before I met him and could recite parts of his history as though I knew him. He was part Finn, part Russian, and though he would not admit it, he was also a quarter Aleut. He had grown up on Alf's Island, a small, now uninhabited island about five miles from Larsen Bay. He was a fisherman, had never married, but he had many friends around the island. Years before, in 1958, DeWitt's first summer as a fisherman, Eddie was one of the first to show DeWitt how to set out a net, how to mend, how to drop anchors. Many felt protective of Eddie, too, because he had never finished second grade and could not read. His more famous traits were his simplicity and goofiness, his love of pranks. Everyone in the bay had a bank of Eddie stories, Duncan included. When Eddie needed an oil rag when working on his engine, he'd reach for his knife, cut off a piece of his trousers, from the bottom up, until his pants flapped at his knees; when he suspected someone was stealing his fuel from the drum behind his cabin, he poured sugar into the drum, then gloated at the beauty of his justice, forgetting that he had ruined the entire drum for himself. He kept all the money he made from fishing in a secret hiding place, not trusting banks, not even having access to banks. One night he had company, and the next morning when he checked his secret vault, he found the money gone. He chased down his guest and tied him up in a chair until he confessed to the theft. One time he was painting the bottom of his skiff on the beach and a bear came by, as they frequently did. This one, as though a circus bear, leapt up on the skiff, miring his feet in the wet paint. Eddie, before he ran, got in a few choice swipes with his paintbrush. For the rest of that year, a certain bear ambled about the village dump, easily identified by its blue fur.

I brought all this into Eddie's cabin with me, and was not surprised that I hadn't been told everything. I found out that the backroom of his three-room cabin served as his clean-up room. Whenever it was time to clean up the cabin, he simply opened the door and threw everything into the backroom and then shut the door. When that room got too full, he would open the back door to that room and throw everything outside, onto the bank of a lagoon. Others had had this idea before him. The lagoon was a kind of graveyard for boats, a few still floating, but most languishing, hulls half in, half out of the murky waters.

But there was news this day. Eddie was very excited. "Did ya hear about my toilet? Ya gotta come and see d'is!" He turned around, and with his grin wider now, opened an obviously new door right in the middle of the front wall of his house. How had I missed this coming in? It was a closet-sized room with a black-seated toilet square in the middle. "Ya, it flushes real good, too!" and he leaned over and pushed the metal handle to demonstrate while we all oohed and ahhed appropriately. We didn't feel too patronizing—after all, we didn't have one, did we? I knew it was a historic moment: at fifty-something, Eddie Paakkannen had his first flushing toilet, ever.

PETE AND JAN DANELSKI'S PLACE, some ten miles from us, was down toward the narrowing headwaters of Uyak. They shared a shallow beach and two cabins with their fishing business partner, Henry Z., and together were known as "Pollack Point." Pete and Jan had three young children: a set of twins and an older daughter. Henry, though married, was there by himself most of the time. In his late fifties, with the coloring and enlarged nose of the alcoholic, he greeted us with a drinking joke, beginning an endless stream of dirty jokes, profanities, and ethnic insults that he found loudly amusing. He was not in the least bit concerned with his audience's response, which was mostly cold and silent. During this barrage, I looked over at Pete and Jan, both visibly impatient, nearly rolling their eyes. How did this work, I wondered, all of them sharing their nets and this small beach? It would be like being marooned on a desert island with your worst relative. Later, I found out that Henry's health was declining, and they were hoping to buy him out. I felt enormously relieved for them.

Pete and Jan lived in Kodiak during the rest of year, where Pete was a longshoreman and Jan was a high school English and Spanish teacher. The bookshelves in their cabin showed them to be serious readers—not a Louis L'Amour or Danielle Steel among them. I was determined to get to know Jan better.

Heading back toward home now, just a few more stops. Ten minutes later, around a corner to Rocky Beach, the Haugheys' place, Al and Jeanine, and their three teenage children, Sam, Adam and Katie. They were set in the middle of a beach studded with rocks, their small green cabin almost hidden in the birch and cottonwood trees. Al had been a schoolteacher in Kodiak, but then moved back to his home state to run a family sheep ranch in Texas during the winters. He had built his cabin in the sixties, with nothing but hand tools since they had no generator then. Their cabin was bigger than Kay and Eddie's, but the same basic style: open shelves, hooks on the walls where everything needed—tools, tide books, fishing needles, gloves—was easily accessed for the dash out the door to the nets. Efficiency and immediate visibility were the prime decorating motifs of all these places. I looked at the food on their open shelves: Spam, canned bacon, canned corned beef, canned peas, carrots, corn, Krusteaz mix, fruit cocktail, canned sausages—all the same foods that still made up much of our diet and that I had seen at all the other places as well. But, unlike them—and Kay and Eddie and Tom Keck as well—Bear Island had a freezer, brought out just a few years before, and we had our own cattle, so we had a ready supply of real beef. I was most grateful that the canned meats were gradually descending the Bear Island food pyramid. To everyone else in the bay, it seemed, the Vienna sausages, corned beef, and canned bacon and ham were simply foods, neither good nor bad, valued equally and simply as necessary fuel for necessary work. For me, still the child of a health-conscious mother, I could see them only as cans of salt, fat, and sodium nitrate, all enemies to the body. Obviously, I wasn't a true fisherman yet.

Then on to our closest neighbors, the Franciscos, Leon and Judy and their four children, all teenagers as well. They lived two miles from us, in a cluster of cabins, pale green with white trim, set in a cove. As we walked up the beach, then followed the trim gravel pathway, lined in stones, then across a curved wooden bridge spanning a creek, I forgot for a moment that I was in bush Alaska. The cabins were neat, perfectly painted and trimmed; the yard was mowed and landscaped; with flowers, bushes, pruned hedges. Even the wood was stacked in perfect symmetry. Though a mountain rose up behind them, and a forest of unbroken green wilderness and open ocean surrounded them, on their plot of ground, the wilderness was tamed and subservient.

We took off our boots to enter the house, the usual Alaskan custom, but ignored in most fishing cabins. Hardwood floors, original artwork, bright white walls trimmed in green—I gazed around the rooms as I had at Dan and Sandy's camp. Perhaps it was possible to make a real home out here. They were warm, shaking hands and hugging us as we entered.

THERE WERE MANY WAYS of living here, I was learning, many dialects spoken, many versions of "camp." Everyone was here to fish, of course. That was a given. But how did they live on land? How did they fit their lives on land around their lives on the water? I did not register any of the shacks as examples of poverty, nor were they repulsive in any way. Nor were the Franciscos' and the Earles' beautiful places to be envied. The conditions that people lived in were so dictated by place, setting, that it was all beyond judgment and comparison. One had a spring, so they had running water. Another place had a well, so it was carried. Some had generators and so had electricity, lights, refrigerators, at least in the evenings; others had generators they ran all day; others had no generator at all. Flushing toilet or outhouse, bathroom with a shower and hot water or just a bathtub and carried water or maybe just a banya. Laundry washed by hand or by wringer washer or by an automatic washer, then dried in a real dryer. Some slept in sleeping bags all summer; others had cotton sheets. I realized that out here, where the pipeline of civilization that delivers water, sewer, and garbage disposal did not extend, each camp was its own community, its own country; each camp had to design itself from the ground up. After making the rounds, it seemed the people of Uyak Bay, and probably other bays around Kodiak Island and Alaska, lived anywhere within the last two centuries. I figured Bear Island was somewhere in the 1930s.

There was some degree of choice involved in it, though, too, the decisions of how much to spend, of how much to box up and truck down to the dock to load onto the tender, how much of the other world's goods you wanted to cart away and load and unload seven times on its way to your world in the bush. How much time and energy did you want to expend just to get it there, not to mention then maintaining it for the rest of its prolonged life? And then, how did all that fit into a life built around fishing?

As we faced our first summer together, we would live more simply, we decided. After all, we were only there for the season, and our primary reason for being there was to fish. Besides, there weren't many options. All the buildings on Bear Island were claimed and filled with either people or fishing gear, or food, but it did not matter. I felt confident that we would have a good summer together. In six months we had figured out how to live as married college students. We would do the same now—by the end of the summer we would know how to live as married fishermen.

The first week we slept upstairs in a little attic loft above Duncan's parents' bedroom in their three-room cabin. After only a few nights, with DeWitt staying up past midnight every night listening to a radio that blared through the ceiling, the trivial became monumental. In whispers late one night, we decided to claim a corner of the loft of the old warehouse as ours. It was a small square building set on pilings at the higher end of the beach with a steep-pitched tin roof, built sometime in the 1930s. It held all the net-mending gear, as well as old nets, miscellaneous tools, spare outboard parts, and old outboards.

By the second week, when Weston and Wallace went off in the skiff to drop anchors to get the sets ready for fishing, Duncan stayed behind. Weston and Wallace were not happy to lose his help. Why couldn't we just put a mattress down in the warehouse like Weston and Bev had for several summers? Duncan had not given in. I was relieved, and proud of him that he had stood up to his brothers on our behalf.

In three days' time, we were done. We cleared out the debris; stapled up insulation to warm the 38-degree nights; put up plywood, trim, and stained it all brown and red. For a dresser, I painted some old wooden fish crates and stacked them against the low, slanted walls. We found an old mattress and springs up above the gear shed; a little white desk came from the warehouse, and a tiny little wood stove, the smallest I'd ever seen, was reclaimed from some other storage. There was no room for any kind of cooking, eating, or washing; we'd eat with Duncan's parents and brother Wallace, which sounded great to me, and wash up at their sink. No house meant no housework, which seemed a stroke of brilliance to me. I'd be too busy fishing to do much else, anyway. Our summer home was complete. We could stand up in the middle of the room; the bed was comfortable enough; there was one window over the bed for light—what else could we need? It was perfect. Let the summer begin.

3

First Pick

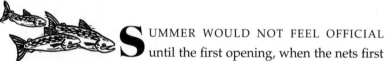SUMMER WOULD NOT FEEL OFFICIAL until the first opening, when the nets first sank into the water. It is 8:00 A.M., June 14, on the official start of the season. In the next few minutes I will start to become a fisherman. This will be my first "pick," my first time working in the skiff with the men. Breakfast is over. Duncan and I are standing on the porch of his parent's cabin surrounded by neat rows of canned carrots, creamed corn, tomato sauce. All of the rain gear and boots are here as well. He is already geared up, looking every bit the fisherman—rugged, strong, almost overpowering, somehow. Though he is not tall, five-foot-seven, he is so muscled from a lifetime of fishing and his years as a wrestler that I always think of him as much bigger than he is. I am used to seeing Duncan in slacks and collared shirts at college and jeans on the

weekend, not in a green rubber suit and layers of tattered sweatshirts. No matter. In a few minutes, I will look the same.

I already had my hip boots, an old pair I found in the gear shed that no one had claimed. Black, made of thick rubber, not like the olive green ones I had seen sports fishermen wear—these were serious. Another whole pair of legs. They were two sizes too big, though, necessitating three pairs of wool socks. "You'll need the socks to keep your feet warm anyway," Duncan assured. There wasn't much I could do about their length—they were designed for someone with legs about three inches longer than mine. I folded the tops over as best I could.

The first time I wore hip boots, I watched Duncan and Wallace carefully to learn the etiquette of these strange items. Sometimes they wore them with the tops folded down below their knees, where they flared out like bell-bottoms. This was the preferred position for walking. Or they would fold them down, then pull the tops back up six inches or so, so that they almost looked like buckets on their ankles. I wasn't sure of the advantages of this arrangement, but it did lend a swashbuckling air to their appearance. Though I had been wearing them off and on for a month, I still was not confident of my hip boot judgments. I would have to keep watching.

On my upper body, I was wearing two thick hooded sweatshirts over a wool shirt, all per Duncan's lead.

"Are you sure I need all this?" I ask. It is cool, in the low forties, which seems a ridiculous summer temperature to me—hardly summer at all—but surely once I start working I'll warm up.

"It's a lot colder on the water than onshore. And you got a wind chill, too. When we're traveling between the nets and you're wet, you get cold. Trust me!" Duncan says in smiling imitation of one of our professors from college.

"Okay, but I hate being hot," I mutter.

"Now, let's find you some rain gear." Duncan shuffles through the array of orange, dark green, and yellow vinyl hanging from hooks on the porch. "How about this?" as he offers me a yellow pair.

I check the size—men's small. I shake them out in front of me, clumsily insert one booted leg, then the other, and jerkily tug them up over the boots and all the sweatshirts. They are like bib overalls, fastened with elastic straps, like suspenders. Duncan tosses the straps over my shoulders, and as I hook them into the slot I wonder how I will ever move. The rubber and polyvinyl together seemed to be synergistically designed to prevent movement. Next comes a life jacket, standard issue, made of foam with a zipper up the front. Now this feels good. It snugs my layers of sweatshirts to my chest and pulls at least my upper half together into a single, manageable unit, unlike the rest of me. I can do this.

Then Duncan hands me a dark green raincoat. "Here, use this one."

A raincoat, too? I look up at the sky: It is overcast, as it has been for several days, but it doesn't look like immediate rain. "Do I really need this?' I ask as I pull it on reluctantly. It is stiffer even than the rain pants, as though it had its own skeletal system, and I were breaking its bones. I feel smothered as it tents over my life jacket and then swallows my hands in four extra inches. "I can't move in this thing. I'm not going to wear it," I announce, expecting resistance.

"Okay," Duncan shrugs. "I don't like to wear them either, but Weston and Wallace always wear them. It's not just for rain, you know. You'll get wet from spray, too."

"I don't care; I'd rather move," as I begin to pull myself out. "Am I done yet?"

"Almost," Duncan says, still officiously hovering over me like a butler. "Just a minute," and he disappears into the cabin, emerging a minute later with a spotless white hat and equally white gloves.

"Is this what your hats look like new?" I ask, disbelieving as I examine it. Duncan and his father and brothers all wear the same hat, small-brimmed, with a poofy top that snaps over the brim, pulling it into a cap like the ones worn by newsboys hawking papers on street corners in old movies, or like the hats I had seen golfers wear on TV. The new hat scarcely resembled what the Fields men and other fishermen I had seen in Kodiak wore, theirs a grimed blend of gray and brown stains, stiff with who-knew-what, except for around the band, which was oily and molded exactly to the shape of the wearer's head. I can fling Duncan's like a frisbee.

"Are you making fun of my hat?' Duncan asks with mock hurt as he fingers his brim.

"Why don't you get a new one? I'd say it's time to trade that one in!"

"Don'cha know it's good luck to wear your old hat? The older the better!"

I smiled tolerantly and put my new hat on, tucking my hip-length braid underneath.

"Your gloves, m'dear," Duncan bows, handing me white cotton gloves. These are not elegant elbow-length evening gloves. They are more like porous gardening gloves. I had worn these out in the skiff before and knew that their purpose was not warmth, since they were as waterproof as sponges, but they gave traction on the slippery fish, Duncan had said. You couldn't pick a fish without them.

I stood there now complete, aware that some kind of transformation had just occurred through Duncan's hands, but the end product—my 115 pounds stiffened and nearly doubled in bulk—was hardly Audrey Hepburn's Fair Lady or Pygmalion's marble goddess. But it wasn't looks that concerned me. I had seen each of the brothers leap about in all this gear like ballerinas—springing between skiffs, toeing the rails with perfect balance, pirouetting from the stern to the bow as they caught a buoy. How did they do that in this getup? Could I ever achieve an ounce of their speed and grace?

"All right, let's go. Dad's waiting for us."

It had been decided that I would fish, at least to start, with Duncan and his father. Since the men work in pairs, my presence as the fifth person made me odd man out, or rather, odd woman in. Weston and Wallace would pick together in one skiff, and Duncan, his father, and I would pick together in another. I was slightly disappointed, thinking it would be fun for Duncan and me to have our own skiff, but on the other hand, as an apprentice, I wasn't ready to shoulder all the tasks of a crewman alone just yet.

I MARCH BESIDE DUNCAN down the grassy slope to the beach, legs swishing. Because it's high tide, it takes us a full ten minutes to get out to the skiff, first pulling ourselves out in a rowboat to a mountain of a rock they call the running-line rock, and then pulling the skiff in with a pulley system they call a running line. I am staggered at how much energy must be expended just to get our feet into the skiff to begin the morning's work.

The first net we motor to is close to the cabins, just offshore. I am so glad that Duncan's family does not fish the way I first imagined, the way I thought all fishermen fish, with large boats out to sea, gone for weeks at a time. I learned, even on our first dates, the mechanics and details of this fishery. These are setnets, attached to shore, which makes them more or less stationary. The net is fixed—it is the fish that move and swirl around it. The nets are tied onto lines that are anchored and remain in place after the nets are pulled up. The lines that form the skeleton of the arrow-shaped nets are tied to shore, then extend out anywhere from 50 to 150 fathoms, 300 to 900 feet. The setnetters' fish are not encircled by nets and then scooped up, as the seiners do; instead they are gilled. As the salmon journey home to their streambed to spawn, the green ocean-colored web strings out invisibly in front of them, the meshes sized to snag on their gills and body as they try to pass through. The work, then, is to come along in a skiff, pull up the net and extract each salmon from the meshes by hand. Hands, like a violinist or world-class pianist, are the precision tools used. Not machines, hydraulics, traps, pots, or any other kind of technology—just hands.

DEWITT IS RUNNING THE MOTOR, a 40-horse Johnson. It moves us efficiently over the water, which is a milky green this morning. I have been watching the water since I got here; every day its hue has shifted from the day before, even the hour before. I don't know if I will ever tire of these colors. As we approach the corks of the net, I follow Duncan's lead, and with him lean over the side of the skiff and plunge my arms into the water to pick up the net—the ocean's frigid forty-something temperature a shock to my skin. We pull the net laboriously from the water up over the railings and into the skiff. I am surprised at how heavy the net is. As Duncan and I are standing, holding the net, DeWitt has shut off the motor.

"Just hold it right there," Duncan instructs as he lets go of the net and turns, looking for something. "Okay, Leslie, you'll stand in the middle and be the hooker." Duncan turns and grins at me, handing me a line with a metal hook at the end.

"Oh great," I moan. "I come to Alaska to be a hooker. What do I do with this?"

"You hook the net here on the corkline, and it frees our hands for picking." I hook the clasp over the line, which is tied to the railing on the other side of the skiff, and it does indeed hold the net in place.

"Okay, that's easy enough," I say, but it isn't, actually. Even though it is calm, the water still rocks the skiff. I am continually thrown off balance, but I can't use my hands since I need them for the fish and the net. While I am learning these other skills, I must attend to the messages sent by my feet and legs. If I don't obey their signals immediately, I will be on the floor in a single move.

DeWitt and Duncan now begin pulling the net into the skiff, hands open like rakes. I pull too, leaning my weight against the weight of the net. The water is still green, but it is so clear and clean I can see silver splotches—salmon—way down near the lead line.

"C'mon, fishy," DeWitt says in light falsetto as he is pulling. He pulls a fish up to his hand. Duncan has one too. And now my first fish appears over the rails. It is snagged just behind the gills. It's still alive, thrashing, bending spasmodically into a C. I am surprised by its power and size. It's the length of my arm, and as meaty as a thigh. This one's a red, I know, having been through Duncan's school of salmon identification before I came out: pink salmon were the smallest, four pounds on average, small-scaled, spots on the tail. They were the easiest to identify. Reds were six pounds on average, with large, shiny scales. Chums and silvers were larger, averaging nine pounds, both with a spray of opalescent silver on their tails. Kings were the biggest, up to as much as a hundred pounds, which I could hardly envision, but those were incidental.

"Okay now, Leslie, this one's easy. Just grab it by the gills and pull it through."

I took it from his hands, clasped my thumb and forefinger over its head and pulled. Nothing happened.

"You have to hold the net with your other hand so you're pulling it against something."

I anchored the net steady with my other hand and pulled again. This time, the fish, fighting against me, slipped out a few inches, then stopped.

"It's stuck on the fin there. Just give it a twist and it'll come free."

I gave a quick twist and a jerk and the fish came free. For a moment I held it, both hands grasping the tail, appreciating its heft and energy as it wriggled wildly.

"You did it, your first fish!" Duncan cheered.

"No sweat," I answered, wiping my brow, then dropping it into the bin behind me.

While I had been concentrating on that single fish, DeWitt and Duncan had both picked several more.

"That's all she wrote here. Let's go up," DeWitt says.

I am guessing that means I need to unhook the net. I do. Then, following Duncan, I help pull us along the net another skiff length.

"Okay, Duncan. How on that?" DeWitt asks.

I look at him to figure out what this means. I decide he's checking with Duncan to see if this is a good place to stop. He must see fish down there.

I hook the net again, and the momentum of the skiff's forward movement nearly wraps the hook line around me. I see that I am not only the hooker but the brake and anchor for the skiff as well. We pull the net up here, and the first fish that greets me is in some sort of sack, twisted a hundred ways. I begin to try and extricate the fish from its prison, but no matter what I do, he remains hopelessly balled up. Duncan sees my trouble. With three movements, he has the fish spinning counterclockwise, then a mesh over its head, then the bag opens up and he pulls it out and drops it to the floor behind me. I look at Duncan as though he has just performed miraculous surgery.

"How did you do that?"

Then Duncan leans over and tells me his secrets. "You see this fin here . . . ?"

Just that morning, I saw and began to learn most of the other ways the gilled salmon can confound the hands and eyes, and the ways to snap and pull and twist them free. Each fish was a geometry problem. The solution began with the diagonal angles of the net itself, learning how it hangs, the pattern of the meshes taut over a fish's body, knowing when to pull the fish through and when to back it out, snapping the gills, twisting the knot over that fin there. . . . I began to see how to do it, but most of all, I could see that what really mattered was attitude and energy. Whether the fish was dead or alive, whether it was four pounds or ten, the length of your arm or the length of your leg, you had to be aggressive, believing you were stronger and smarter than this imposing creature. But how to do it so fast? And how to keep your hands nimble in the 42-degree water?

It is peak high tide now, and the current is running hard. The net floats out in front of us as if there is no lead line weighting it on the bottom. Now when we pull the net up to pick the fish, it is twice as difficult. The three of us pull in concert. My shoulders are straining; even DeWitt, with all his extra weight and thickly muscled shoulders and arms, is leaning against the tide's force. I wonder how I will have the strength to do this when I am working alone with Duncan or DeWitt, as I will later in the summer.

Now, at this stage of the tide, everything I have learned about picking has changed. With the net this taut, the fish hang differently. In fact, some fall out as they approach the skiff.

"Get it, Leslie!" Duncan calls as a salmon drops through the meshes back into the water. But the net is in the way and I can't get under it.

"Ohhhh," DeWitt says in genuine disappointment as he watches the fish, rigid, sink beneath us.

"A big red, too."

I look at Duncan, expecting him to smile, but he frowns mildly at me.

Okay, I think. *This is one of the rules of fishing. You don't lose a single fish.*

We finish pulling down the line and come to the hook of the net, which sits like a big triangle. It's much more complicated here as we spend half our time bent over the railings, pulling, grunting, muscling and maneuvering the skiff in the narrow comers, over the buoys and lines, the boat now heavy with our own weight and the fish we've already picked. Surely there must be an easier way to do this, but I have no brilliant ideas.

When we finish with this net, I look at the fish in the bins at our feet. Maybe seventy-five fish. Is this a lot or a little—I don't know. But it looks like a lot to me. Just pulling those fish from the ocean to our boat took far more energy that I would have guessed. This is so personal, so primitive, I realize—our hands have touched every single fish. And no matter how many fish there are in the nets—100 or 300 or 3,000, we still touch and hold every one. One day Wallace commented to me, "Do you realize that, except for the outboard, we're fishing the same way people have for hundreds of years."

WE GO NOW to the next net on the other side of the island. The tide is not as bad here; the net is looser as it hands. I am bent over a fish when suddenly I hear a loud, watery snort behind me.

"What was that?" I spin around and see where something has been, the water smooth where it has just swallowed something—something big, I think.

"Sea lion," Duncan says, with a bored, irritated tone, still picking fish. "Let's see what he does."

I can't believe Duncan's manner. A sea lion! I scan the water around the skiff, anxiously awaiting another appearance. Then it comes again, a blast, a roar just feet from us. There he is, by the bow! He looks like a brown blubbery glob under water but his head, out of the water, is sleek yet broad and square. He is just a few feet from the skiff now. He lifts his head and roars a throaty roar, his yellow teeth bared to us and the sky. Yes, the sea lion epithet is indeed accurate. DeWitt and Duncan have stopped working and are watching him. He slips under the water again, and just seconds later he is in the net in front of us, tugging at a salmon. The water shatters again as he erupts with a fish, bloody, in his mouth; then, as though performing in a sea-life show, he flings it up into the air and catches it, biting into the soft belly, then tosses it behind him into the water.

I am enthralled. Duncan is not.

"Look at that! He's just playing with it. He'll wipe this net out," Duncan says with disgust.

"What do you mean?"

"I mean, they can eat as many as thirty fish a day—that's one sea lion. You get a herd of them, and your net's wiped out for the day. See, he's not even hungry anymore." Duncan gestures back to the net, where the sea lion is again snapping another mangled salmon playfully into the air.

"What are you going to do?"

"What do you think? I'm going to try to scare him away!" He leans over the side, waiting.

The sea lion, as though on cue, comes up just ten feet from Duncan, near the stern. Duncan raises his arms menacingly and shouts "Yaaaa!" like a cowboy trying to start a stampede, but the sea lion seems to know he poses no real threat. He rolls over on his back and roars back derisively. Duncan continues shouting and waving his arms. I join him to double-barrel the defense, but it appears useless. We give up—he does not. For the next ten minutes, the huge creature rounded our skiff, charging us with great blasts and bellows, apparently trying to chase *us* from the net. Finally, he seemed bored with this entertainment, and with a flick and roll of his bulbous form, he was gone.

IT'S ALMOST NOON NOW. We've been out four hours and I'm hungry. I have to pee, and so does Duncan and his father.

"Well, I guess I gotta shake the dew off my lily," DeWitt intones in a homey father's voice, his Oklahoma accent still traceable, though he left during the Dust Bowl of the early thirties.

I smile at Duncan, he smiles indulgently and I turn around. I like this, that we can live together this way. When they're done, it's my turn.

"Let me off on that rock over there, Duncan." I point to a cove with a shelf of rock jutting out.

While I am balancing on my private rock, struggling to undo all my layers, Duncan and DeWitt pull out the candy bars and pop.

"What do you want, Leslie, a Hershey's or a Uno?" Duncan asks, after picking me back up. He's sitting on the seat in the stern, with a root beer beside him.

"Hershey's, of course," I say as I reach for it. "Ugh!! How can you eat those things! They're just chocolate-covered Crisco." I roll my eyes as he takes an exaggerated bite. It shocks me, still, the consumption of sugar and fat here. My mother, for years, never even bought white flour or white sugar, nor any kind of sweet or treat, though we longed for it, and contemplated lives of petty crime to obtain it. I take the offered Hershey's with a faint twinge. On shore, I would never consider eating a candy bar or drinking a pop, but it's different out on the water. When I can see for two hundred miles, when more than half a mile of net filled with kelp, grass, and fish who have swum thousands of miles waits for our hands only, when the work subsumes even time itself, how is a candy bar significant in an economy like this? I unwrap my Hershey's and pop my Coke.

DeWitt sits, his head down, munching his bar. He appears to be studying the salmon. He looks up at me and says, straight into my eyes, "Those are beautiful fish, aren't they?" He picks one up with both hands, holding its silver body out lengthwise in front of him, and with the wonder of a boy, he shakes his head. "Beautiful fish."

I look at him, trying to hide my amazement. How is it that after twenty years of seeing and smelling and handling these creatures he can still see them? Why hadn't they turned into faceless objects, or pieces of money? I hoped then that in twenty years I could do the same. And he was right—the salmon were beautiful. I had never seen beauty in a fish before, but neither had I pulled them from the ocean and held them in my hands as I did now. They shone like foil in the sun, even underwater. The reds and silvers had blue, iridescent backs; their eyes were blue, or yellow or hazel. Their scales were arranged and scalloped so perfectly. And they had tongues! I had never thought of fish having tongues.

What if I had married into a family of cod fishermen, and

had to handle cod with their belligerent eyes and thick-lipped grimace, with the pallid, dull-skinned body trailing behind like a distasteful afterthought? The search for beauty would have been futile, I am sure. What if I had to fish for crab, who were hardly creatures at all, just spiny machines? Or, what if, by some horrible turn of fate, I now had to catch sculpins for a living? They were the worst. They would occasionally catch at the lead line, the bottom of the net. Their faces were monstrous, all spines and bumps, with a mouth more than twice the width of a body that ended in a venomous horn at either end, the eyes nearly invisible. The mesh of the net would hook over the mouth and the spines, forcing hand-to-hand combat. They were nearly always alive, it seemed, and though the body behind them was disproportionately small, as though its only purpose were to ferry about the oversize head, it would thrash its spikes in protest until the job was done. When finally extricated and thrown back, it dove with purpose toward its murky haunts. I imagined that when God made this fish, He did not consult a thesaurus of adjectives he wished it to personify; He simply said, "This fish will be *ugly!*" I do have to pick them from the net sometimes, but at least I am not making my living off their ghastly forms.

IT LOOKS LIKE this pick will be over soon. I realize that I am saying the word "pick." I am even thinking the word "pick." That four-letter word seems to fill in for nearly everything done with the nets, and it is my word now, too. There are two picks a day—meaning we leave shore and go out on the water to the nets two separate times, coming ashore in between for lunch and a rest. In this case it is a noun, as in "How was the pick?" or "This pick shouldn't take too long." But "pick" is a verb as well—we go out and pick the nets, referring to picking the fish out of them. The men also say, as we approach a net, "Okay, we're going to pick up here," meaning the person in the bow is to lean over into the water and lift up the approaching net from the corkline and bring it into the skiff. It becomes a noun again when we talk about the people who do this. They are fishermen, but more specifically, fish-pickers, as in, "Are you going to be a fish-picker, too, Leslie?" as one of the neighboring fishermen asked when he first met me in Larsen Bay. The terms conjured up discordant images in my new-from-New Hampshire mind, where "picking" meant an excursion into the garden or orchard or field to pluck apples, blueberries, beans, or corn from their green growing stems. There, it meant fruit or vegetables heavy in the hand, warm with sun. Here, in this country, the same word meant a fish hanging from your hand, cold as death from the cold sea.

WE ARE ON THE WAY to the tender now, like farmers to market with the produce we have picked. I smile as I sit on the stern seat next to DeWitt as Duncan, running the outboard, stands over us. I look up and we wink at each other, proud of ourselves for this skiff full of fish, both of us happy that we are working together, just as we imagined and planned back at Cedarville. After these hours in the skiff, the boots, life jacket, all the gear that seemed to remove me from myself when I started already feel natural, just outer layers of my own skin.

I like this summer uniform, I decide. It's much better than the one I wore at HoJo's all those other summers. A single year separates me from that place, and a single year separates me from being a teenager. I would be there right now had I not married Duncan, but I am now 3,000 airplane miles away and I do not even know that former world yet as memory, not good or bad or anything—it has simply vanished.

4

Hurled to the Shark

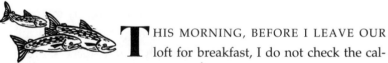 THIS MORNING, BEFORE I LEAVE OUR loft for breakfast, I do not check the calendar. I know what day it is: July 26—put-out day. This is the day we load our nets from the mending racks on the beach and drop them back into the water. I am grim. I have done this four times by now in this, my first season, which makes me still a nervous greenhorn, since Duncan, his two brothers, and his father have been fishing for more than twenty years, yet I know exactly what will happen in the day and night ahead.

Now I stand in the beached skiff as it sits sideways, loading each of the eight nets into the skiffs. We are clawing the net with our hands, pulling the green webbing from the racks over the sand and up and over the skiff sides. Duncan is pulling the leads, the heaviest weight; Wallace is pulling the corks, the most awkward job; and I am in the middle pulling the fine thread of web into a silken pile at my feet. The nets must be stacked precisely in the skiffs so they will drop clean into the water, lie where intended, spin out over the stern without a knot to pull our boat, or all of us, after it.

All the nets are loaded now, eight nets in three skiffs. The skiffs with the nets in them have no outboard; they will be pulled by the skiffs powered with the 35-horse outboards. We step out of the last skiff, and I glance behind me as I leave the beach, our little battleships loaded and ready. The opening begins at 6:00 P.M. Though it is only three, we will put on our gear and head out.

"LESLIE!" Duncan yells back as he starts down to the beach toward the waiting skiffs. Everyone is ready before me. "Get some candy bars!" I am searching frantically for my life vest, hands on every hook, frisking the extra raingear draped around the porch, feel a familiar sponge, grab it. I push into my mother-in-law's cabin, into the tiny kitchen, rummage the cupboard till I find the hidden supply—Uno's, Hershey's, and Snickers. I run down the grass yard, onto the sand, leap into the skiff and we are off, the five of us, all looking alike in our raingear, out to skiffs painted red, white, and black. Because of our uniformity, not only our clothes but our gear, the skiffs, the cabins all painted red and white, it feels like an industry, an enterprise so much larger than the facts at hand: a core of three brothers, a father, seven skiffs, and eight nets. For a moment I see us, Weston in the stern running the kicker, eyes squinted in concentration as he maps out the afternoon and evening. Duncan solemn as he watches the water, Wallace, just seventeen, with the same air as his brothers, and their father, DeWitt. And me, my face no different, not because I am strategizing, as they are—who puts out what nets, in what order, will the NE get worse?—but because I have taken this world on like a face, except it goes deep already. I am one of them, I think, then no, I am not, but I will be, if I can.

THAT 6:00 P.M. MINUTE has enticed us through weeks of scraping and painting skiffs, mending and pulling the hairy weeds out of last year's nets, dropping anchors. It is all for this, now, Duncan standing in the skiff with the 35 kicker, eyes on his watch, DeWitt and I in the skiff with the nets, poised for his word, and then "Let's go!" as the second hand hits the twelve and it is official, the opening has begun. I have already tied the net in the skiff onto the line in the water. Duncan gasses the kicker now, and his skiff, like a racehorse out of the gate, charges ahead free until the line to my skiff suddenly goes taut. We freeze for a split second, then my skiff jerks forward behind his, the net playing out with a hiss and tumble behind me over the stern. My job—not by my choice—is to clear the net should it catch or snare as it pulled out behind us. I nearly cringe as the skiffs lunge yet faster. What if the net tangles? I realize I have absolutely no control over this mess, and then—a cork snags, the skiff jerks to a stop, begins to swing sideways, the cork creaking threateningly. "Clear the cork!!" Duncan shouts, and I lean over, punch the cork jammed in the corner, and the released tension yanks out fathoms of net. We are nearing the shore keg and it snags again, the skiff pulling against the locked net—"Leslie! Get it!" I kick it this time, and then just as we come up to the buoy, Duncan shouts, "Okay, get ready to grab it!" and we are over the skiff sides, leaning out as far as we can keep our balance, gripping the running line that holds the net in place while Duncan jumps over and leans his full weight on top of us to tie the net without losing any of the tension. "Hold it, hold it . . . !" he warns, as DeWitt and I pant over our balled fists; I screw my eyes up tight, count my breaths, and when I hit eighteen, he says, "Got it!" and we relax, let go, stand up, and then the next is easier as we spell out the net in the hook. Here Duncan kills the kicker and we pull it by hand. This is fine, this is good, I say to myself, as we pull—the pressure is off here. When we are done, and the net hangs in the water like a curtain, the row of corks blinking in the waves, I feel good.

"We've got some corks, Leslie. Come on back here and let's get 'em," Duncan says, the tension gone now from his voice. Some of the corks have caught under the net, and need to be freed. This is one of my favorite jobs. So simple, yet some kind of elegance, even poetry to it. I wedge myself in the corner of the stern while Duncan backs down the net, keeping as close as the tide and wind and waves will let him. As we idle down, I lean over and, with a quick dunk, palm the submerged cork out from under the net and clear so it bobs up instantly. Lean, dunk, pop, Duncan watching as we go, and if I get every one first try he doesn't need to stop. We just motor down, lean, dunk, pop, all the way down the length of the net, one hundred fathoms, until every cork holds its part of the net and it sways and blinks with every wave, graceful.

Then on to the next net and then two more. We will put out four; Weston and Wallace will put out four.

When the nets are in, then it happens, what all of this is for—the fish. Sometimes, as soon as the net is wet behind us, we see silver lifting it back up out of the water, a furious thrash of anger as three, four, a group of salmon hit together. And we stop, no matter what we're doing, smile at one another at the instant logic and mathematics of it—yes, a year of ordering supplies, a month of fourteen-hour workdays for this moment, for these salmon behind us and at our feet.

But if it is early in June, or late in August, or in any low year, there may not be much to marvel over. The net may soak for hours and days without a fish, blank. Duncan told me about this, about the early years, how few fish they caught. His family sometimes left four months of work with a slip from the cannery that would pay off their living expenses, but not much more. The risks never lessened over the years. I see that this is a fishery built on faith. There is so little control over so much. Setnetters are not hunter-gatherers who stalk and chase their prey, not even farmers who till and plant and tend what rises. The nets are plunked out here in hope leavened with experience, strung out into the ocean, yet tied to shore, like some kind of giant arm motioning "Here, swim in here." There is no way to urge or chase them in. We can only wait for the salmon that choose this place at this depth on the days that the nets are there, and then hope for their blunder into the meshes, and that their blunder gills them fast enough that they hold against the currents and riptides until we come to pull them into the skiffs. When I have been picking for many hours, so that my back aches and my hands are stiff, they are the enemy, and I don't care if the nets stay blank. But then when I am rested, and Duncan and I look at college bills, when we estimate our living expenses, I know those fish, every one is sent. If God knows the fall of each sparrow, then He knows the path of every salmon. Sometimes I remember this.

IF THE FISH are hitting that night, and they are this night, we pick. I would like to go ashore and be done for the night. What perfect closure, move on from one task to the next, a night's sleep in between. But we don't work that way. The time clock for fishing follows Alaska's summer sun; in May and June, night and day are twins, one a slightly paler version of the other. We nap in the day and work in the night; pick fish in the day, pick fish at night; these nets, these fish, are no respecter of person or sleep or fatigue.

After the fourth net, five hours since we started, we declare it dinnertime, pulling out the candy bars and pop. We sit there, the three of us, our skiff tied to the net, slapping the water gently. This is the only break we will have tonight. Duncan and I are sitting together as we eat, our rubberized and reptilian legs pressing against each other on the seat. Duncan leans over and gives me a kiss, leaving a wet spot on my face where his nose dripped. He's got a couple of scales on his cheek, and a smudge of fish blood on his forehead. I've got something dried on my jawline; my gloves are a blend of blood and gurry. I'm not feeling romantic. He's yelled at me three times already this put-out. I know later he'll explain that a job's got to be done no matter who it is, wife or crew or anyone. Then I'll complain that he treats me like a crewman and he'll say, *Well, you are.* Then I'll say *no, I'm your wife and you can't step in and out of marriage just because you're climbing in and out of a skiff,* and so it will go. I did not expect the skiff to be run democratically, but neither did I expect such a pronounced hierarchy. I'm not sure what to do about this, how to establish in this geography the kind of balance and equity we have in the other.

WE WERE DRAWN to each other not by physical prowess or my potential as a fish-picker, but, among other things, by a mutual love of philosophy and theology. After meeting in college on a road trip to Maine, we began a dialogue of impassioned notes and letters when apart and discussions when together about the nature of God, about the puzzles of predestination and election, about man's free will or is it only free moral agency? How far does God's sovereignty extend? How can God hold us responsible if in fact He is the primary and sufficient cause of all events?

How does evil fit into God's plan, or is evil outside of it? These questions were life and death to me. Though I had considered some of them before, at eighteen, I understood their enormity and could not proceed with anything until I found some answers. Duncan, the fisherman from Alaska, who was also class president, cared as deeply as I did about these concerns. We talked, wrote notes, studied philosophy together, took classes together, prayed together. The bond ran deep. Where was all of this now? Our most abstract question was likely to be "How many reds do you think this skiff'll pack?"

For now, though, I'm not wishing myself anywhere else. Not because of supreme contentedness; rather because the world we are floating in is so complete and has wrapped me in its cloak with such strength, I can think of no other place or way to live than what we are doing this moment, and most, what we must do to finish before we can get to bed.

FINALLY, the nets are judged done for the night. Weston and Wallace come up beside us in their skiff, both looking tired, but wearing the same expression I see on Duncan. They do not even glance at me as they decide the mechanics of who will take what skiff to the tender to deliver, and I am hoping they will not need me. I won't ask to go ashore, though. "You can go in," Duncan finally says to me in my ear. "I know it was a tough one, but you did great. You really worked hard. Thanks, Leslie."

At the beginning of the season I might have protested, but in these weeks I have become grateful for any concessions Duncan makes for me, but at the same time, I felt weak and guilty that I need them. I never needed them before. I could always match my three brothers on most tasks. Why can't I work as hard and long as these men? I was the one out of a hundred ninth-grade girls who could climb the gym rope to the ceiling in six seconds, beating everyone else. In tenth grade, I was the one chosen out of my class to heave the twenty-pound medicine ball in our Winter Carnival Olympics. Here I felt defeated.

I slide out of the skiff, trudge through the black night water up to the beach and the long hill up to Duncan's parents' house. The lights are on. How glorious, like a star! Duncan's mother has hot soup on the stove and grilled sandwiches waiting. I am so grateful as I spoon the soup with numb hands. In five minutes I am done, back outside, walking down to the old warehouse on the beach, to our loft. The wind has not abated any, and though it is sucking sound in the opposite direction, I can hear the skiffs straining under their loads, still going in the dark, just arriving at the tender. I have no energy left to pity them; indeed I do not, for haven't they grown up with this? Doesn't Duncan profess love for this? And is there anything these three brothers cannot do? Then up the ladder and into the tiny room. It is cold in there without heat, about 45 degrees, and the tin roof is banging, and something else is whistling with the wind, but I don't care. I notice as I pull off my sweatshirt that I have fish scales stuck to my arms. I leave them there, climb under the three sleeping bags, and sleep. It is 1:00 A.M.

THE NEXT MORNING, the alarm rings at seven, the usual. Duncan is trying to wake beside me. I didn't hear or feel him get into bed last night. I don't want to get up, don't want to put on raingear and face the nets again. But the wind has come down. "Thank you, Lord," I whisper. "Are you awake, Leslie? We've got to get up," Duncan mumbles, rubbing the palms of his hands into his eyes. I won't ask to stay in. How can I? I got in earlier than any of the men last night. But I'm so stiff from trying to harness the ocean last night, I can barely move. We both roll out of the one side of the bed, then fumble for clothes in our wood crates, and in a few minutes we are down the ladder and up to my parents-in-law.

Duncan gives the door one rap as he enters.

"Come on in," Wanda calls from around the corner. She is just putting a bowl of hot muffins on the table. DeWitt and Wallace are already here. DeWitt looks up and smiles kindly at his new daughter-in-law.

"Good mornin', Leslie. How'd you sleep last night, my dear?"

"Oh, it was a little bit noisy with the roof flapping in the wind, but I was so tired I didn't really hear it," I answer as I sit at my place. Then I think, oh, dear, did that sound like I was complaining?

"Yeah, it was blowin' pretty good last night. Wandy, you ready to sit down?"

"Just a minute," she called as she bustled from kitchen to table, setting down another amazing banquet: fresh blueberry muffins, scrambled eggs, coffee, bacon, canned pears with sprinkled cheese, and juice.

"Where's the fried potatoes?" DeWitt asks, looking around the table as Wanda sits down.

Wanda looks from me to Duncan, then to DeWitt. "I didn't make any this morning," she says, defensively.

"We haven't had fried potatoes for three days now. You know we need 'em when we're workin' hard. There's nothin' like fried potatoes in the mornin,' " DeWitt says, like a slogan. Wallace and I exchange covert smiles. I nudge Duncan under the table. How will this end? I'm not too worried.

"Well, you can have them for lunch, then. How does that sound?" Wanda cajoles. The cloud has passed. We bow our heads and DeWitt prays, "Heavenly Father, thank you for this good food which has been prepared for our nourishment and enjoyment. Thank you for all your many blessings. Thank you for the fish. Make us grateful in our hearts for these things. Amen."

We eat quickly, every one intent upon the food. It will have to last us for at least six hours. Lunchtime is ideally at two, but when the fish are hitting, it could be three or four or later until we stop for lunch. Wanda's and Beverly's rule was, "For every extra hour that they're out, fix another dish." So we would come in to a table crowded with beef roast with potatoes and carrots, biscuits, green beans, Jell-O, applesauce, with chocolate cake for dessert. The table was always set perfectly, with every utensil, napkins, casserole dishes instead of pans. It was a marvel to me. My family had given up on mealtimes long ago, the food left on the stove for anyone to eat when and if they wanted. I admired Wanda, and saw how tirelessly she worked, hauling her own water in buckets, though she was fifty-eight then, the unending piles of dishes, the bookwork and accounting she did for the family business, mending net. The one thing she didn't do was work out in the skiff. I envied and admired her, but didn't want to change places. That was all women's work, I thought. It smacked of domestic slavery.

I wasn't sure what I was, and neither was anyone else. I came in often to generous meals, and afterward, knowing no one would help Wanda with the dishes, and because I was a female, I felt elected. While the men rested and talked over dessert, I collected and stacked plates, began the cleanup. "Leslie, you don't have to do that," Wanda would protest. I still believed in sharing the work with Duncan, but it was clear by now that the sharing was not going to be mutual. My motives in still carrying the torch weren't entirely pure, though. I worried that Bev and Wanda might resent my working more with the men than with them. They needed help with the shore work too. But the life of that family, the life of the island revolved around the work on the water. Nothing else mattered, and I wanted to do what mattered.

WHEN OUR NETS weren't working us, we were working the nets. On closures, when Fish and Game closed fishing for a few days to let the salmon up the streams to spawn, we untied the nets and pulled them up, this time using not the kicker to unravel them, but our arms, dragging them up from the ocean floor, heavy with kelp sometimes, sometimes fresh fish just hit. The nets had to be out of the water, not a shred remaining, by 9:00 A.M. To keep everyone honest, Fish and Game flew over regularly. Take-ups were just as intense as put-outs, with one ameliorating factor. The speed was our own, not motorized, and so within our control. The take-up of a single net was like the 400-yard dash. Not a sprint, because you couldn't poop out halfway and then just walk the rest. And even if you paced the first net perfectly, so that you made it to the end, there were still three more nets to go.

I was usually the first one in from take-ups, let off on shore by Duncan, who knew I had nothing left to give. I knew it as a gift. He and his brothers would go on to the tender to deliver the fish caught before the nets came out. I would trudge up the hill in varying states of emotion, sometimes tearful, sometimes angry, always tired. Often Beverly would be there on the porch, ready to offer sympathy, a hug. She was seven years older than I, and was my sister-in-law, Weston's wife, but we were closer to each other than we were to our own sisters. At the end of one take-up night, near eleven, as I pushed my body laboriously up the beach, my limbs like deadwood, she came down to greet me.

"Leslie!" she called. "How did it go?" She peered anxiously into my face and put an arm around my shoulder.

I sighed carefully, trying the quell the emotions I was now

allowing myself to feel in the face of such kindness. I couldn't hold it in any longer. The night had been intense. I had made a few mistakes, one running line had broken, the nets had too many fish for us to pull them as quickly as we needed; we had almost gone over the deadline; Duncan had stepped on my back when I had fallen to get to the net. . . . Every loss, every shout had registered somewhere deep inside my chest and it was choking me. Until now. I erupted into sobs, heaving, tears blending with salt water and gurry, my arms over Bev's shoulders. She stood there quietly, letting me cry. When I was done, we walked up together to her house, where she made me hot chocolate. Sitting at her table, in a kitchen still unfinished, floors bare plywood, walls unpainted, she handed me a piece of paper, marbleized, with sweeping calligraphied letters.

"Here, Leslie. I thought you might like this." She smiled as my face lit up. It was a verse from the Old Testament, from Isaiah, one we had talked about before. I read the familiar words again: "They that wait upon the Lord shall renew their strength. They shall mount up with wings like eagles. They shall run and not be weary; they shall walk and not be faint." I had memorized it a few years ago while in high school, but had never needed it as much as I did this summer. I wanted to clasp it to my breast, transfer its hope and promise directly through my clothing and skin.

"Thanks, Bev. It's beautiful. I'll put it up next to my mirror, by 'the poem.' "

Bev laughed, knowing this as the place of honor. "Tell me the poem again. This seems like a good time for it. Do you know it by heart?"

"Only the last stanza." It was a poem I had found early this season in a poetry anthology from college—"The Leg," by Karl

Shapiro. The moment I read it the words became my own. In a quiet voice, I recited

> *The body, what is it, Father, but a sign*
> *To love the force that grows us, to give back*
> *What in thy palm is senselessness and mud?*
> *Knead, knead the substance of our understanding*
> *Which must be beautiful in flesh to wake,*
> *That if Thou take me angrily in hand*
> *And hurl me to the shark, I shall not die!*

I say the last two lines again, and we fall silent.

"It reminds me of your poem about Job," I say finally, breaking the moment.

"Yes, me too. Remember what Job says? 'Though He slay me/ yet will I trust Him.' "

We are quiet again. This verse scares me profoundly, and yet it gives comfort, too. I don't want to leave, but it is nearing midnight. We hug one more time.

"See you on the nets tomorrow."

"Bring one of your new poems!"

"You bring one too!" We smile like conspirators.

ONE MORNING, near the end of July, it happened, the run of pink salmon forecast by Fish and Game came running, and so did we. Fifteen million were forecast, and when we stumbled up the hill for breakfast, Duncan looked out in his usual visual check of the nets visible from shore, then, "Hey, where's the hook of the third? We've either got a shark in it or it's sunk with fish!" It was sunk with fish. And the derby began. We had fished and caught healthy amounts of salmon up until then, enough to keep us tired and reasonably sure of making our tuition payments that next year, but we hadn't made enough for rent and living expenses. I had hoped for the flood of fish along with everyone else, but now, as my heart fluttered and my stomach turned, as though I were about to go on stage, I wondered, *If we haven't been catching many fish yet, what will it be like when we do?* And then the answer: what I thought I knew about hard work became a romper room memory. There were pink salmon swarming all over Kodiak Island, filling the seiners' nets, sinking ours, the ones that got away choking the spawning streams. We stood in our skiffs in salmon up to our ankles, then our calves, then our knees, walking on them, falling on them as we still bent to pull the net in for more. Three weeks of days and nights nearly indistinguishable from one another, eating and sleeping around the fish, lunch twelve hours after breakfast, my hands so sore and bleeding in the deep cracks between my fingers I tape them before putting on the cotton gloves, a shoulder that hyperextended with any stress at all, Duncan and his brothers' arms going dead-numb at night, their hands locking with carpal tunnel, the dreams—Duncan pulling the covers off me hand-over-hand shouting "coil the line!"; mine, that the net snares my foot while putting out the nets and I go down, drowning over and over because of the fish, the overflow that runneth from our cups, our fish overfloweth, our cups run away, the fish, the fish, and I'm not listening anymore, can't hear anything, I just want to sleep, to hear the sound of sleep curling up into my ears, and only that.

WHEN THE SEASON was over, in mid-September, we flew from our island back to Kodiak. The first Sunday back in town, I stood beside Duncan in church, singing hymns, my eyes closed and face uplifted. After four months at fishcamp, the congregational voices washed over me like milk. At the end of the service, a family friend strode across the aisle to greet us.

"Duncan! Leslie! How did your season go?" he boomed, his hand extended to Duncan. I knew he was a business executive for a local Native corporation. We had been invited over to his house once for a potluck, where I had heard his latest fishing stories—he fished a short subsistence net one day each summer to stock his freezer.

"Oh, we got a few fish." Duncan smiled, a bit wanly. We were both still shell-shocked.

"A few fish, I bet!" He grinned knowingly. Then he turned to me. "Leslie, you pick any fish?"

"A few," I said, in the same killer understatement, too tired to care about accuracy or making a good impression.

"Did you? Well, let's see your hands! You know, you can tell a lot by someone's hands," he said, smiling a wink at Duncan.

I held my right hand out, palm up, looking away. He placed one hand beneath to steady it, with the other he pulled lightly on my fingers, then brushed his fingertips over what was left of the skin. His smile dimmed. "Yeah, I guess you did pick a few."

"She picked more than that," Duncan said, putting his arm around my shoulder proudly and squeezing.

I smiled blandly at them both, unsure of what to say, only knowing that I had survived, that there were now nine other months before me to return to college and live a different life, and choosing then to believe that though the seasons would circle around again and chase me back to those waters, that island every summer for the rest of my life, surely I would live, again.

5

Houses, Houses

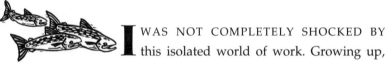 I WAS NOT COMPLETELY SHOCKED BY this isolated world of work. Growing up, we lived "out" too, on tar-patched or dirt roads in rural New Hampshire, not for a romantic ideal of rural life, but because that was where the work took us. Our work was the restoration of old colonial houses. They weren't valued much then, in the late fifties and sixties, the era of the subdivision and the low-riding, efficient ranch home. There were no shows on television yet dramatically documenting for appreciative audiences the discoveries and recoveries of these historic hulks. We began almost by accident, as something my mother stumbled upon by desperate necessity.

One source of our troubles was my father. He was a traveling salesman, like his father before him, but he could not seem to sell anything to anyone. I see him coming through the door carrying his latest booty: this time a burglar alarm system, a contraption with bells and red lights that we weren't allowed to touch. Another time brochures for steel Butler buildings, his latest hire. One day, when I was nine or so, he came in with a large black trunk and a funny expression on his face. Or maybe it was on my mother's face. We all gathered excitedly in the yellow-carpeted den, while he fiddled with the unfamiliar locks and openings. Then, for a few moments, as he bent over the trunk while we squirmed with anticipation, my father was a magician, and I thought anything possible of him. It was a wild thought I would never think again in my life, nor anything even close. It was open now. We strained for a better view as he straightened, now holding in his hands something red and filmy, see-through, with black lace and strange straps. Our eyes grew round—did we laugh? Then followed one after another—this one white, this one black, red again, each one flouncy and feathery, as light as air, as though made for flight: bras, underwear, suggestions of nightgowns. I knew nothing of these things, but I instinctively felt this show was dirty, a striptease act no less obscene for the invisibility of the women who would inhabit these non-clothes. I giggled behind my hand along with everyone else, but I was embarrassed, humiliated as I looked at my father, who held each object up for view with a smirk on his face. He was to take these store to store. I don't know how long that job lasted—probably only weeks, like many of the others. Between jobs, months, sometimes years went by without another.

In high school, I had heard of Arthur Miller's *Death of a Salesman* and the character of Willy Loman. I knew he was a pathetic figure, a weak failure of a man who could not sell enough to support his family. I thought of my father like this—a Willy Loman. Years later, when I saw the play for the first time, I knew there was no fit. My father appeared to have no goals for employment except to stay out on the road. The purpose of work, for him, seemed to be leaving home and spending the day or week out on the open road unencumbered by a harassing wife who needed money and six children who wished they had a father. He would never have gone into his bosses' office and fought for a raise, even fought for his job. He expressed no aspirations for his sons—or his daughters. And we did not, we could not, suspect him of cheap, on-the-road affairs. This for the same reasons he could not sell.

Though handsome, with a strong, square jaw and regular features, deeply tanned skin from his days driving in the sun, and a still athletic physique, there was something gravely deficient in his personality. He was empty somehow. He seldom gave eye contact, and when he did, it felt mocking. No matter the occasion, he chose to be alone most of the time. He had not a single friend for as long as any of us knew him. When present at home, his attention was saved for the newspaper or a book or magazine exclusively. He seldom conversed with us or my mother; his primary iterations were long readings from the paper, which he insisted we listen to. More than this, behind his brown eyes, there was a wall that seemed to flatten everyone in his gaze into an object. He radiated not malevolence—there seemed no premeditation in it—but absence, his muscled body, his handsome, expressionless face no more than a carapace sheltering a cavernous void. He had no apparent relationship with his wife, apart from siring six children. I suspect that he did not know our middle names, nor did he know our ages or grades. When my sister, ten, gave him an embroidery of a little sailboat she had made for his birthday, with all of us gathered to see this gift given, he looked at it for a moment, then tossed it in a drawer, saying, with genuine puzzlement, "What would I want this for?" Sometimes he tried to hug us, but the three of us girls did not want him to.

YEARS AFTER I left home, I found some of his writings from college. He had told me once that he had wanted to be a writer, and that he had been editor of his two-year business college newspaper. I was astounded, unable to imagine him in any leadership position, making any sort of decision. In another sense, though, I was not surprised. He had always been a reader. We had a good showing on our bookshelves, two hundred volumes, perhaps, many of them classics, most of them his. I felt as though I had grown up on his books, reading Tolstoy, Dostoevsky, Hemingway, Mann, Dickens. I never forgot that they were his—many of them had an elegant bookplate on the first page with his name carefully printed in a right-handed slant, "Howard S. Leyland." Mother occasionally said he was smart, that his IQ test score was high, but that was usually an accusation, a point of ridicule after he had done something wrong.

On one of my visits home, she came into the living room with a sardonic look on her face and an envelope in her hand.

"Here, Leslie, here's your father's work I found." She handed me a once-white, now yellowed folder, her mouth creased in distaste.

I was sitting on the couch. I took the folder hesitantly, not wanting to find out that he was an inept writer, or that he was more pathological than we all thought. But then, curiosity surged and I began to open the metal clasps.

"There's one in there I think you'll find interesting. About a young man at the beach. See if you recognize him. . . ." her voice trailed off as she left the room.

There wasn't much in the folder, a few editorials, a few short stories. I found the one set on the beach and began reading, almost fearfully. There were only two characters in the story, a young man, a not-even-disguised version of himself, and his wife, unnamed, with two unidentified little children. They had been at the beach all afternoon, and now the wife was leaving with the children, turning back and calling him to come. The man did not want to leave, and even more so now that she and the kids were gone. His feet were planted in the sand; he felt the sand pulling him back to quiet and safety as she walked off into the horizon, still calling him. And the story ended there. He had written this while in college, almost ten years before he married. It was all there already. My theory that the demands of wife and family somehow alienated a once-normal person, that he had slowly been changed by his failure as a salesman and as a husband was shot out of the water. Why had he married, then? And why did he have children, let alone six of them?

WORKING ON HOUSES, fixing and selling, was my mother's idea. Though she had trained and worked for a short while as a dental assistant before she was married, now, with all these children, it was impossible for her to return to work. But she could work at home. She was not intimidated by the fact that she had no experience in building and little experience with tools. Somehow, she simply began. It all started before I can remember. . . . by the time I was five, we had moved five times, from one town to another, my mother with four of us under five then. One place a little dairy farm, my mother and father milking the cows by hand and selling the milk. Then we lived in a country-club town, near outcasts, down a back road in a big yellow colonial. It was two hundred years old and the worse for its age. We lived there for five years, my mother managing six of us now, from ten years old to an infant, and working on the house every moment she could. She replaced the floors, using wooden pegs as nails, as the early colonial houses did. She scraped layers of old wallpaper and replastered and repapered every room in the twelve-room house, hoping she could sell it for a profit. By herself, and with such help as we gave, with some weekend help from my father, she completely rebuilt the house.

During those five years, somehow she was able to buy a series of small derelict houses in other towns—Gilmanton, Dunbarton, Barnstead, South Effingham—where we would go to work on weekends and during summers The six of us kids called each house by the name of the town. I remember one weekend at "Gilmanton," a house that sat sideways on a hill overlooking a lake. It was a center-chimney colonial that had been empty for years, too derelict to attract any buyers. This weekend we were replacing all the windows and painting the exterior. My job, at eight, was to scrape and repaint a stack of many-paned windows.

After that house was sold, we spent a few weekends at South Effingham. This house, unlike all the others, was not a colonial and had no historic value; it was a beach cottage off on a sandy road near a lake. We worked on that house through part of one summer, but not unhappily: the lake nearby had a beach, and if we had worked hard and the weather was good, we would go swimming. That was enough to move us through the longest, hottest day.

Dunbarton began as an adventure, but became our least favorite house. Uninhabited for years, standing alone on a dead-end dirt road, it had been entirely engulfed by vegetation. We all felt like jungle explorers the first time we came, whacking our way through to the doors, then the break-in to the mysterious interior. It was dark inside even on this sunny day, the rooms empty, cavernous, and cool. The six of us kids alternately ran, tiptoed, peeked from corner to corner, not knowing what we would find, excited at the secrecy of this house. "Look!" we heard Mother call, "Indian shutters!" They were the original ones, solid boards that pulled out from pockets beside the windows for protection when under Indian attack. It was a secret, magical place. But not for long. It was time for work. The machetes came out, one for each of us old enough to use them: Scott, Laurie, Jan, and I, in that order, ranging now from thirteen to eight, and then my mother and father. For the rest of that hot summer day, and for other summer days after, we were bent to the ground, sweat rolling off our faces, hacking at an immense stand of bamboo that towered over our heads. It grew so fast we could hardly keep up from week to another. Even as I cut it, I was sure its hollow stalks were shooting up behind me.

FINALLY, after several years with a "For Sale" sign staked in the front lawn, the yellow colonial sold. We promptly moved next door for the summer to a tiny house we called the Chicken House because it had been originally built to house scores of chickens. Four of us slept in one bedroom, two in another; my mother and father slept in the living room.

From there we moved an hour's drive north to a village of eight hundred and a 150-year-old Cape set on a high hill. We worked hard on the house, restoring it to some form of its original luster. Because we couldn't afford to hire out any work, my mother learned to do it all herself: plumbing, wiring, masonry, finish carpentry. I never knew what tool I would see in my mother's hand from day to day: a shovel, a chainsaw, a tape measure, a hammer, a trowel. . . . Though small, five-foot-four and not much over one hundred pounds, it seemed she could do anything she set her mind to do.

The best feature of this house was an add-on wing that allowed me, for the first time, to have my very own bedroom. The wing wasn't heated, though, so it was intended for summers only. I stretched the season as far as the blankets on my bed allowed, on into October, the temperature dropping lower and lower. When I tired of seeing my breath and shivering into my clothes each morning, I reluctantly moved back to the pitched-roof room in the main house with my two sisters.

It was there in my summer room that I began to try to pray. It was there, in that house, that I began to need to pray. There was something missing in my life. Not mine only, it seemed to me, as though my life were singularly defective, but the world I could see through my eyes felt flat, two-dimensional, like an elaborately decorated screen that, if I tried, I could surely pull back to reveal . . . I didn't know what. One veil had already been rent. In this house, the six of us came to know about our financial woes: the bank was about to repossess the house; our money from the sale of the last house was nearly gone; my father disappeared after taking the last bit of money left in the bank that we were living on, to rebuild the engine in his car so he could make his getaway. Mother was in school at the time, training to be an occupational therapist's assistant. Groceries, always thin, got sparser and sparser. The early childhood belief that adults were in charge, that they held the world in their strong, broad hands, and that nothing bad could ever happen to us—was gone. If no happy-ever-after, then what? Surely there was something more. Was it God? Whatever it was, it hovered near me, behind me; I could feel it sometimes just at my back, and if I turned around fast enough, it would still be there, the rest of the world, the pieces, the fullness of what was missing. I felt certain that if I tried hard enough, I could have access to this other place. But I didn't know how. I lay awake many nights, looking up at my ceiling, sending up urgent prayers for my father to get a job, for the house to sell, for Mother to be happy, for things to be right. One prayer was answered—the house eventually sold after three years on the market.

WE MOVED ON, this time to a 175-year-old colonial, another center-chimney, near the end of a maze of back roads in another town. Though we were immeasurably thankful to leave the other town behind to start afresh, and though we loved our new surroundings—open fields and pristine woods with not another house in view—this house was the worst of all of them. It had been thoroughly Victorianized in the late 1800s and nothing was more anathema to my mother than the Victorian architecture she had grown up with. Our first task was to jack the house up and replace a rotten sill, which my mother had discovered to her dismay when tearing up the old floor. For weeks we had no kitchen floor and balanced about on joists, with the dirt cellar underneath us. For months after, the outside wall was only partially repaired, since we had run out of money already. There were holes in the walls as it snowed. We sat around our only heat, a woodstove in the kitchen, with blankets wrapped around our heads.

Over my high school years, on weekends, and when we got home from school, we worked under mother's charge and changed all the windows in the house, tore off a front porch, knocked down walls built later to add more rooms, tore off the plaster that sealed off the three original fireplaces, scraped and steamed off seven layers of wallpaper in each room, laid new wood floors or sanded the old ones down, put up Sheetrock, and taped and painted it. The house was restored gradually, with no joy or even relief. There were discoveries along the way that punctuated our work with excitement: a massive front-step rock found when tearing down the porch with the date 1795 and the initials "J.P." carved into it; a beam with "1795" etched into its grain; under the wallpaper, in the dining room, original stencilings called "poor man's wallpaper" of birds and weeping willows, their colors still faintly discernible; the original brick bake oven beside the six-foot brick fireplace, all found behind the thickly plastered walls. But the house's authenticity extended too far—it had no insulation. Each of those four years, as winter approached, the work slowed, then stopped as the winter cold moved in. Our single heat source remained the one woodstove set in the kitchen/great room. We never had the money to put in a furnace. The bedrooms, and every room but the kitchen, were not appreciably warmer than the outside. We slept under piles of sleeping bags, took hot bricks from the stove up to bed with us on the coldest nights, wore hats, mittens, scarves, and two pairs of socks and buried ourselves underneath our covers every night with just our noses sticking out. Those cold mornings, I was so grateful to leave for school, where I could spend the day in a heated building. As I slid behind the wheel of my 1964 station wagon—the "goat barn," because we sometimes used it to transport our goats—I would think guiltily of Mother alone in the cold house with nowhere to go for warmth but bed.

There were times when we resented and resisted her push, when we wanted most to be like other families, but we knew it was not possible. It helped us knowing that what she required of us, she required of herself, at the least. The almost monastic austerity of our living conditions—our clothes, rooms, and table—were hers as well. She allowed herself no luxury except a single quarter-pound block of butter she rationed to last a week to flavor her bread and cereal.

When spring and summer came, we reveled in the warmth, but then the work began again in earnest, now converting the wing of the house, which had been a stable and outhouse, into a family room. When not working there, we spent hours out in the half-acre garden, from which we froze and canned our winter's supply of vegetables. Beginning in the summer and later, during the fall weekends, we moved into the woods to our own land, where we chainsawed down maples, birch, oak, sawing and stacking them into an old truck, then to our shed, working from morning until the summer light faded. On sunny days, when the fields were dry and the grass long, my mother joined us out in the hayfield mowing and raking a winter supply of feed for our ten goats. We didn't have a tractor, and had no money to buy one no matter what the vintage, so my younger brother Todd and older brother, Scott, rigged up a Leyland special, the engine and hood of our father's old Mercedes with the back half of a wood wagon attached. We hand-scythed the hay or used a walk-behind sickle bar, then returned later to fork it up into our "tractor." We laughed at our contraption and were glad we lived so far out. No one would see it. If they did, perhaps they would begin to guess the truth. It served as the perfect symbol for our lives. Outside we wore the veneer of the middle and upper class: my mother drove a black Mercedes; our dog was not a spaniel or a mutt but a Russian wolfhound; we lived in a gorgeous-appearing house. Yet, the reality: the Mercedes was six years old, haggled down to less than $3,000; we had only purebred dogs as pets in case we needed to sell them; our house was below freezing five months of the year; our food was painfully doled out; and we spent much of our time, when our friends were playing and going to movies, out in the fields and woods, in the house, working.

6

Falling Off the Face

I WAS PROFOUNDLY GRATEFUL TO HAVE made it through my first fishing season; I was equally grateful to leave. After two days spent in a series of airplanes, Bear Island felt a continent away, and my other life began. As soon as Duncan and I returned to Cedarville College for our last year, the school year of 1979 to 1980, I began to shed my first fishing season from my body as quickly as I could. I saw the other women wearing dresses, heels, mincing daintily about campus. Forgetting my own similar attire, I felt moments of disdain for their exaggerated femininity, but as I walked from class to class, trying not to swagger, I didn't like the way I looked either: my clothes swelled taut with too much work, muscles I didn't need now. For the next nine months, I'd be carrying only books—not fish, not nets, not heavy boxes and lumber up steep beaches. Just paper.

THE YEAR PASSED QUICKLY as Duncan and I lived out packed schedules and too many classes, trying to fill in the gaps we had overlooked in the last two years of indiscriminately indulging our curiosities and mental hungers. Finally, in May, we stood outside the chapel in our graduation gowns.

"So, what are you two doing now?" Duncan's friend Dale asked as we posed for another photo. I was anxious to get this over with, the whole day, the graduation dinner, the baccalaureate. I felt mostly embarrassment at the ceremony, though I had worked tirelessly and obsessively through my four years and was graduating magna cum laude. I wasn't accustomed to celebrating and didn't know how.

"We're going to live out next year," Duncan replied. Then, seeing Dale's blank look, "Out on our island, you know, where we fish, in Alaska."

"Oh, yeah!" he replied finally. He quickly looked over at me in my makeup, heels, and nylons, checking to see if this was all right with me. He knew I was an English major, devout in my studies.

I smiled and said, "Yes, for a year at least."

"Oh, gee, that sounds romantic." He glowed now, relieved that this was a joint venture. "But what will you do out there?"

"Just survive, probably, try to keep warm," Duncan said, serious. "How about you? You going to go for your CPA?"

"Yeah, but I've been thinking about law school. Well," as he turned to go, "have a good, uh, live-in, whatever!"

OUR FRIENDS were going on to graduate school, to seminary, to jobs as teachers, pastors, commercial artists and musicians, and we, Duncan with a degree in history and social science with a teaching certificate, and me with a degree in English and minor in biblical studies and Greek, we were going on to "living out," shorthand for living out in the bush. We would work through another fishing season, and then stay the winter at Bear Island. Those who didn't know us well had their suspicions confirmed: we were out of step, definitely. No career or education or ministry advancement or experience. Off the racetrack. It was as good as falling off the face of the earth. It posed an interesting question: What would happen if suddenly you just stepped out of your life, walked away from everything and everyone you knew, if you were just—gone? That was not our question, that was not the experiment, and yet, I thought of it.

I had felt that same sensation every day from sixth grade on. When school was out for the day, then out for the summer, and my brothers and sisters and I returned to our house, it felt to me like stepping off a high building, with vertigo all the way down. It was a disappearing act performed twice daily, emerging in the morning from the dark door frame of our huge colonial house, then a long walk to the bus stop on the dirt road, then after school, waiting to find a ride or way home. Once home, at the end of the dirt road, we would see no one from our other life. No one was welcome; no one ever came—we were too embarrassed by our deconstructed house. The two worlds were distinct, which saved us in some ways, but left me feeling lonely and invisible. This year on Bear Island would be different, I hoped.

MY MOTHER was not happy with our plan. "You're going to stay out, alone? Just the two of you? Why?" my mother asked pointedly.

"A couple of reasons. We're saving money for traveling next year—"

"Where are you going?"

"We're not sure yet. Somewhere in Asia. But if we stay out, we can save enough money to go for the whole year. We won't have many expenses at the island. And we're building a house. If we don't stay over, we'll never get it done. There's no time in the summers."

"What if something happens? There's no one there to help."

"We'll take care of it," I responded, trying not to sound ignorant and blithe, but competent.

"No, I mean something serious, like when you're working on the house," she continued. I knew what she was talking about. I was five or six, playing out on the lawn with my sisters, with the whine of the power saw in the background. Suddenly we heard terrifying screams, and then saw Mother running out of the shed next to the house holding her hand, still screaming while thick blood streamed down her arm. Her fingers were hanging, the blood pumping out. She fell to her knees, curled up with her head between her knees, the hand, still held in the air, blood everywhere, rocking back and forth. My father was there, unruffled. He drove her to the emergency room, and because she was crying, he would not be seen with her once he got there, embarrassed by her emotional display. She nearly lost three of her fingers. They had been sewn back on but they weren't the same. I remembered probably more than she knew.

"We've got a good first aid book, there's a Health Aide in the village, and we can call the Coast Guard if we need to. Other people live out too, Mother. We're not the only ones," I said, trying to be reassuring.

"Well, I suppose it's not much different than when you're out there for fishing. Still, you've got to be so careful! Well, write me." She sighed, and then she didn't say any more. She knew it was pointless.

STAYING THE WINTER was not a good idea to anyone, though. No one in Duncan's family had ever spent the winter on the island. They were not thrilled. There was plenty of substance to the warnings. We were young; Duncan was twenty-three and I was twenty-two. I was inexperienced. We would be completely isolated, the nearest person eight miles away by water. There was no technology for telephones out there; the nearest was eight miles away by water, again, to the village, where one hundred people shared a single phone in the Community Center. Our only real voice to the outside world would be through mail, which we retrieved once every seven to ten days, since it was such a major expedition. We would catch a lot of winter weather there on the Shelikof Strait, our backyard, the 40-mile-wide and 200-mile-long stretch of water between the west side of Kodiak Island and the Alaska Peninsula. Both sides are flanked by mountains: on the Peninsula side, 2,000-to-3,000-foot mountains lift straight up from water, and behind these, another range that escalates to 12,000 feet. On the Kodiak side, mountains from 1,000 to 4,000 feet line the Strait. The result, a 40-mile tunnel that corrals winds, chutes them into velocities that spin our wind gauge to the hurricane mark several times a year.

We'd have to carefully plan our food, fuel, and medical needs for the year, as well as our building supplies. For food, we would stock up with cased goods on a last run from town in the fall, prompting profound discussions on cornmeal, oatmeal, barley, baking powder: How much would we eat in a year's time? How many cases of canned peas should we order, if any? (Duncan voted two, I said none; we ordered one.) How many varieties of beans did we need for a decent pot of chili? In addition to those staples, I'd make my own bread, yoghurt, sprouts; we'd have deer, fish, and our cattle there for meat; we had hens for eggs, and anything else we'd either do without or make do with what the little village store had. For fuel, we had 55-gallon drums of number-two oil for our oil stove, three drums of gasoline for the outboard, and three drums of diesel for our generator, all of it brought out with the tender from Kodiak, along with all our building materials.

We felt little concern about these logistics. Duncan had planned and lived by such estimations every summer and some falls since he was four years old. And I had a taste of it from my first summer. We were not planning on suffering any extreme deprivations; this wasn't some kind of dare, or test, man against wilderness. It was much more important than that.

ON SEPTEMBER 2, 1979, we stood on Bear Island's stony beach waving the last family off to their other jobs and selves, the second half of their schismed lives now reclaiming them: Weston to the seminary in Indiana where he taught Greek and Hebrew; Beverly to her life as mother, musician, and poet; Wallace back to college; DeWitt and Wanda to Kodiak where he longshored, ran cattle, and where Wanda taught piano, and would finish her twentieth and final year of teaching second grade. They were loaded now in the skiff with the garbage bags and boxes that always comprised our luggage out here, and we stood there, waving, feeling as though we were the ones on a voyage, we were the ones with our white handkerchiefs out, fluttering them in a last good-bye before our ocean crossing. The skiff faded into its own wake, and that was it, we were alone, utterly alone to navigate this island through every day of the next nine months, until they all returned for the next salmon season.

"Okay, where do we start?' I asked, putting my arm around

Duncan. I felt giddy, free; released from the schedule of salmon and openings/closings/net mendings. I could do anything I wanted, a hundred thousand things and all of them possible on this sixty-acre, empty, treeless island. We were Adam and Eve, and this was paradise.

"Let's move into Mom and Dad's house now." His arm was over my shoulders as we walked up to his parents' cabin.

"That won't take long. We've only got about four boxes of stuff up in the loft, and then our books." Then I stopped and took his hands into mine. "We get to start all over, Duncan," I said, suddenly serious, staring meaningfully into his eyes.

He sighed. "Yeah, I know. This wasn't a great summer, Leslie. But we made it through. And if it weren't for all those fish, we couldn't be here this year, and we wouldn't be able to even think about traveling next year. It was worth it."

I was silent, not knowing what to say. He didn't know, he had no idea what it had cost me. And I couldn't think about it now, or even this winter.

"I don't know, Duncan. I just want this winter to be good for us." I was determined not to spoil the months before us. It would be best to try and forget the season behind me. Though we had taken a few days to rest, one of them when we skiffed around the bay visiting other fishcamps, my second season here hadn't been appreciably different from the first. And little wonder—nothing had changed. There were still only five of us trying to manage too many nets.

One of the last take-ups, when we pulled all our nets from the water, had been one of the worst. It was blowing about 20. We had five nets to take up; the last three nets had filled with fish the one time they weren't wanted, just as we were pulling them. We had no extra time to deal with them, and had had to haul in nets and fish and kelp and all as fast as our fatigued arms could drag the whole mess in. My job was to pull the inside webbing and then pick the fish instantly as they came in to make room for the rest of the net. Under this pressure, and after picking two skiffs full of fish with Duncan just a few hours before, my hands were in no shape for this action. Picking fish requires a pinching and grasping motion, done with a rapidity and repetition that leave the hands stiff and weak after just several hours. It was the early and temporary stages of carpal tunnel syndrome. Weston, later, would lose the use of both his hands, necessitating a painful, slow-healing operation on both wrists.

"Grab that line!" Duncan shouted. "No, not that one, the yellow one! If we go over it, we'll twist the net completely. Get it!! Leslie, get those fish there. Hurry! We've only got twelve minutes left!"

I couldn't get them. They were balled up hopelessly, and my fingers wouldn't work anymore. "I can't," I said, both apologetic and angry at the same time.

"Get out of the way, then. Take the leads while I get these fish. See if you can do that," he shot at me.

We made it on time, as I knew we would, just from sheer push from Duncan. I had already seen that no matter how impossible the situation, Duncan would do what needed to be done out of will alone.

After the nets were in the skiff, we pitched all the fish into two empty skiffs, bending to the skiff floor, grasping them by the tail, one in each hand, and flinging them over two by two, bending and flinging some 300 times for 600 fish. It was dark by then. We had five skiffs and five people. "Leslie, can you run this skiff up to the island?" Duncan had asked. We were down on Russian Dick's set beach and needed to run all the skiffs the two miles back to the island. After two summers, I had run the skiff lots of times, in the dark as well, but not loaded this low in a NE blow with miles to travel. But what could I say? The only other possibility was for one loaded skiff to tow another, a far more dangerous proposition. "Okay." I sighed, feeling pressed from all sides but not knowing any way out. I stepped reluctantly into the "Humpy Hearse," heavy with three nets mounded in its length. "Just follow Wallace if you can't see!" Duncan shouted as last instructions. Engines all around revved, and I could just make out the other skiffs as they pushed forward. I joined the train at the last, following the spume of wake that glowed white behind the skiff in front of me. I stood in the stern as I drove, as all of us do, to see over the bow as we travel. Though I was exhausted, every sense was on overdrive, listening to the drone of the engines ahead of me, trying to trace their outlines in the black air, watching for rocks and kelp patches that signal rocks, wondering the stage of the tide and if we would try to make it through the spit or if we had to go around the back side of Bear Island. The answer came a few minutes later. Though the wind was blowing away from me, I heard the skiffs circling up ahead and heard Weston yell, "Can't make it through the spit. Go around!" "Thank you, Lord," I whispered, relieved from the dread of threading through a cut in the spit in this dark. We turned and made the longer trip around the island. As I came in close to the beach, behind another skiff, my stomach sunk—they were taking the skiffs onto the back beach rather than the front. I hated that back beach.

"Leslie!" I heard someone shout over the wind. "Bring the skiff in here! In here!!" Then someone turned on a spotlight, and I saw it was Duncan waving his arms wildly at me, signaling me into this unfamiliar landing.

I had been relatively fine up until then. Though stressed, the task had been manageable, but now, I had to find my way in there. I knew it just well enough to know there were rocks everywhere just below the water, huge boulders, and sharp pinnacled rock to the right of the larger one I could see, but how far away was it? Even at high tide, we only came in here occasionally, watching for the rocks every second.

"It's too much!" I shook my head angrily. "Why do they ask so much of me? It's not fair! I don't know the way in there!" I voiced, furious, the wind grabbing my words and dispersing them, empty. It was never right: Either I was the initiate who was patronized, or I was asked to do far more than my experience warranted. I throttled down and tried to idle in carefully, but the wind was stronger than I realized. It was pushing me back out into the deeper waters, away from the light. Then, because I had throttled down too far, my engine quit. Quick, as I started to drift back out, I palmed the shift back into neutral, then pulled the cord as if I had a single pull to start it—and it did. I nosed back in carefully again, stomach churning, my hands locked on the throttle, trying to balance enough speed to move against the wind but also to keep control as I moved through the rocks, hoping desperately I would not hit them.

"This way! No, you're going too far!" Duncan screamed over the wind. "No! No! You're going to hit those rocks! Don't you know anything? Come in here!" Duncan was frantic, his arms pointing a path I couldn't see and didn't know, as the wind kept blowing me off course. I was completely disoriented in the dark, with the spotlight, and a night far too long. Now others were yelling and waving at me above the wind. I couldn't see their faces, just dark bodies running and voices shouting and it was some kind of nightmare that part of me stood outside and watched.

I made it in finally, after hitting the rocks, gouging a solid ding in the prop. When I trudged up to the loft, I felt dead inside, not just my body.

I DIDN'T UNDERSTAND IT, this slavery to an occupation that consumed all of us, even those ashore working to support those on the water, demanding everything a person possesses, every muscle twitch and fiber, every ounce of perseverance. Who made up this work? Who decided that we should stick our puny hands into the massive currents of ocean and salmon and try to tame it, to snare and wrest it all in with skin-thin nets? It seemed such audacity, and yet my new family was doing it. Others were doing it. I was doing it. But for how long? How long could I survive this single devotion?

But now, a whole winter here without fishing. We'd be keeping our own schedule. And what could be better than building together, something I knew about, and creating our own kitchen and bedroom, where we could cook our own meals, eat alone together, and sleep in sheets instead of sleeping bags? I would find a way for us to *live* here on this island, more than just fish. Surely if we built a house, we would find a way to live in it.

WE WERE EXCITED about building our own house, but nervous about proposing it to the family. Our plans represented a major expansion to the island and operation. Except for Weston's house, the other buildings—a smokehouse for smoking salmon, a banya, a gear shed for storage of buoys, lines, and anchors, Duncan's parent's cabin—were either the old original buildings here when DeWitt bought the place in 1960, or Duncan and his brothers and parents themselves had built them out of driftwood and washed-up logs from the beach. It represented a major expense for the family since all the buildings were financed by the fishing operation and therefore all costs were shared. We were proposing another building, a sizable one, and this one entirely new.

"Leslie, I've got it! I know how we'll build our house!" Duncan said excitedly one afternoon at the end of our first summer.

"What? What are you thinking?" I said cautiously.

"We need a workshop area, right? Someplace to keep our tools and paints and all our maintenance stuff. We'll build a two-story building, have the upstairs be our place and the downstairs the workshop. That way we'll get two things we need at once!" Duncan was ecstatic.

"That sounds like a good idea. What do you think everyone else will say?"

"I think they'll like it. They won't mind paying for a building that everyone will get to use. Besides, we don't need a whole house to ourselves when we're out fishing all the time anyway! It's just the two of us," Duncan persuaded.

I liked the idea. I wanted to walk softly with my new family, and yet I didn't want to replicate Weston's and Bev's marital history on the island. They had shifted around for five seasons, from one shed to another, from a bed on the floor in the gear shed, to a one-room shack on a lagoon thick with bears. When their house was finally built one slow fishing season, it then took seven years of slicing time from the fishing to make it livable. I had grown up that way, moving from place to place, eating in dirty sawdust, using a sawhorse for a kitchen table, and I wanted no more of it. We would build the house, finish it over the winter, and be done.

AS WE MOVED our few boxes into Wanda and DeWitt's house, we felt like we should be whispering or tiptoeing, or looking around our shoulder for someone disapproving. But this had all been arranged, that we would live here in the only finished and livable space on Bear Island while we worked on our upstairs apartment. The goal was to be done by next fishing season. It was a modest goal; it would not take us the entire winter, so we would have time for other pursuits. I had an idea for a novel I wanted to write, and had a whole notebook of poems that were percolating toward some kind of finish. Duncan and I both had brought up boxes of books from college that we'd been anxious to read, all the "should-have," "ought-to" read books we hadn't had time for. I was determined to keep up my Greek, after investing two intensive years of language study; Duncan had a collection of history and theology books he meant to digest from the bookstore he ran from our college apartment.

I didn't know what to expect from winter here. Duncan had told me about the dark, that on the shortest days, it wouldn't get light in the morning until nine thirty or ten, and that on cloudy days, which was most of the time, it would get dark again by three thirty or four. I looked forward to the dark, and watched attentively as each day faded sooner, so that by November we were losing five minutes of light a day. This was the price, of course, of long, long summer days lit past midnight, and only then did night blink, once, it seemed, just a hazy dusk before light again at 3:00. It was a fair exchange, I thought, going into it. Just hang until December 21, and then the hourglass is flipped and light spills the other way.

We would not have a lot of snow, probably, Duncan forewarned, knowing I liked snow and the turning of New Hampshire's four distinct seasons. It was different here at this far north latitude because of the Japanese current, a wide, warm swath of air and water that circulates around the Gulf of Alaska, melting the snows from the arctic air that finds its way down as well. The Japanese current blurred the lines between seasons, made the calendars and their pronouncements of the arrival of fall, spring, summer, something to joke about:

"Duncan, it's the first day of spring. What's the temperature?"

"Uhhh, it's forty degrees, same as yesterday."

Three months later, we say it again. "Today's the first day of summer, June twenty-first. Can you believe it?"

"Well, it's warming up. Look, it's forty-four degrees," Duncan would say, mock defensively, somehow feeling responsible for the weather.

Fall came fast after the brief summer, making a dramatic and symbolic entrance the first week of September as it does nearly every year, with gale-force winds corresponding to the biggest tides of the season. After that, snow, hail, rain, a brief Indian summer—anything was possible all the way through the calendar until the end of May, when it was fairly safe to cross snow off the list.

Still, even without subzero temperatures, fall was cold enough. Cold enough to feel the damp and chill through layers of thermals and wool pants and wool shirts and parkas when outside. The air always felt wet. The six-hundred-square-foot cabin, though small enough, could not keep out the chill. Heat from the oil stove stayed huddled in the kitchen, unwilling to turn the corner to the other two rooms. Our year's worth of canned food up in the loft would freeze without better heat, and our chickens, our winter egg suppliers, would freeze as well. Our first task was to build a sturdy chicken house, then to pull out a window from the outside wall of the living/dining room and mount a wood stove on a temporary brick hearth in the middle of the room, where the dining table used to be.

We settled into a comfortable routine almost immediately. With a wood stove now, we needed a ready supply of fuel. The beaches were bountiful. Logs of cottonwood, fir, pine, spruce, even cedar found our shores and the shorelines around us regularly, an unending supply just floating in, drifting in with the currents. This was even more amazing to me than the schools of salmon running the currents past our island—they still had to be caught. The wood washed up steadily with no lure or connivance of our own. Every trip in the skiff, regardless of its first purpose, served for log hunting.

"Leslie, do you see that log over there, the yellowish one? Does that look like cedar?" Duncan directs to my ear, his arm out. We're on the way back from a supply trip to Larsen Bay.

I follow his pointing finger to a splintered log bumped up among the rocks of a knobby beach. There's a tumble of wood, smooth and whitened like bones, cluttered around it, along this whole beach, in fact. But we're looking for bigger quarry, like this. "I don't know my woods that well, Duncan. It looks like a really good one, though. Doesn't look like many knots."

"Okay, let's get it. You let me off on the beach and I'll tie the line to it."

"You're sure we can pull it off? It's awfully far up the beach." I hesitate. "Why don't we come back at high tide and get it then?"

"By the time we pass by here again, it could be gone. Someone from Larsen Bay or Karluk could come by and snag it for their wood stove. I'm sure I can get it down to the water. Okay, take me in!"

I wonder briefly where this confidence comes from and how to obtain it. Duncan believes in machines far more than I do. We switch positions in the skiff, me taking the handle of the kicker, Duncan stepping to the bow with the coil of line we always keep in the skiff. It's dead flat today, no breaking surf to speak of— perfect log-hunting conditions, except for the stage of the tide. I idle in until Duncan leaps out, always smooth, without a splash. ("Think like a seal," he told me the first time I had to leap out in hipboots to slow the skiff as it hit the beach.) I reverse the skiff into deeper waters while he ties an anchor hitch, a simple knot that won't pull out, about two feet from the end. He's done. I slow back in, he hoists himself in and ties a double-clove hitch in the skiff, and the tug of war begins. In a single twist of the wrist, the kicker spits us forward, the line stretches taut, the log sits, the engine whines higher, spinning a tornado under the skiff, and just when I think the engine will self-destruct, the metal parts zinging off into space, the log lifts slightly, slides, bounces off the rock in front of it, rolls, then plows the gravel as it heads straight for the water, and it's launched.

We found another, a fir log, and then a creosote piling, a real prize. We labored back to the island with a long raft behind us, as happy for the wood as we'd feel for the meat from other hunts. At the highest point of the tide, we beached them, then pulled them just past the highest tide mark with the tractor to ensure they were ours for keeps. We worked them at our leisure then, between other jobs, or as a late-afternoon activity—Duncan with the chainsaw snarling them into stackable rounds, then me swinging the maul, cracking the wood into fresh wedges. When thinking through the winter, we had not planned on this extra labor, but it was not onerous. It was work I had done for years at home, and I could feel my back and arms strengthening daily.

Most of our other needs did not change significantly from our summer routine. The water was still hauled in on our shoulders from the well, a level 100-foot walk straight out the door. The outhouse was farther, a good hike, some 300 feet, and continued to serve us well. Nothing to break down there. For electricity we had a generator, the "light plant," which we turned on as late as possible each day to conserve fuel. I washed weekly in an old wringer washer, hanging the clothes out on the cold lines. We wore the same clothes for days, until the jeans had memorized and recorded our every bend and move, and our shirts and sweatshirts wore the fruit and stains of all our labors: sawdust, flour, paint, mud.

We had expected to continue our summer bathing routine in the banya, a weekly steam bathing ritual (named and lent by the Russians in their colonial days) we used in the summers, but it was too wasteful. In the chilled fall winds, it took far too much of our wood supply to keep the entire building warm, so we moved our once-weekly head-to-toe bathing into the house. In the morning of the designated bath day, we put the aluminum tub I used for rinsing laundry on top of the oil stove in the kitchen and hauled six buckets of water to fill it. It took hours to heat, but by evening, it would be steaming deliciously. We would wash in another aluminum tub set on the floor. Not complete immersion, though. If I scrunched, I could fit all of me into a compressed circle, but most of the time, like Duncan, I tented my knees over the sides with my feet on the floor.

Sometimes after a bath, I would look at my face in the mirror. I was struck by how young I looked, how boyish and plain without makeup, how at twenty-two I looked no different from the girl who grew up in those New Hampshire houses. In fact, no different from a photo my mother had sent me, taken six years earlier when I was in high school. My younger brother Todd and I were standing in the hayfield, each chewing on a piece of grass like a gangster, arms on our pitchforks, looking away in profile. I was wearing a cut-off tank top and cut-off frayed jeans that showed tanned, muscled legs and well-biceped arms. My hair was back, the ends hanging sloppily around my face, just the way I wore my hair now. The message was clear: Don't mess with me! Todd, next to me, held the same pose, but he was spindly, skinny back then. I was the one to be reckoned with. It was a joke, of course, Ma and Pa cutthroat farmers at work in the bitter fields.

I had tacked the photo over my desk at college as a reminder of my former life. I didn't look much like that then. The college had a dress code that made us all look like pastors or corporate professionals or Southern belles, depending on personal style and interpretation: during class hours, dresses or skirts for the women, slacks and collared shirts for the men. I never complained about the dress code, though others, particularly the women, did. Dresses and nylons had been a form of both rebellion and disguise for me since high school. At home, while we worked, and for the preservation of our school clothes, we wore ill-fitting out-of-style jeans, ripped shirts, clothes we would be ashamed to be seen in by anyone. At school, then, when most from the blue-collar town wore patched hip-hugger bell-bottomed jeans and body suits, with little or no makeup for the natural look, I fought back with mascara and eyeshadow, with skirts, jumpers, blouses, sweaters, whatever I could find and alter to fit from the clearance racks of Kmart. Since I really couldn't sew, it was a cooperative effort between my sisters, a tin of safety pins, which held an amazing number of outfits together, and my mother's twenty-year-old Elna sewing machine. Because of our sleight of hand, and because I was a good student and did not party, or swear or engage in the other visible vices of high schoolers in the seventies, we were enviously and sometimes resentfully viewed as offspring of a rich and highly cultured family.

The deception was complete, though not entirely intended. Only my biology teacher, Mr. Carlson, suspected. During our three-hour labs once a week, he drove us out to local rivers and lakes, where, under his direction, we gathered data for an environmental profile of the area. One winter my sophomore year, we took ice core samples on a lake. It was bitter cold this day, in the low teens with a crisp, biting wind. I was wearing my only coat, a thin, mustard-colored men's golfing jacket, which the label indicated since it had a logo of a man and a set of clubs. For some reason when my mother took us shopping that year at Mammoth Mills, a giant five-and-dime with creaky wooden floors serpentined in an old mill building, I was insistent in choosing that for my coat. It was too big, and it was meant for spring, not a New Hampshire winter. For those three hours out on the lake, I shivered quietly, hugging my coat to myself as inconspicuously as possible and trying to work. I had brought neither hat nor gloves, so keeping warm became a full-time concern, yet I didn't want to call attention to myself. Mr. Carlson saw me, though, near the end of the field trip.

"Leslie! Are you cold? Well, no wonder! Why are you wearing such a thin coat on a day like this?" he chided. "Here, you need this," and he took off his neon orange–ruffed hat and plunked it on my head.

I was deeply embarrassed, yet grateful for the hat. "Thanks," I muttered. It would have to be orange, I thought. Like wearing a billboard.

Later the next day, when I was taking a makeup exam in his classroom, he came over to me. After a preamble, he said softly, "Must be pretty cold at home, huh? I guess you don't have any heat."

"We have a wood stove," I responded defensively, feeling exposed and embarrassed again. How did he know? Then I guessed. The other biology teacher, Mr. Kallgren, lived down the road from us and sometimes gave us a ride home. He probably knew. Mr. Carlson, thankfully, didn't pursue it any further. I was glad that he knew, somehow.

The disguise continued into college, though it was more difficult yet. After paying tuition, room, and board, I had just enough money to slide into the washing machine slots once a week, and then enough left over for one pack of gum from the bookstore, the five pieces rationed to last the week. Yet somehow I pulled my wardrobe and toilet together enough to be viewed as a contender in the college female parade. I would forget about the chasm between my house in New Hampshire and college in Ohio until friends visited my sparse, undecorated dorm room and wandered over to my desk. They'd see the photo, laugh out loud, then "who's this?" Then the double-take: "Leslie! Is that you?" The response from anyone who saw it, particularly men, was the same—disbelieving. I would say impatiently, "Yes, of course that's me," marveling at that person's simplicity, as if I or anyone else had only one way of dressing, one way of moving about in the world.

THE HIGHLIGHT of our week was mail day, which was whatever day within a six-to-ten-day span that met several criteria: Our work needed to be at a stopping place; the weather had to be calm; and we had to need to go. "Need" in this case meant not any external imperatives, such as paying bills or returning polite responses to relatives and friends; "need" meant a compelling hunger to confirm the existence of the rest of the world, and that that world had not forgotten us altogether. Our mail was voluminous. We subscribed to about thirty journals and publications, but among those, the real treasure was letters from friends, from my mother, from former college classmates and professors who had extended their homes and friendship to us. The first month of our sojourn, we would look quickly through the mail as we dropped it from our post office box into the black plastic garbage bag, and disciplined, we'd seal it tight with a twister and ride home, even more awake to the gulls and terns, the puffins, murres, and bald eagles swinging around us because of that hard, bright spot within, that letters awaited. Later, as winter settled on us, my discipline wavered, until finally I would tear into the letters and devour them the whole way back, blind to the water, the sea otters, and dolphins, whatever swam or flew past.

"Listen, Duncan! Dan and Martha are going to have a book published!" I reported this day, glancing up appreciatively to Duncan, who stood behind me on task with the kicker.

"Wow, that's great. Let me see. What do they say?" He glances down at the letter in my hand as I start reading, shifting from water to paper, then back again as we find the details.

Next I open the one from Ron Grosh, my English professor/ mentor. "Ah, Ron says some of the faculty are retiring early next year."

"Who, does he say?" Duncan asks, his voice above the engine.

Then a letter from Pete and Kathy. They were in seminary and thriving. Peter and Diane sent us a picture of them with their baby; they all looked deliriously happy. Dave and Sue were settling into the pastorate in a little farming community in Ohio; their congregation was growing rapidly. What were we missing by being here? What would our professors, our friends, my family say to see us here, wrapped to our noses, plowing along a cold ocean in a tiny skiff, me holding a letter with hands pinched into my jacket sleeves, my face sometimes greased with Vaseline as protection from the wind; Duncan bearded, in fat clothes and thigh-high boots. They would not have recognized us. Did they even think of us at all? I wanted them to know we were not dropping out, that we hadn't fallen off the face of the earth, that we meant something by living here; it was not an escape, or an excuse. I wanted my brothers and sisters to know that I was not here on this island in hiding, as my siblings and I had been at the end of the road all those years. Though I was wearing the same clothes, that same bare tomboy face, this was not a fall.

There were other places to stand and move. I could be here on an empty island in Alaska with Duncan, invisible to the former worlds we had lived and moved in—college, libraries, museums, churches, conferences, the worlds I cared about—but still students and artists and engineers of another way of living. And most amazing of all, in God's Providence, I knew how to live that way already. I knew what kind of clothes to wear, how to wear a plain face and messy hair, how to work and not stop or rest until the job was done; I knew how to carry water, how to live outside. . . . Surely it was possible to inhabit wholly different worlds, and move and step between them gracefully, without a fall.

7

Killing and Eating

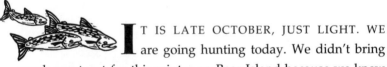 I T IS LATE OCTOBER, JUST LIGHT. WE are going hunting today. We didn't bring much meat out for this winter on Bear Island because we knew we could easily get deer. This morning, the fog still wisps the air, lisping over the calm waters. It is hard to get up. We briefly reconsider, knowing we could go tomorrow or the next day or the next, but this morning is calm, and we will need meat soon. There's not much for preparation, just dress warmly, pull on hip boots and life jacket over our coats, check the gas tank, get the rifle, pull the skiff in, start the engine, and we will be hunting. It is hunting mostly in the sense of looking very carefully as we parallel the shoreline, eyes skinning the beach for the stray deer or two that has wandered down to munch on kelp and sea greens. Sometimes we will see whole herds, huge bachelor packs of thirty to seventy that rove the long beaches, ganglike, moving

from island to lagoon to the mainland over to the other side of the bay. . . . They are Sitka black-tailed deer, not native to Kodiak Island, but planted here in 1924 from southeast Alaska. With no natural predators other than man, they are plentiful, so much so that some years the hunting limit in the bush is seven per person. They are more beautiful than their cousins, the whitetail deer I knew back East, delicate beyond just deer-ness, because of their size. They are small, often no bigger than a goat. The hoof of a big buck easily fits in my hand.

When we are settled in our skiff, we decide to go down to a long several-mile stretch of beach not too far from our island. The ocean is a pool this morning, and as we zip through it, I can see myself leaping in like a silver fish, all point and no splash. But when we arrive, there is a swell—"as usual," we roll our eyes. It can be tin-pan flat everywhere but action is always guaranteed on this beach. We skim the shoreline, and see a fox slinking around a rocky stretch we know is good for clams, and farther down, we see otter lounging among the kelp beds, but no deer. We decide to go farther, down around Rocky Point, where we seldom go because our sixteen-foot skiff feels so small and the waters so big below the 2,000-foot cliffs. It's a dry run there, too, and we start back, scanning the long beach line one last time as we head home when we see them. About eight deer, all bucks, headed down the beach as if on some kind of schedule. They hear us and watch us as we slow to change positions in the skiff, now me at the 40-horse outboard, Duncan poised in the bow with his gun, ready to jump out onto the sand as soon as his hip boots allow. The surf is not too heavy, but I am new at this, and getting it just right, just close enough for him to leap, then reversing full throttle stern-first through the breakers without taking on too much water. Duncan is ashore now and I am back out in stiller water, watching, catching up on breath. He stands on the beach, quiet, rifle in hand, while the deer, too, watch. He is ready now, the ones we want are out in the open. He drops to his knee, aims, fires. The herd runs wildly, and Duncan has just moments to squeeze off one more shot as they scatter, leaping up the cliffbank to the dense brush above. Seven have run, one is down. My turn. Nervously, I throttle low and ease the bow back into the surge and break, while Duncan stands there with the deer heavily draped over his shoulders. He catches the sink of a wave and rolls the body off into the skiff as it dips before him, and we are on the way home.

I WOULD NEVER have done this, even three years before. Hunting season in New Hampshire was for us a time of war and near mourning. A week before the opening, my mother would tramp the boundaries of her land, posting the largest neon orange NO HUNTING! signs she could find, adding them to the NO TRES-PASSING signs that were nailed generously along the dirt road that adjoined our acreage. We always lived in rural areas, surrounded by woods and forests. We grew huge gardens, had chickens and goats, but we never ate our animals, except once— Harry and Larry, two pigs we guiltily fattened through one winter. At the last, my mother balked at the slaughter and released us all from the deed, hiring it out instead, the whole thing, from live pigs to packages in the freezer. She hated the hunting and killing of any animal, but saved her greatest scorn for deer hunters. They would come, park their truck along the dirt road, and for several weeks we would walk about in fear, fear of being shot, fear of letting the dog out, whose fawn colors would surely catch a bullet. If we dared a walk at all, per mother's instructions, we kept to the road, wore loud red and sang and talked as if with megaphones to advertise our presence. They were nefarious, mysterious beings, these hunters, our enemies. Every newspaper story of a hunting accident was read aloud and we all would shake our heads at the tragedy, murmuring, "What else could you expect? They were hunting, weren't they?" Occasionally we would hear a distant gunshot, and then we knew all our cautions and fears were justified. Even more occasionally, we would see a truck emerge from the woods with a deer in the back—crumpled, neck broken, legs splayed. Even then, I could see its magnificence. And I would be angry.

HOW WAS IT I was so easily converted after just two summers and now a winter here? It started with the salmon, I think. It didn't bother me to kill them, first, because of their sheer numbers. I knew from reading *The Alaska Fisherman's Journal* that the red salmon runs in Bristol Bay were anywhere from 20 to 40 million salmon strong. Here, around Kodiak Island, the pink salmon return alone could be as high as 25 million. It was a tribute to the Alaska Department of Fish and Game, who managed the resource so successfully. Knowing those numbers, and that the fish in our nets were themselves on their way to spawn and then die, settled any qualms I might have had. Near the end of the season we would pass by Humpy Creek to watch the spawning fish. They were hideous: their noses and teeth grotesquely hooked, their backs humped, their flesh withered and rotting, skin black-and-white mottled, coming off in shreds. They were the embodiment of death itself, and yet, still, they lived until the eggs were set and milted. It seemed a marvelous thing that though many of the fish were just days from the freshwater streams they were bound for, we could snatch the salmon from the salt water in all their silver beauty, their scales like perfect armor, their flesh a gorgeous red, before they drank of the poison of fresh water. We caught them not only for ourselves, but for others. *I am feeding people*, I would think, sometimes, as I pulled the fish from water to air. *Feeding them beautiful, perfect food*.

I WATCH THE DEER now dead in our skiff, my hand grazing its coarse hair. It is hair, not fur, I realize. I have never been this close to see the difference. Suddenly the dead animal begins to stir. Just a leg. Muscle spasms, I think. Then it begins shaking its head; then it lifts its head, kicking all feet, trying to stand. Duncan and I look at each other, horrified. "Sit on him!" he yells at me. Without hesitating, I jump down hard on his neck and straddle his chest. Still unbelieving, I look his body over carefully from my prime seat, realizing there is no blood to be seen anywhere, just a nick in his antlers. As he struggles beneath me to rise, we run through our options in short, breathy phrases. We are still ten minutes from home. If I let him up, he can do serious damage with his adrenaline-powered hooves or sharp antlers. Someone could easily be knocked overboard in the fracas. It is too risky to try and shoot him in the skiff. There is only one choice, it seems to us. I will hold him down until we get to the island, and we will let him out there. At this point, I longed for the code of chivalry where Duncan would graciously and on his own initiative offer to trade places, but a switch, however equitable or chivalrous, was not possible.

I rode the bucking deer all the way back to the island, managing to keep us all in our respective places. When the beach finally came into view, Duncan aimed straight for the softest sand and gassed the engine. We braced for the hit, jerked to a stop farther up the beach than I'd ever been in a skiff. I rolled off the deer and with one leap he was out, up the beach; Duncan was down on one knee again and this time the bullet hit true.

WE SLICE OPEN his throat and angle his head downhill, to bleed him as best we can. Duncan removes the scent glands on the backs of the legs. Now the gutting; for me the worst part. Though there is something very primitive about it, still, it is done with delicacy. It is a form of reverse surgery, our care with the knives and incisions not for the sake of the animal but for us and the good of the meat: the intestines, bladder, scent glands, and stomach must not be punctured or the foul gas and bacteria will contaminate the meat. Deftly, yet cautiously, Duncan severs the membranes holding them to the cavity, then at the last, I squat down and pull out the bulging stomach and ropes of intestines, still warm. We need to remove them from the scene as quickly as possible, before the bears follow the scent of blood to our beach. The heart and liver we save. Duncan has brought the ATV over, trailing a piece of plywood tied on behind for a makeshift trailer. With both hands, I grasp the slippery, gelatinous organs and slide them over onto the plywood. They ooze to the edges of the wood and we immediately realize there's no way they'll stay on for the five-hundred-foot downhill run out to the spit, where the tide will carry it away. I say I will do it. Using my body as a shield, I kneel on the plywood, spread my arms to engulf the still steaming viscera, my face just inches from its membranes. And we are off roaring down the hill, going too fast, the plywood, the guts, my own spread arms and legs rattling over rocks, logs, wanting only one thing—to get there, and to keep my face out of it all. It is nasty, I am shaken as we land on the beach and need a minute to catch my breath before pulling these parts of the deer I now know so well into the water. The salt water stings the scratches on my hands with a purifying bite, and I hope I will not have to ride the entrails of any other animal again. It is far too personal.

I HAVE SEEN DEER often here during summers and this fall. They swim on and off our island at will, propelled by instinct or searching for better grazing or more plentiful water. One night Duncan and I went for a walk toward a flowered meadow and points beyond, the goal to be filled with evening air and watch the eagles along the way. Around the first corner we saw a deer, alone, on the hillside above us. She was intent on grazing, and though there was no path and the slope was steep, I felt compelled to approach her. She saw us; we did not try to whisper or sneak. We were in the open and were simply advancing and conversing as we went.

"Look, Duncan, what is she eating with such relish?" I asked.

"Those yellow flowers. What are those?"

"Uh, coastal paintbrushes. It's okay," I cooed reassuringly, as we edged closer. "We won't hurt you." Then, "Isn't she pretty, Duncan?"

"Yeah, so delicate and feminine."

She continued to glance our way as she ate, but clearly the forage was of first concern. Finally we were within ten feet of her. This close, she stopped for a moment, lifted her head, regarded our company with some interest, still chewing madly, and, finding no cause for alarm, went back to her berry bushes and paintbrushes. We could have touched her with just a lunge. I have nearly touched many deer like this. They do not act like any wild animal I have ever known. Their unconcern for our presence does not serve them well.

ONE MORNING late that summer, just a few days after the deer season opened, we were finishing breakfast and saw what looked like a covey of ducks, very large ducks, all swimming in an orderly row, but with strange heads. They came closer, about thirty of them, and then I could see they were not ducks, but deer. It was my first sighting of a waterborne herd. They were swimming across from another island about a mile away. They were remarkably buoyant and obviously very experienced in such crossings. And though the island was obviously inhabited—our red cabins could be seen for half a mile—still, they were steering directly for our beach. As their hooves touched ground, they gingerly stepped ashore, still together, and all of them began walking quite calmly toward the house and us as we stood on the porch, watching. Just outside our door, as they walked past, Duncan just as calmly got his gun, lay in position, we chose the two bucks we wanted, and like that, it was done: our hunt for the year, our supply of deer meat was provided. There was no sport in it, and that was good. The killing of an animal held no thrill or fun for either of us. Had Duncan been a hunter because of the joy of the kill, I would have turned away, repulsed. I was glad this was done now, but I hated it, too, and wished they had come ashore somewhere else, and had at least fled from us in the two-legged bound of fear. Let them at least know who we are.

AFTER THE FISH came the cattle. My father-in-law had ranched on Kodiak Island since 1952. It was a skirmish for every year of it. DeWitt's federal grazing lease of 32,000 acres bordered what he came to call the "bear hatchery," a federal refuge protecting the Kodiak bear, a huge subspecies of the grizzly. The cattle, open-grazing in steep valleys and hillsides, had no defense from the predator save a panicked gallop that didn't even wind the bear. Two years before I joined the family, he loaded a herd of twenty onto a barge and out to Harvester Island, the island just a mile from us, where he also had a grazing lease. Here, he reckoned, they would be safe from bears, and so they have. The herd has flourished, nearly doubling in size, fed only by the grasses and greens of this place. This has become our main meat supply, these cattle. They feed twelve of us in the extended family all through the year. Every fall, two or three animals are chosen to be culled. From now on I will stand with the others for three days parsing flesh into portions and packages. Though it is all bloody work, it is so reasonable. Almost since the day I came it has appeared so. This is a necessary part of living out, of ranching, of commercial fishing. This is what it costs to live here, and this is how we feed so many. When the gun comes out and I brace for the shot, I remember this.

NOW THAT THE DEER is gutted, it is lighter, and we carry it easily into the warehouse. It's good-sized, about 130 pounds. We hang it from the rafters to finish the bleeding and to ready for skinning. Knives come out now, knives that were sharpened the day before or that morning, and we begin skinning the hide from the still-warm body that seems smaller now than on the beach, even smaller than when it lay in the skiff. Duncan brings out an ulu, an ancient skinning knife used by the Inupiat for whale, sea lion. I'd seen documentaries of babushkas in parkies wielding their ulus and moving through a walrus hide with a deft, slicing speed. The original ones were made of bone and stone. This is a castoff, an old rusted iron blade found among the refuse of the island's previous resident, an old Swede named Henry Landberg. I try it, and find the handle comfortable. The blade feels wrapped around my hand. If a hand were a knife, this is the kind of knife it would be, I think. I want it to work, as if there would be some kind of purity or cultural integrity to this, to do something ancient. But the balance is not right, and the blade is too thick and dull. It's a poor imitation of a real one, I decide with disappointment, something made for tourists, and give it up for a handmade bone-handled knife from Texas.

We slide the knife under the fat of the skin as the other hand pulls the hide taut. Out of habit, we try to keep the hide intact, though we have no plans to tan it.

When the hide is finally off, with a combination of cutting and then pulling it over the head, it becomes meat now. I am glad to feel this sudden distance. But it is not the way cattle become meat as they are skinned and then hung. The old bulls are so massive, that once inert, quartered and hung, it is impossible to imagine them again as living beings. Not so the deer. Even as it hangs, it is still lithe, fragile, the muscle between bones is spare, efficient, not thick and fleshy. We will let the meat hang for four days, to season. I consider for the first time how good it will taste.

I have friends who are vegetarians. Two have come to visit, neither one partaking of our meat or fish. I want to explain to them about how many salmon there are, about the winterkill of deer every spring, sometimes just a few, sometimes many—the flesh gone, just the hair and hide tenting over bones, and some just-new fawns. Too many deer for the island, too much winter. In the fall, before the snow, a large herd of deer began a swim, a swim from somewhere too far away. The weather got bad as it often does in September, the seas heaved, and somewhere out in the Shelikof Strait it happened. They washed up on a beach just a mile from our place, about ninety of them, strewn along a half mile, locked in the contortions of their drowning. Annie Dillard wrote, "Creation carries on with an intricacy unfathomable, and apparently uncalled for." Part of that carrying on and that intricacy seems to be slaughter and waste. I would like to stop it. I have tried in small ways—the murre just this month. . . .

We were traveling in the skiff on the way to Larsen Bay. Goldeneyes, a few puffins, murres were about, all busy with morning feedings. Then, overhead, an eagle dropped from the sky and snatched a murre from the water just feet beside us, then rose up into the air, the bird still struggling in its talons. Shocked, we watched the eagle ride the currents against the mountain to lift its heavy prize to its nest. An execution had happened before us with such startling speed and in such grotesque detail—we saw it all, the talons, the eagle's hard eye and calculated swoop, that it hunted with such fluidity and grace, and maimed or killed without even needing to stop, as though it didn't matter. I was appalled and, in an equally instinctive move, grabbed the gun from the bow and fired it vertically. The eagle, startled, released its hold as it flew, and the murre dropped, slowly tumbling down the hillside to the beach below. I had not planned this, but now we both felt a desperate need to this bird, more than that, a responsibility, because now we were a part of the whole snarled web. With the eagle circling us, screeching, we raced to the beach, tenderly lifted the duck. His sides were pierced and bleeding, eyes open, but he was still alive, still struggling. He could live. We could nurse him. We brought him back to our island, found a cardboard box, lined it with grass, then waited. The ending is no surprise, how we found him the next morning, how wrong the whole thing was from the beginning. The eaglets went hungry, our consciences were not assuaged; the murre's death was wasted. The universe could not be so tinkered with.

IT IS DINNER. We are having roast eight days after the hunt. The package we took from the freezer said "deer roast," not venison. We never call it venison. There is no living creature with that name. We do not pretend anything other than what we have done—we have killed a deer and now we will eat it. It is tender, though a touch gamey. With potatoes and carrots and home-made bread, it is a modest feast, and we begin by thanking the giver of the deer.

8

Winter Travels

A MONTH LATER, NEARLY THE END OF November now. It is just light, about 9:30 A.M. The gray light pales the bedroom enough for me to slowly wake. I rise to my elbows, look out to flat gray water, high clouds—mail day! "Duncan!" I'm too anxious to wait for him to wake. "We can go!" We haven't had mail for two weeks, too busy with our work to take the day. But the last week has left footprints up my spine; it's Friday, and I feel the weight of waiting now on my neck. I had sent some poems off to a few journals a month or so ago and, though I knew it was much too soon to expect a reply, I couldn't shake that expectant feeling that somehow, if I were extremely lucky, I might win the lottery.

"It's not time to get up yet," Duncan mumbled. We had stayed up until two that morning, both reading, too engrossed in our books to go outside in the cold to the generator house

and turn out the lights. It was far easier just to keep reading. "See if you can go back to sleep," Duncan sleepily urged as he turned over.

By ten thirty we were both up, and after a breakfast of oatmeal and toast, we started to get ready. Mail runs, or any traveling for that matter, had become much more complicated as of two weeks before.

A horrific NW blow had screamed in. We were expecting it, having heard its official forecast on the sideband radio: "Shelikof Strait, gale warning, gale warning," the voice had droned. "Northwest winds to sixty, gusting to seventy and higher in bays and passages." We pledged a skiff alert. When the winds came, we were posted at the window of the house all day as the wind gauge edged higher and higher, to 40, then 45 gusting to 50. Everything went white and gray, no matter its color before, as if the wind had peeled back every layer down to the substance common to all organic things. The skiff out on the running line tossed and struggled valiantly, and held. By that night, though, the wind was yet stronger. We could not sleep for the noise and the loose ends of the cabin rattling and banging and knowing that our only transport off this island was under attack. Without it, we were marooned, quite literally.

Every thirty minutes we took turns running down the hill in the dark to the beach and the running-line rock, wrapped in a coat and shining a huge army flashlight out to the water. The skiff was taking in too many waves, riding low and sluggish in the rollers. What we feared had already happened: The skiff had swamped. Everything in it was probably gone as well—our one backup outboard, a box of survival gear, gas cans, and oars. The skiff was too heavy now with water to pull it on the line. This was disaster. We had no other way of getting off the island except for a punt, a child-sized rowboat you had to kneel in or risk toppling over the sides. It was used on occasion to row out fifty feet to the running-line rock at high tide, and nothing more. There was nothing we could do then but wait.

The afternoon of the next day, the storm was abating enough for Duncan to risk launching the punt. Duncan put an outboard on it, a 35 horse, the smallest we had; it was like putting the engine of a Mack truck on a go-cart. Both of us were strung with anxiety, both for the punt's maiden voyage out on the relatively high seas, and for fear of what we would find: a too badly damaged *Chum Chagrin*. It could have been funny, the sight of Duncan solemnly squatting in the toy boat, his frame filling the entire space, and the tiny hull now powered and making a real wake as it buzzed up and down the waves out to the larger skiff. The *Chum* was indeed damaged, but not beyond repair. We both went out later that evening when the water had calmed enough to risk two people squatting in the punt, and bailed the skiff with six-gallon buckets until we could tow it back to shore.

After that near stranding, and after losing too many nights' sleep for worry, we started up the tractor, a 1948 Ford dressed in slick red paint, and, with a snatch block and rollers, we hauled the *Chum Chagrin* up onto the lawn and parked her. She was the oldest and smallest of our fleet of wooden skiffs, all built by Jake Laktonan, an elder Alutiiq known locally for his workmanship. The skiffs were flat-bottomed for beach landings, generally an eighteen-foot length, a five-foot beam, the sides low, just two and a half feet high, with a sleek, flaring bow that lifted under any power. The skiffs seemed almost alive to me with the borrowed life that wood grants to everything fashioned from it; they were warm, pliant somehow, yielding in a following sea, firm as a surfboard when coasting the rollers, soothing over white-water lumps. All the skiffs, each painted meticulously in white, trimmed in red and black, were further personalized with names, most bearing a salmon species and an alliterative description of its fate: and so the *Coho Calamity*, the *Humpy Hearse*, the *Sockeye Sorrow*, the *Salmon Spasm*. I would miss all of that later, as we gradually phased out the wooden skiffs with all their quirks and leaks and laborious upkeep for a new generation of maintenance-free aluminum boats, cold tin cans identified by number, not name, that move over every patch of water the same, with the nondistinct authority of metal.

Of all our possibilities from that year's fleet, we chose the oldest skiff, the twenty-three-year-old *Chum*, because, though it leaked the most, it was also the sturdiest. It was our only remaining planked skiff; the others were all built of plywood. That, and its smaller size, sixteen feet instead of eighteen, would make it easier for the two of us to handle, we reasoned. In truth, behind our purely rational decision lingered an affinity on both of our parts for all things old and in need of care and restoration. Of course, when we had made that decision months before we had had no idea that the planks would further separate in the cold, necessitating constant bailing, and that we would be shoving and pushing it about as we now had to do.

We stepped into our respective launching roles. While Duncan went to start the tractor, I gathered the letters and cards ready to mail, stamped them, put them in a bread bag with a twister, then in a larger garbage bag that would serve as our mailbag. I was already geared up in all my layers, but held off on the raingear and life jacket, knowing there was work to do first. I was done now, why didn't I hear the tractor? I poked my head out the door and saw Duncan still bent over the engine.

"What's wrong?"

"The battery's low again. I've got it on a charger, but it'll take a little while. It was really cold last night."

"Shoot. How long do you think?"

"Oh, let's give it thirty minutes or so."

It took longer than thirty minutes, but finally it did start. It had a rough purr, like a tiger, not like a cat. Duncan manned the tractor—I wanted nothing to do with something so old that was needed so acutely. It hauled nets, anchors, drums of fuel from the beach; anything too heavy to manhandle was somehow pulled or dragged by this tractor. My role, then, was to run the rollers, three smooth logs that had originally washed up on the beach. With a snatch block, Duncan hoisted and raised the bow of the skiff for me to get the first rollers underneath, then as he moved forward and the skiff rolled off the rollers, I would run back and pick up the roller just past the skiff, and run it up to the bow as the skiff kept moving forward. Like this, like a juggling act, running three rollers under a skiff that never stopped moving, we pulled the *Chum Chagrin* out to the water. By the time she got there, I was sweating under my layers. I learned to launch the skiff first, *then* dress for the trip.

IN WINTER we tried not to travel on windy days, knowing that even on the calmest days the chill of our own wind as the 40-horse outboard propelled us over the water would instantly drop the felt temperature by 40 degrees, our bodies bearing the full force of our speed. If the thermometer read 20 degrees, it was minus 20 while we traveled. In the dead of winter, no matter how we dressed, it never seemed warm enough: three pairs of wool socks, thermals, wool pants, wool shirt, down parka, then raingear from neck to ankles to break the wind. Still, our faces were exposed, and our hands. When Duncan was driving, I would hunch down in a near curl on the wooden seat and turn my back to the wind. Duncan, though, had to stand to drive, to see over the bow—our usual position for driving. There was no wind break for his face other than a beard. On particularly cold days, I would bring a piece of Visqueen, a heavy clear plastic, and sit back to the wind, inside this giant bag, an opening just at my face.

Because it took so much effort to step off the island even for five minutes, mail days became an excuse to travel. It felt wasteful to ride the thirty minutes up to the village just to then turn around and go home again, so we lingered in the village, visiting Dora Aga, Eddie's sister, a sixtyish Finn-Russian woman with high Slavic cheekbones like her brother's who dwarfed most of the men in the village for size and strength. She was one of a very few who still kept the old ways, subsisting as much as possible on the land's offerings. We would come to her house, a sagging gray-shingled structure, and she'd be in the kitchen, putting deer intestines in a bucket to soak, or splitting salmon to brine before smoking. She'd offer us raw herring roe, spooned into margarine containers for lunch, pickled octopus. When we butchered our cows, we'd bring the head and hooves to her. She knew how to eat anything.

Dora was married to Johnny, a little, wiry man half her size who salmon-fished in the summers and assisted in bear hunts spring and fall. The rest of the year he mostly drank and gambled away his money, despite Dora's hulking presence and their frequent fistfights. Both were commercial salmon fishermen, but because she and Johnny couldn't inhabit the cabin of a small boat together, or agree about where to fish, how to fish, when to fish, they fished separately, each running their own seine boat. Dora usually caught more.

WHEN WE FELT like traveling farther, we'd skiff down to Parks cannery, another thirty minutes away, where Eddie Paakkannen was winter watchman. We stayed two or three days each time. He kept us up past midnight every night playing his favorite game. When Eddie asked, "You guys wanna play some gin rummy, eh?" right after dinner, Duncan would kick me under the table and say, "Sure t'ing, Eddie! We'd love dat! But you're not gonna beat me tonight!" Eddie would laugh back. "Oh, ya! Well, I got dem lucky cards, so ya bedder watch out." The first time I heard Duncan talk to Eddie, I turned and stared at him. What was this recidivist dialect? Why was he talking this way, "dis," and "dose" and "over deres." Duncan didn't even seem to know he was doing it—"I don't talk like that!"

Duncan would launch into those rummy games with such gusto, and I would have no choice but to follow, though I hated card games, and gin rummy in particular, but I admired Duncan's kindness. I knew he was doing it just for Eddie. With three decks, it would take us all night, past midnight to finish. I would have been lost altogether if he hadn't had a radio and a good line on an Anchorage station that featured a *Desperate and Dateless* Friday show. It was a 1980 Alaska-style radio version of *The Dating Game* where the dull, the flashy, the macho Alaska mountain men and the bored-on-a-Friday-night law clerk called in and eventually chose from among several equally graced suitors for a Saturday date. I don't know if it was a hit in Anchorage, but for me down at the Parks cannery in Uyak Bay on the west side of Kodiak Island in the cold of winter with a wall of cards in my hand and the whole night still before me, it became a veritable theater of human tragedy and comedy, a sweeping epic, Shakespearean in scope. I hung gratefully on every foolish word.

When Eddie had finally won, he'd say, "Well, I guess dat's it for tonight. I gotta get up at four dis mornin' so I'll see you guys in da mornin'."

"We know better dan ta try and beat you outta bed, Eddie. We're gonna sleep in!" Duncan would announce, still playful though it was long past the playful hour by my clock. Then

Eddie would go into his room with its queen-size bed and we'd go into the room he used as a guest room, a tiny alcove with a single twin bed in it. We could fit only if we both lay sideways the same way and didn't move. Despite our discomfort, we chuckled at Eddie's decorum with guests and knew it was not out of rudeness or insensitivity that he lounged while we labored to sleep; it simply never occurred to him to do otherwise.

OUR WORST WINTER TRIP was just after Christmas. We didn't want to have Christmas alone, so we invited everyone in Duncan's immediate family out for a Bear Island Christmas, promising adventure, solitude, and escape from tinsel. To our surprise, everyone accepted. Weston and Bev flew up from Indiana with their daughter Tamie, then three, and their nine-month-old, DeWitt. Wallace flew up from college in Ohio, and Duncan's parents, DeWitt and Wanda, flew in from Kodiak. Duncan and I wanted everything ready for them when they arrived. Our first obstacle—no Christmas tree. No tree of any sort, for that matter, on Bear Island. It is distinctly treeless. The hills and surrounding lands are bushed with dwarf birches and bush alder mostly, nothing Christmassy enough for our eyes. On one of our mail runs up to Larsen Bay, we telephoned and asked his parents to send us out a Christmas tree on a boat that was coming this way. It came about ten days before Christmas. We got the call late one stormy afternoon, blowing dead easterly, straight down the channel.

"Bear Island. Bear Island, you got it on there?" the radio crackled. I jumped from my seat—I had been writing in my journal, excited just to hear another voice. I looked out the window and saw, down by Harvester, a fishing boat coming into view.

"Duncan, someone's calling! I think it's the boat from town!" I rushed to the radio. "Bear Island back to the call."

"Yeah, this is Santa Claus making a delivery. I've got something on board for you," the radio drawled.

Duncan came in, his face quickened just as mine was to speak with someone new.

"Roger, Santa Claus. Glad to see ya. Those reindeer gettin' seasick at all?" Duncan jibed. Though it was a mile away, we could see the boat, about a sixty-five-footer, pitching and swaying in the blow.

"Nah, these're sailing reindeer. Say, I got a tree for ya and a few other packages. No rush, though. It's kinda nasty."

"No problem. We'll come out and get it now."

We knew the skipper didn't want to anchor up for a few days just waiting for us to come get our tree, and no time like the present. It was high tide, too, which was perfect for the beach launch.

We knew the routine, and now had as good a carrot in front of us as our weekly mail—maybe even better. In five minutes we were geared up, with less than our usual toilet, since we were traveling a mere two or three miles rather than twenty. Down to the beach, me rounding up the rollers as Duncan started the tractor and putzed down to the parked skiff. It was blowing about 25, rain spitting sideways, and a huge swell coming down the channel, but it had come down a lot since yesterday and the day before, when it blew 50, gusting to 65, our wind gauge said. I ran the rollers, everything went smoothly, the last shove out and we were off. It was slow going since we were bucking straight into it, the waves large enough to raise us high, then sink the larger boat out of sight. When we got there, we loaded our Christmas cargo in a hurry, dispensing with the usual amenities with the skipper because of the swell banging our two vessels together.

The skipper, a friend of the family's, returned to Kodiak and gave a report to DeWitt and Wanda, shaking his head. He thought we were crazy for going out there. He watched our return through his binoculars as we rose, then disappeared in the trough of every wave for too long, it seemed, then he'd see the tips and then the branches of a Christmas tree slowly rise up, and there we were, the little red-and-white skiff, the two tiny figures in it anchored to the tree, then down again in the water. He watched us, worried, all the way to shore.

IT WAS INDEED a Bear Island Christmas, complete with blizzard, a frozen well, quick long-distance chugs out to the iced-up outhouse, our only communication a sideband radio that didn't have much of a chance against the weather, games around the wood stove, a turkey feast. With not a sound from the outside world, no one telling us what to buy or wear or do or say, the holiday was ours alone. We weren't especially creative in our celebration, but it all felt new to me since my own family had not celebrated the holiday since I was nine, both for religious reasons and because we had no money for presents. We decorated the tree on Christmas Eve with ornaments Wanda had brought out from town, munching cookies and slurping hot chocolate in Santa Claus mugs they had used for as long as anyone could remember. Christmas morning, before we opened the presents, DeWitt continued a tradition begun when his boys were young. He ceremoniously reached for a heavy Bible, settled down in the one armchair in the cabin, and while we scrunched on the one couch and few wooden chairs, he opened to the passage in Luke and began to read in a deep, sonorous voice:

"In those days Caesar Augustus issued a decree that a census should be taken of the entire Roman world. . . . So Joseph also went up from the town of Nazareth . . . with Mary, who was pledged to be married to him and was expecting a child . . . and she gave birth to her

firstborn, a son. She wrapped him in cloths and placed him in a manger, because there was no room for them in the inn. . . ."

We all sat silent, most of us bowing our heads, lost in the words. *"And there were shepherds living out in the fields. . . . An angel of the Lord appeared to them . . . peace on earth, goodwill to men on whom His favor rests . . ."* I loved it all, not just the majesty and rhythm of the language, but I was astonished again at God's chosen entrance into the world, that He would come to His people, not with pomp and purple robes, demanding obeisance, but through the ripping flesh of a woman to lie naked and helpless in a dirty barn. I could not understand it, nor did I want to. As I listened, something in me opened, just a crack, and I could see into a vast dark space so thick and encompassing it took my breath, as if I didn't need it there. It was the other place, the other dimension I looked for as a child. I had found it six years before in the words of that book, words I knew to be alive, inhabited by holy breath.

When DeWitt finished, *". . . the shepherds returned, glorifying and praising God for all the things they had heard and seen, which were just as they had been told. . . ."* we slowly raised our heads, opened our eyes to each other, dressed in woolens and flannels, and the room, the little cabin, the snow falling in the morning dark out the window, and beyond that, only ocean and mountains, not another Christmas light for miles and miles.

THE DAY AFTER CHRISTMAS, tired of being shut-ins, we seized a mild break in the weather and loaded into two skiffs for a trip down to Parks cannery to see Eddie.

The trip down was everything a winter trip on the ocean should be—cold and utterly beautiful. It was about 18 degrees when we left, the wind light, and as we moved down into the head of the bay, we felt the air chilling yet further. If Bear Island was the refrigerator of Uyak Bay, this was moving down into the freezer as the bay narrows beneath 4,000-foot mountains, a straight rise from the water. The mountains produce their own snows and weather and usually wear white even through the summer. Bev, tense, held little DeWitt, wrapped into a huge cylinder, as tight as she could against her own bundled figure; she was not too enthusiastic about the trip, about bringing a nine-month-old out in a skiff in winter, but neither did she want to stay alone at Bear Island. I didn't understand her anxiety, then, not knowing anything about what it meant to be a mother.

We stayed overnight with Eddie, as we planned, but the next morning when we rose for breakfast and then to return to Bear Island, the weather had turned nasty again—cold, blowing snow, and a stiff wind to keep it all stirred up. We tossed it off lightly to the vagaries of life on the water, admired our own flexibility and waited, played gin rummy until even Duncan wore out, and after the third day of the lock-in, we were all crazy to go. We had read every sentence on every printed page we could find in the whole cannery, which wasn't much. There was nothing else to do. The cannery, pegged to the foot of a 3,000-foot mountain that rises vertically behind the last building, offers no beach to walk, no trails or hills to meander in a blizzard, just indoor cards and food. The next morning, the thermometer still read 8 degrees, but the wind had come down some, and the sky was clear, so we decided to go. Easy to reason: if we stayed, another front was likely to move in and we'd be here for a week or longer. We were all in agreement, even Bev, who had no relish for the hour-and-a-half trip ahead. We wore nearly all the clothes we brought, two days' worth, and then our winter clothing, heavy parkas, over that. It would be cold, but it was now or never.

We were traveling in two skiffs for better speed. It was bitter cold with the wind chill plunging the 8 degrees far below zero. Within twenty minutes the spray from the bow began to freeze to the skiff, and soon its effect was apparent. We could not see it on our own skiff, but I watched Weston's and Bev's skiff next to us, Bev hugging the baby as tightly to herself as possible, her head down, and below her, the planks icing up steadily. Ours had to be as well. The skiffs had slowed considerably now, so much heavier in the water, and yet we had another forty-five minutes to go. We couldn't make it. Duncan, who was driving our skiff, slowed and pulled parallel to Weston's skiff. They both idled down and turned to talk.

"What do you think?" Weston asked Duncan, his own face almost fully concealed underneath his parka. But I could hear his voice—tight.

"We're icing up bad. I don't see how we're going to make it like this," Duncan answered, equally tense.

"I think we'd better go on in to Larsen Bay and wait out this weather," Weston answered.

"Yeah." Duncan paused. "We've got the animals, though. They haven't had food for a couple of days now and it's been so cold." We had a dog, Nugget, a goat, Gretchen, that we were babysitting for the winter for a summer neighbor, the two pigs on Harvester Island, and a house of hens. "I think we can make it if we lighten the skiff, and just take two back, me and Wallace."

"I'm going, too, Duncan," I announced quickly. There was no way I wanted to be stuck somewhere for another three days.

"I don't know, Duncan. It's awful cold." Weston shook his head. This was not a group decision, as was common to all arrangements decided in the skiff.

"We can't just leave the animals!" I piped up.

"With just us and no baggage, we'll be light enough. We'll call you on the radio when we get there," Duncan continued.

"Okay," Weston conceded. "Be careful. I don't know where we'll stay, probably with Stella and Victor. Call us on sixty-nine."

"Okay. We'll see you tomorrow or when the weather warms." After handing over the garbage bags serving as luggage, we parted slowly, his skiff turning now toward the village.

Duncan adjusted his parka so the ruff closed over his face as much as possible. He had a beard, which would help what couldn't be covered. It began to snow as we parted, and within a few minutes the snow came at us like bullets, not the soft light flakes of a Christmas Eve. Duncan stood up in the stern, his visibility now further limited, and faced the full bite of the single-digit temperature now blown so sharp we couldn't breathe it direct. I turned my back again, wishing for the Visqueen, the polyethylene sheeting I usually sat in. Duncan waved Wallace up front to better balance the skiff for a smoother ride, and so we went, Wallace in the bow, his back to the wind, his face huddled low nearly to his knees, me in the stern, back to the wind, hiding my hands inside my hip boots, and Duncan standing, his eyes squinted nearly shut, and ice forming on his beard. The skiff was sluggish, still icing, but we were close now and knew we'd make it.

When we landed, we were too cold to be happy. We were nearly paralyzed to our places, and stiffly, uncertain, stumbled out of the skiff and onto the snowy ground.

"You okay, Lessie, Wallace?" Duncan shouted in a slurred voice, his chin too cold to articulate, his beard almost completely frozen over.

My nose felt frostbit, and my face and hands, when I touched them, felt like someone else's, like after novocaine at the dentist's.

"I'm okay, I think," I answered finally.

The thinnest of the three of us, Wallace got the coldest and could hardly walk. "I think my cheeks are frostbit," he said softly, his hand to his face.

"Le's get up to the house and start a fire in the stove," Duncan urged, and we hobbled awkwardly up the hill, beginning to be thankful because we saw a fire and warmth in our future, but not feeling it yet.

The others came late the next day, when the air warmed to the twenties and all danger had passed. I did not check the wind chill chart. I did not need that number to know what it meant to travel in the winter. Each time we skiffed the frigid waters those cold, sharp months of too little light, the beauty we fed on was the beauty that threatened us.

9

Boundaries

EVERY DAY AFTER THAT CHRISTMAS of 1979 brought tiny packages of light: just seconds, at first, then a minute, then two or three more minutes of dusky light a day, then slowly lengthening to four and five minutes a day. We knew those minutes were gifts. We measured them not by the clock, though, but by the tasks we could begin to finish. The weeks cycled past, spun by the light and the work that grew to fill it.

It was spring, April now, but the weather, to my consternation, had changed little. I was dismayed, too, to find that Bear Island had shrunk over the winter. I had walked and hiked every inch of its perimeter. If I walked on the outermost edge, I could extend the walk to forty-five minutes. On days I had excess energy, I would run up and down the steepest grassed slope I could find ten times, twenty, then on to the next slope, for an hour or longer. When I had tired myself enough to rest, I would sit or sprawl on the moss and lichen, watching the world swirl around me. Everything in motion: the water speeding across the Shelikof to the other side, pushed by the wind; the clouds following the water, traveling in their own currents, the grasses swaying, birds kiting, only the far mountains stationary, and this island, and me.

SOMETIMES I was there because of a fight. Fights were inevitable, and my two-and-a-half-year-old married soul knew this, but I hated them, hated any kind of conflict with the passion of those who grow up in its locus. This was a small one, about the kitchen cabinets we were working on, but then it festered to the whole topic of decision-making. There seemed no escape from my position as the novice on this island. Many days we worked together smoothly and efficiently. On these others, I had an overwhelming urge to run away, as I did as a child, when my father would come home for the weekend, and the fighting would start. All six of us would run off down the dirt road to the frozen pond in the woods with our skates and sleds and stay until dark, playing with a pitched fervency, not wanting to return, ever. The urge was just as strong now, to run, to hide, to call someone on the phone, to go visit a friend, to hear other words and lives and let my own fall into a broader space. But there was no way out or off this island.

I THOUGHT I KNEW SOMETHING about boundaries growing up, and I feared them terribly. One Christmas, we were on a camping trip to Florida—compensation for no presents or Christmas celebration. We had no money for gifts, but we could travel as cheaply as we could live at home. We thought it a more than fair trade; along with our mother, we came to despise every gaudy light and tree, every image urging us to buy what we could not.

I am seat-belted in with Todd, my younger brother, which was okay with me since we were good friends and football-baseball buddies. I've just turned fourteen, Todd is twelve and a half. My youngest brother, Clark, is double-buckled with Jan; Scott is in the passenger side of the front seat—the navigator's position—and Mother, of course, is behind the wheel. She is driving the Mercedes she had bought for little more than a dance. Laurie, three years older than me, and the second oldest of six, is not with us; she ran away from home last year. My father is not here; he seldom came on our trips, which was a great relief.

The trip started with frantic final packing that night, then at midnight we started off, Vivaldi's *The Four Seasons* blaring from the stereo speakers as we whisked away into the night. It was a classy getaway, I thought, as the violins carried us down the potholed dirt road. Mother had been planning her route for days, trying to time her circuit of the big cities—Boston, New York, at dead times, if such a thing existed. We knew we were fresh meat, with our green-and-white "Live Free or Die" New Hampshire plates that signaled "backwoods hicks" to wily, speed-crazed Massachusetts drivers. Mother was terrified of Boston drivers in particular, so we were, too, seeing her white knuckles on the steering wheel, all of us on a 360-degree lookout for the dangers that zoomed and hurtled around us.

By early morning, four or five o'clock, Mother wore out and proclaimed a rest. The first rest area we found she steered us off the highway and eased in among the semis, huge caravans that dwarfed our overloaded black beetle.

"I've got to sleep. I don't want to hear a peep out of anyone," Mother warned as she leaned her seat back against my knees.

We were quiet for a moment, heeding the tone in her voice, then, inevitably, with six jammed into a car built for four and all of us needing sleep, we could not be still.

"Okay," Mother turned around accusingly. "Todd, go out on the roof."

Todd began climbing over our legs. "You'd better take your coat." With two long steps he was up on top of the roof rack where all our camping gear and food was stored—two tents, a green one that smelled like oilskins—the boys' tent—and the other, a light beige—the girls' tent. Then the Coleman stove, the air mattresses, a box of food, sleeping bags.

We heard Todd over our heads, scuffling and settling down. I sighed inwardly, hoped Mother would sleep. Quiet and still for a minute or two, good. Then the jiggles. The car almost vibrating, small shakes, then shaking front to back. Mother banged on the ceiling. "Stop that, Todd! Lie still!"

"Okay!" Todd answered back, muffled.

Again, a jiggle, small, but detectable, and another, this time the car vibrating left to right. Mother unrolled the window now. "Todd, get down!" she shot up, disgusted. This was getting serious now.

"I'll go, Mother," I volunteered, knowing I could lie still if anyone could. I just wanted Mother to sleep. She was the only driver. This trip, like all of our trips, was only possible because of her energy and initiative.

Todd jumped down and slunk back into the car as I ducked out the other door. The night air was so clean, I felt freed from the stuffy car and the brewing crisis. With two lunges I was on top. I wrapped my coat around me, and lay on the boxes on my side, looking at the lines of trucks, all parked at the same angle, and the stars. The boxes were hard and lumpy—we hadn't packed them with a bed in mind—and I had no pillow. There was just enough room to curl tightly, letting my feet hang off the back. I lay as still as I could, awake for the first time since we had left. I would not sleep up here, I knew. I moved not a muscle, let my ears open like eyes and willed my body to relax, Mother to sleep. Yes, this was working. I didn't hear any sounds underneath me. Then a truck pulled in, his lights scanning the car. What should I do? What would the driver think? Embarrassed, I covered my face, hoping I would look like any piece of luggage, then the lights passed and I was alone again.

It was strange to be there lying on top of the Mercedes, but I didn't think of any alternative. There wasn't one. Not a hotel. None of us had ever stayed in one; we didn't even know what they looked like inside. Another truck came, and another, as I melted into the boxes, discomfited. What would I say if someone came over? Then rapping on the roof and Mother calling up, "Leslie, get down! For Pete's sake, you can't be still any better than Todd," and we were back on the road again, all of us quiet now.

I slept finally because I felt myself wake. Where are we now? New Jersey, it is light, and the vacant highway landscape is suddenly filled with houses, toy houses as far as we can see, all in precise rows, each one just missing its neighbor, close enough to share paint, and behind each one a wire-fenced plot. Mother, despite her fatigue, begins singing a song about "ticky-tack houses." I can't join in the song; I am too horrified. Do people really live here? No, these are the houses where statistics lived, not people, surely. And it is all the worse for the precision, the premeditation of the act. I found a new image of failure. This is what would happen to you if you failed. If the centrifuge of life spun and you didn't hold on you would end up here, on lot number 347 in a tiny box with a little square centimetered lawn in back, and there it was, your whole life in a flash, caged within the metal fence. It was the bleakest landscape I had seen in my fourteen years. I vowed secretly and deeply as we drove past the suburbs that I would never live there in such entrapment, that my life would be different, that I would not be flung, faceless, into those precisely measured hovels.

AS A FAMILY, we traveled to escape our own boundaries. We felt the strictures the keenest during our four years in one particular town, where I spent my tenth through fourteenth year. We were nearly as cut off there as we were at Bear Island that winter. We lived high on a hill, almost a mountain, surrounded by a moat of woods and forest, shared by only one other house. It was three miles to the village center, on a combination of bouncy tar and dirt roads, the last mile up the hill a narrow, snaking road so steep the school-bus driver refused to make the trip. This was not a country club town like the one we had left: This was like Appalachia. Our geographical distance, and our perch on the hill, were no protection, though. Each day, in an exquisite mockery of travel, we spent two hours on the road in the school bus getting to and from where we didn't want to go. It was a maddening circuit that took us into dark pockets of woods and houses and people.

Our daily travels began every morning before 7:00 when, after a breakfast of lumpy twelve-grain cereal—if my mother caught us—we began the walk down the hill. If it was spring or fall, we would run the whole way down, books stacked in our arms, legs braced in a constant brake. If winter, we could slide on our feet the whole way down. Todd and I usually ran or slid together, pacing ourselves to match each other's every step. At the bottom of the hill, we would wait for the bus. Todd and I always sat together, and we always chose the back seat, since we were first. The first twenty minutes of the ride was ours alone. We huddled together, often ducking behind the seats out of the reach of the driver's mirror—and we sang. We sang every song we knew: The Supremes, "I'm Going to Make You Love Me"; the Jackson 5 chorus, "I like the little wiggle in your walk," inching our voices up into falsetto. Folk songs: "Early One Morning," "The Ash Grove," Joan Baez songs from our mother's records. We didn't know how to sing harmony, and our voices weren't that good, but the acoustics in the backseat of the bus pleased us. Some days we brought our recorders, mine an alto, Todd's a soprano, and played together, heads below the seats, embarrassed that the driver would hear us, but determined to play away these long minutes.

We traversed a maze of dirt roads, one long stint on ribbony route 3B, past the two houses with garbage layered to the porch ceilings, the house with a deer hanging by its neck each fall, then off into another corner of woods and houses. The kids climbed on singly, in groups, each one finding their cluster for the morning.

Todd and I sat together in the back for another reason—for protection. There were rowdy high schoolers who came on, and though any one of them might choose me for entertainment, one in particular I dreaded. Randy Bouchee, with oily brown hair hanging past his shoulders, skinny, with dirty teeth and a perpetual sneer, would swagger onto the bus, then scan the seats. On my unlucky days, he would select me as the object of his attentions and would throw himself casually into the seat in front of Todd and me. Then it would start.

"Are those supposed to be bell-bottoms you're wearing? My, aren't we getting groovy!" he would mock.

I had no comeback, and just sat there stoically, having discovered some time before that it was best to just be quiet. I learned this at my other school, where my sisters and I were ridiculed often for wearing brown lace-up boy's shoes when the girls all wore pointy-toed little sneakers and Mary Janes; for wearing boys' boots—the galoshes with the buckles all the way to the top—when girls wore pull-on go-go boots; and boys' raincoats, the yellow ones with the buckles and head piece that made us look like fire hydrants when everyone else wore shiny slickers. We knew what our mother's defense of this garb was—boys' gear was cheaper and better made. We knew without trying it that this retort would only make them laugh the louder. So we perfected the ignoring gaze. It usually worked for Randy, too, eventually.

He leered in my face now, just inches away, apparently enjoying the effect of his words. "You've got crooked teeth. Did anyone ever tell you that? I bet you think you're pretty, but man, you look like a witch with your long, stringy black hair and your ugly teeth."

I felt my insides go cold. How did he know what I hated most about myself? I looked out the window, nodded reassurance at Todd, who, two grades younger, sat wide-eyed, looking scared.

"Your sisters are much prettier than you. You're fuckin' ugly, a real witch! You won't even have to dress up for Halloween!" he snorted.

I sighed inwardly—this again. I knew it was true that my sisters were prettier than me. Much was made over my oldest sister's beauty, and my next sister, a year and a half older than I, had begun to grow her hair and was suddenly being noticed by the boys. Like every twelve-year-old girl, I longed to be pretty, but most of all, I longed for my mother to think me pretty. She had often been complimented on her handsome children from the time we were all babies, but I felt sure I was the exception. My compensation was that I was good in school.

I continued to gaze impassively out the window, registering no emotion. The boys across the aisle of the bus, third- and fourth-graders, began doing an obscene imitation of my science teacher, who was daily jeered for the way his pants fit. I was relieved for the distraction, but couldn't watch them, either. The window was the only out.

Randy was just a year older than me, in eighth grade, in my sister Jan's class, while I was in seventh. He was part of an infamous cadre of eighth graders that terrorized the teachers, the students, the rest of the school, and even the town. Half of the fourteen or so in the grade were one and two years older, having been kept back in younger grades. The boys already looked like their fathers with flannel shirts with ragged cut-off sleeves and tight jeans. They shaved and drove souped-up cars or motorcycles. Two sisters, Betty and Dora, both of them five foot eight to my five feet, had tried to beat me up in the girls' bathroom a few times, over a contested sweater one time, and over a perceived insult to one of their friends another. Everyone but my sister and her one friend, Cheryl, smoked at least cigarettes, and more, on the weekends. Drinking was habitual; sex was not only a recurring topic of classroom discussion but it was also a favored activity before and after school and during recess. The thirteen in my grade were somewhat tamer, but were clearly headed in the same direction. The younger classes were no better. At recess, the fourth graders regularly threw snow and iceballs, hitting their preferred target, their teacher, a four-foot-ten, eighty-pound, sixty-something woman who had a severe form of scoliosis. They called her Chicken Legs to her face. The third graders would arrange fights between the first-, second-, and third-grade boys nearly every day after school. A first and second grader were sent home one day after they attempted to copy the seventh and eighth graders' sexual recreations.

I didn't know how to fight back against this. Sometimes I did fight—chasing down and beating on one of the eighth-grade boys who had stolen my hat, protecting my younger brother Clark on the playground, ending up in the principal's office. But it wasn't the physical violence and the threats that so unnerved all of us—it was the sordid and predictable perversion of every word and thought into verbal pornography that hurt us most.

After school, the return trip home was worse. Ours was the last bus of the day. We waited forty-five minutes after school to then begin the forty-five-minute ride to the base of our hill, then the final hike home up what was now a mountain. The last year there, even this too-long journey was prolonged when, in ninth grade, I joined the rest of the high school students and was transported to a regional high school, adding another hour to the trip. We had a single recourse against this: We could walk, and we did so gratefully. The five miles a day was a small price to pay to keep our dignity. We often ran the whole distance, at least until the final mile, our feet pounding the taint of our school hours into the dirt, books bouncing on our backs, racing each other, or pacing ourselves to run in unison.

Despite this, there were compensations for living there. We were surrounded by a forest of crisp hardwoods and sweeping evergreens, all of it ours alone to wander and hike. Summers were spent on and under their branches as we built forts, swings, and raced each other up and down the highest trees. Todd and I constructed several original domiciles, one we called the salt-box; another dug into the ground then domed over the top with pine boughs; others hammered into triangular clusters of trees, where three boards became the foundation for an almost uselessly angled hut. There, the two of us also created our own gym with a pine branch nailed between two trees for our respective chin-up bars, where Todd and I worked out nearly every day, competing to see who could do the best gymnastic routines, the most pull-ups. My older sister Laurie, already into clothes and boys, would wander out occasionally into our spot of the woods, observe my grimacing face as I pulled up for the twentieth chin-up, and warn, "You're going to build up huge muscles, Leslie. You'll be sorry!" There was a pond down the dirt road a half mile away where we would all go swimming on the hottest summer days.

In the fall, our favorite time, the entire hillside would flame into hot oranges and reds. The first half of the road that plunged down our hill was lined with old maples. We would run down the hill on our way to the school bus splashing through whole running rivers of leaves, our ears filled with a shushing like water over rocks. In the spring, the maples were tapped for syrup, as many as three buckets on each tree. For those weeks, we saved the paper straw from our carton of milk at school, and as we climbed the last part of the hill home, thirsty and hungry, we pulled our straws from our crumpled lunch bags, and furtively, though no one was around, we climbed the bank to the trees and stuck our straws in the metal buckets, sucking great gulps of the slightly sweet liquid until we were so full we could hardly make it up the last rise of the hill.

Though we loved what each season on that hill brought us, all of us wanted desperately to leave this town, my mother included. But the house wasn't finished yet. And once it was, after renovating the wing and doing all the major reconstruction, the house took three years to sell. We were trapped. My mother felt it perhaps more than we did, seeing our classmates, fearing her sons and daughters would end up in the hot rod cars that blasted down the dirt roads, shimmied around the sharp corners of the twisting paved roads. Already the cars and their long-haired drivers had found our house, they knew Laurie, and by my last

year there, they were coming for me, too. Mother was determined we would get away. The hitch was our bank account, but
she already knew that if we were careful we could travel for the
same amount it cost us to sit at home—and we did. We packed
our 1964 Country Squire wood-paneled station wagon with all
our camping gear and took off. One summer to Virginia. Two
winter trips to Florida. And one summer, the summer between
seventh and eighth grade, 1970, Mother gamely drove us, sin-
glehandedly, ten thousand miles across the country and back.
All of us, already masters of thrift, took it to a new level, camping only in campgrounds that were free, or cost little. We cooked
our own food over a camp stove. We did nothing that cost
money, apart from eating and buying gas. Our destinations were
national parks, and anything else that was free and educational
along our route: We hiked trails nearly every day; we toured a
pea factory, a tuna fish cannery in Astoria; we walked the docks
of marinas, explored ghost towns in New Mexico, traipsed
through museums. Those two months were the happiest of our
family's life, freed from the town's dark tentacles and our lonely
perch on the hill; freed, too, from the conflict that flared every
time my father came home. I learned that there are ways out,
that if you search, you can find gaps in the fence, holes beneath.
That knowledge served me well on Bear Island, too.

10

Escapes
from Immobility

A T TIMES DURING THAT WINTER ON
Bear Island, I felt as tightly bound as I
did during those years in that New Hampshire village, and as
caged as I imagined were the occupants of the New Jersey suburban ghetto. Instead of those hovels, I was here in this marriage
and on these few acres, surrounded by the waters of the Gulf of
Alaska. I was in both places for good; I meant to be, but sometimes I was perversely grateful for the circling cliffs and moat of
ocean, the fortifications shoring up my beliefs. They ensured,
always, the return down the hill, the slow walk toward the
house, the opening door, immediate or eventual resolution. Restoration was never certain, though. We were too new for that.
Each conflict here presented several frightening options, reconciliation only one among them, but the only one I allowed possible.

Duncan felt the confines sometimes, too, though less often. We talked about it a few times, remembering Lloyd and Edith Swan, the couple who had lived on Harvester Island years ago, in the fifties. I knew a little about them, the stories that take on a life of their own and in the space of a few words the lives and souls of whole people are sketched in caricature. The story most relevant to us was this: Edith and Lloyd were once happily married. They had children and kept busy with their respective projects, hers raising chickens and selling the eggs to the villagers in Larsen Bay, keeping the money for her own. Lloyd tended the sheep on the island, whose meat and wool he sold, and once a week, or whenever the kerosene ran out, he would row out to the navigational marker on the end of the spit and refill the lantern with kerosene. Ah, but their frustrations with each other mounted, until they could no longer share the same house. She moved out to another old building. Mornings, she would bring her eggs to his door and sell them outright to Lloyd, or barter them for coffee and meat, which apparently he was the keeper of. I met Edith many years later, when she was old, her mind drifting. It was not hard to think this of her. Duncan and I would laugh about the story, and then we'd stop abruptly. What a perfect parable for us, and for anyone who lived out.

There were other stories. Joe Maxwell and his wife lived in a lagoon just across the water from us. The warehouse still stands, though barely. He was a binge alcoholic, and she was emotionally unstable, as the story goes. He took to drinking, or kept on drinking enough one time to send her over the edge. She packed a suitcase and walked the wild cliffed edges in her going-to-town clothes, a pathetic figure, miles from any plane or way out, desperate to leave.

Then there was Russian Dick, a White Army Czarist supporter who fled Russia during the Bolshevik Revolution and, after marrying a native woman from the area, founded a home-site on a bank two miles from Bear Island. Always a dark, mysterious figure who invoked fear, he kept to himself for years, secretly mining for gold. He also ran a herd of cattle and would row all the fourteen miles to Karluk and ten miles to Larsen Bay to sell the milk. One year his wife just disappeared. Dead, he said. She fell off an icy cliff. The people of both villages believed he pushed her. His son, Tony, went on to kill two people in the lagoon next to Bear Island. Jealousy, we heard. He was in love with another man's wife—the couple who lived on Bear Island—and he ended up shooting her and a friend.

THESE WERE sobering stories that testified to what could so easily happen out here between two people. We were just beginning to experience then, that first year out, the complexities of marriage in the bush, and the threat of relational stagnancy and worse that paralleled the boundaries of our island. We would face the same set of difficulties again and again each summer as we returned to the island, but it would take years to understand the paradox at the root of our struggles. For now, I had come to realize the source of some of the tension: In this realm we were not equals as we were in the other. This was the realm powered by upper-body brawn. We were equals and competitors in that other world—the world of books and mind. Here my ranking fell. I had little authority in this country because of size, stature, and always, no matter my proficiency, relative inexperience. There were indeed many times of great joy, and a deep, quiet satisfaction in sharing nearly every event, so that our histories were blending and merging into a single story. At the same time, our differences were magnified, our every frustration with each other amplified in the surrounding silence. Without distractions, or other webs of relationships, we were free to tunnel deeper and deeper into ourselves, into our imagined slights. A world, peopled only with two, could be a very small world indeed.

ONE DAY, our world enlarged by two. "Parks cannery, calling Parks cannery, Munsey's bear camp," the VHF radio suddenly blurted. Duncan and I looked at each other. Someone new in the bay—with an English or Australian accent! Company! The next good traveling day, we hitched up the skiff and tractor and were on our way down to Munsey's bear camp, down another arm of Uyak Bay, some fifteen miles away. John and Julia came out to meet us, both in their late twenties, from Australia, and as anxious for conversation as we were. They were making their way around the world, allotting five years more or less to the enterprise. While passing through Alaska, and wanting to stay, they answered an ad for a winter watchman at a small camp, and so became our neighbors. Julia was a chemist, with a Ph.D. from Cornell, and an all-around mechanic; John was a veterinarian, artist, and quilter. A series of back-and-forth visits eased our hunger to talk politics, religion, travel, art, literature. The days, though getting longer, passed more quickly with a nightly radio schedule with John and Julia, who always had news or a bit of trivia for us, and our weekly visits.

ONE WEEK, we realized we had to fly into town to take care of some business. On our next trip to Larsen Bay, we called and reserved two seats on the mail plane for the following day, then drove home in the skiff to pack for our little excursion. I felt unaccountably happy for this weekend in town. The next day, though, the planes weren't flying due to a ceiling of fog all over Kodiak Island. When all flights were canceled, and the fog showed no plans of moving, we sat, deflated.

"Leslie, what do you think about hiking down to Seven-Mile Beach tonight and camping out somewhere down there? Maybe in the old cabin or on the beach?" Duncan proposed, in an effort to cheer me up.

'Yeeaahh," I drawled out, considering. Then, "Hey! Let's ask John and Julia to go with us!"

We radioed them that minute, and it was agreed with enthusiasm on both sides.

They arrived in their skiff in the late afternoon. By five o'clock, low tide, we were on our way, backpacks, Julia and John in knee boots, us in hip boots rolled down for easier walking. This mass abandonment of the island by foot and boot was only possible because of the spit. Bear Island was connected to Kodiak Island by a rugged quarter-mile-long spit that emptied for dry crossings only at the lowest stage of the lowest tides. It was nearly dark now, just past seven. We had walked about three miles and were just considering where to camp when we saw the boat, a large crabber approaching Bear Island. It was still some distance away, but by its lights we knew it was the *City of Seattle*, a friend's 2-million-dollar crab boat. He had said that anytime he was in the area, we could hitch a ride to town. If we called him on the VHF, he'd come in for us. I grabbed Duncan's shoulder—we'd get to town after all! But we'd have to get back to Bear Island to radio, otherwise he'd pass right by. And one more problem: Duncan got out his tide book he always kept in his pocket while I shone the light over the small print. The tide had turned just ten minutes before. In less than an hour, it would be impassable by foot or boot. By peak high tide, six hours later, the water would rise its full twenty-five feet, and the trail of gravel anchored by randomly placed cragged boulders and reefs would be invisible beneath a blanket of water. But if we got there in less than an hour we could make it! We were so thrilled at this possibility we nearly forgot about John and Julia. After explaining the situation briefly, they allowed us to persuade them to an about-face and a near-run the whole way back, the two deadlines foremost in our minds: the spit, and then catching the *City of Seattle.*

We were fast and made it back in half the time. Breathlessly we approached the sandy ramp of the spit, peering into the dark. We couldn't see much, but we could hear it, not just the sound of ocean, but of ocean breaking over rocks. Duncan checked the tide book again to be sure; the tide, a -1.7, had turned just under an hour ago. We could see water from both sides converging in places, but when we shone the flashlight, the rocks out at the lowest point were still visible.

"We can still make it!" Duncan said confidently.

"I can see the rocks in the channel. That's the deepest part. I'm sure we can make it," I urged, turning to John and Julia.

They were dubious, seeing the black waters surging, then breaking white in a rupture of foam.

"I don't know, it doesn't look safe to me," John began.

"Look, we've all got boots on. It's not that deep," Duncan persuaded.

"If we're going to go, we've got to go now. Every minute and there's more water," I added. I was going to get across no matter what.

Julia and John looked at each other. "Okay," Julia relented, though reluctantly. "We have to hold hands so we don't get lost in the dark. Don't let go no matter what," she warned in an authoritative voice.

Duncan went first since he had the flashlight, then Julia, me, John. We held hands tightly, locking fingers over palms as we stepped out onto the rough gravel and into the water. It was only inches deep here, then as we walked, stumbling on smaller rocks, feeling our way, it passed our ankles, then our knees. We weren't yet out halfway, and the channel was still to come. The waves now were no longer benign—they rolled in toward us from both sides. We gripped each others' wrists now.

"Hold on! Don't let go!" Duncan yelled. "We're almost through the worst of it!"

"No! We need to go back!" Julia yelled back. We won't make it in time! The water's too deep!"

"We've got to keep going. It's too deep to go back!"

The water was up to our thighs by now. We couldn't see the waves coming, we could only hear them as they broke, and then, I could see in front of us, like a zipper of white as they broke along the length of the spit.

A rolling hill of water crested over my hipboots, soaking both legs instantly. John's arm began to slip out of mine as another wave hit him. "John! Don't let go!" I shouted, grabbing him harder. We had to keep going, that was all I could think. I had him again, and we kept moving, slowly, trying to find the higher ground, until one step and I rose, the water down to my knees, and then we were kicking the water out of the way as we hit our own beach on Bear Island. We were wet to our waists. We meekly offered apology to our friends, hoping we still were, then excitedly sloshed our way up to the radio and got ready for town.

THREE WEEKS LATER, after our weekend in Kodiak, we left Bear Island unexpectedly again. Our apartment was nearly done; we had added to our construction duties a chicken house, a boat shed down on Harvester Island; and a major remodel of the banya. We had run out of work when we heard that an old cannery across in another bay was going to fire up for the herring season and was looking for workers. Ready for a new challenge, and excited by the prospect of earning money for our Asia trip, we signed on. Duncan and I were hired as general workers, working where needed, first in painting and renovating the old bunkhouses before the workers from Seattle arrived, then later I was cooking in the kitchen, helping to feed a crew of thirty-five while Duncan worked as a foreman.

After two weeks at the cannery, I was restless again. One day rose warm, the sun shining as if paying off its debt. After a long winter on the island, and so little sun, spring seemed possible, and I wanted out on the water, alone.

"Duncan, it's too beautiful. I've got to get out of the cannery. The animals on the island need to be fed. I'll go there and come right back."

"You know the rule—no one travels alone in the skiff. Leslie, we've kept it all winter. I'm not going to break it now," he said in a "forget-it" tone of voice.

"Duncan, I have to get out of here. You know I can run the skiff. I can handle it! And I have nothing to do. I've finished all my work for the day. It'll save you a trip to feed the animals," I said, pulling out all the stops, watching his every facial muscle for reaction. I hated this, having to ask permission, as if I were a child. "And besides, look at this weather! You couldn't get a calmer day. What could happen?"

Duncan sighed with great exasperation, ignoring the mirroring waters of the bay in front of us, then looked at me wearily. "Okay, go! You've got enough gas in the skiff, an extra tank is already there. If anything happens . . . Leslie, are you listening?"

"Yes!" I riveted my eyes back to his face. "If anything happens . . ." I repeated, mimicking his voice just slightly, trying to veil the sarcasm I felt. Why did he have to be so melodramatic?

"If anything happens, find a beach and build a fire. You got it? If you're not back by four thirty, I'll come looking for you," he finished.

"Okay, I hear you," I said impatiently. "Build a fire, find a beach. Okay. I'll be back before four thirty," I shot over my shoulder as I jumped from the dock into the skiff.

I WAS OFF. It was my exuberance alone that seemed to speed my wooden skiff over the miles of smooth water. Winter would be over soon, and then another fishing season to get through, and then we would be off on our year-long trip. That was too far to think about right now, though. To be alone, really alone in this moment was intoxicating. I needed it far more than I had realized. Why is it so much harder to be alone when there's only two of you? But we expect too much from each other, I argued with myself, expect that our every need will be fulfilled by the other. How can we not expect that, or not need that, when there are no other choices? But look at the Garden of Eden. Even in that perfect world, or maybe most especially in a perfect world, Adam and Eve were not alone; God walked with them in the garden every day. But the winter had been good, too. I was growing into this place. It was not just Duncan's house, Duncan's family, Duncan's island; I could be part of all of this myself. And now, the sun on my face, a landscape that moved and changed, the whirr of making my own wind . . . It lasted twenty minutes. Then, as suddenly as the pulling of a shade, a heavy snow squall hit. The mountains navigating my passage, guiding me clear from the Shelikof Strait, disappeared. The snow came fat and fast, the fog breathing white between the flakes—the white-out was complete. All that was left of my vision was my sixteen-foot skiff, my hand shielding my eyes, and a circle of turbulent water that followed me wherever I went.

I slowed in hopes of seeing better. My worst fear was that I would overshoot Bear Island, small as it was, and end up in the Shelikof. The strait is relatively shallow, as salt water goes, much of it less than 120 fathoms. At these depths, and with the wind tunnel, calm can erupt into gale, flat water into twenty-foot boils in minutes. Many vessels, from skiffs to multimillion-dollar crab boats over one hundred feet, have sunk within minutes in the Shelikof. I had to find the island, or at the least the other side of the bay, which would lead me out to the island.

I don't know how long I wandered in the fog before I found land again. If I could have touched it, I would have kissed it. It was as good as home for a few minutes, until I realized, as I followed the line of cliffs, that I was somewhere I had never been. How could that be? These were fjords, like Norway; how did I get to Norway? part of my brain asked, completely disoriented. I clung as close to the shore as I dared, watching for rocks, tracing its outline with my wake, peering at every cropping and cliff face, expecting a flash of recognition at any moment. It did not come. Still, I could not let go of this one anchor—the solidity of land in a world blurred into degrees of the nebulous.

I needed one of two things: something I recognized—a promontory, a hill, anything I could name and follow back to my own bay; and if not that, at least a beach. A voice in my head, it was Duncan's voice, said, "Find a beach, build a fire, and wait." I repented of my earlier judgment immediately. His parting had been delivered with a melodrama and foreshadowing I scoff at in inept novels and that I scoffed at then. And now I was living what was too affected to read! I smiled wryly at myself. But I could not find any sort of beach, not one spread of sand beyond the tide's reach to beach the skiff, to rest. Just cliff and cliff, rocks jutting black rising into fog, the suck and rain of surf as it battered the shale . . . Time was irrelevant, except as it related to the expenditure of gas. That I was conscious of. It was a constant worry. I was almost to the end of the six-gallon tank, and I had another, but how long would that last and what then? If only I could find a beach.

I did, but not until the gas ran out, not until the engine died, not until the pull cord broke in my hands as I desperately tried to start the engine one more time, not until I was nearly against the cliffs in a smashing surf with nothing but oars, not until I was at the end of all I knew to do. Then I stood, helpless, hands at my sides, and shouted a prayer through the clouds to the God I knew was there, a prayer for mercy, a prayer for a beach. This is part of why I know about mercy and prayer: Immediately the snow stopped, the fog lifted, and for the first time in hours I could see. There, somewhere between a half mile and mile across, was another shoreline; among the black rock faces sat one beach. It was small, just a handsbreadth from where I stood, but I could get there with my oars. "Thank you, Lord!" I nearly shouted, head up.

When you're on the water, any beach is home. The slide of the skiff bottom onto sand, that sound, is like the crunch of gravel under your tires as you pull into your driveway. I claimed that beach as home. My first task was to build a fire. We kept a survival kit in the skiff stocked with strips of inner tubes and matches for starting fires, flares, a polyurethane tarp. For the rest of the day, I paced the fifty-foot width of gravel, gathering wet driftwood to feed the fire I had finally gotten started with a thorough dousing of gasoline.

After several hours of this, I could not stand the wait, and the smothering knowledge that soon they would be looking for me. It would not be pretty. I had done something really stupid. I shouldn't have insisted on going. Then an idea—why don't I just hike in to Larsen Bay? It wouldn't be too far, I figured, to follow the shoreline back around to the tip of this point, and then no more than a mile through the alders to the village. I could make it in a couple of hours and get there before 4:30. I could just radio over to the cannery and it would be done. Yes, I had to try.

There were trails all over converging on the beach, and a well-traveled trail that led solidly away and in the direction I needed to go. I began walking, feeling relieved that at least I was doing *something*, going somewhere. As I walked, ducking through the underbrush, a large bear skull lay near the path, and three minutes later, another. I slowed, began thinking about the engineers of this trail, and how warm it was getting, and that Kodiak bears don't just snuggle down for the whole winter, but doze and rise according to the weather. What would I do if I blundered into a bear? Who would know where my remains were? I stopped, agonized by a push-pull so evenly balanced I was paralyzed: If I made it into Larsen Bay I could prevent an all-out search effort—a very strong push. But if I kept going and something happened, like a bear, on the way, I would never be found—a strong pull. I desperately wanted to avoid being the subject of a search, but . . . Finally, I began to pray, again: "Lord, I don't know what to do! Please help me!" And then, it occurred to me to ask, "What would Duncan say?" In a moment, I heard him in my head, his firm voice saying very clearly, "Leslie, no matter what happens, stay with the skiff! Always stay with the skiff!" I didn't remember whether he had said that in his parting speech, but I heard it now, and the words were right; the words were true. I thanked the Lord, and turned back to the beach, to my beach, to await what would come next.

I did not know then, but I was wrong about my location. I was not just around the corner from Larsen Bay; I was two corners over, on the back side of an island, a five-mile-long island where bear guides like to hunt because of the density of bears. I would not have realized my mistake until dark.

An hour or so later, I saw, far across the bay, a tiny white skiff, like a toy on the horizon. I looked at my watch—it was four-forty-five. Duncan. The search would begin now, I shuddered, both relieved and mortified.

WHEN I DID NOT RETURN AT FOUR THIRTY, a good six hours after I had left, there was no way to call or check other than following the same route in the same way. Duncan jumped into another skiff and plowed the shorelines the way he knew I had gone. An hour later, when he got out to the island, my planned destination, he saw I never got there. A search had to be started—now. But there was no way to call or get any word out where he was. He'd have to go to the village. Now he leaped back into the skiff with an urgency fed by the terrible fear that perhaps even then it was too late. Just two summers before, a man and his young grandson had skiffed out into the same bay on the way to hunt deer and had simply disappeared. Their skiff was found floating, unharmed, and the dog and rifle still in it, but both were gone, and were never found. Duncan made the eight miles back to the village, where there was a single sideband radio. Once there, he got Victor Carlson and ran to the cannery to call. He keyed the mike, and as calmly as he could, despite his racing heart, called the Coast Guard, and the vital statistics flew.

From there, Duncan called on the CB the one pilot in the village, Dave Oberg. He fueled up immediately and took off in low circles, eyes on the water. The word was out. Duncan almost relaxed, for a second. Boats were called by VHF radio and began running grids in the Shelikof Strait, a Coast Guard helicopter was launched, and Duncan sat at the center of it all, by the CB, the sideband, and the VHF radio, listening to the reports—"No, nothing here. We'll try over in Zachar Bay again"—and directing the search—"Try down at Seven-Mile Beach. If she missed the island she might have drifted down there!" The reports all came back negative. Duncan desperately wanted to jump in a plane and search himself, certain he could find me, but he had to stay and direct the search from a chair in the cannery.

Back in Kodiak, a coast guardsman who knew me heard the radio transmissions: "Female aged twenty-three, Leslie Fields missing . . ." and called my church. It was Wednesday night, prayer meeting. It was almost 8:00 P.M., nearly over. The pastor was finishing the group prayer when the phone in the back office rang. Someone quietly slipped out and answered, then strode up to the pulpit boldly, whispered something in the pastor's ear. He straightened, then announced, "Leslie Fields has been reported missing in a skiff out in Uyak Bay." Everyone there knew me, and the prayers began.

Eighty miles away, the search had ended for the night. It was dark now. I had hunched down beneath my survival tarp that I always carried in the skiff; it would be a cold night on the beach. Then, one pilot suddenly, impetuously, after tying his plane up for the night, decided to fly one last run, despite the dark. Incredulous to hear an engine in the dark, I flew to the can of gasoline I had thrown on the fire each time a plane had come close. In the daylight, no one had seen the smoke or fire. In the night, though, the flare of the gas-fed flames caught the pilot's eye, and it was over. I chanced to look at my watch as I climbed, weary and grateful, into the plane. It was 8:00 P.M.

DUNCAN WAS on a boat by then, riding back to the Zachar Bay cannery. He got to the cannery at 10:00 P.M., where I was safe and had been waiting for two hours.

How do you greet someone you thought was dead? What do you say when you stand in front of the person you hurt the most, the one who tried to prevent what happened, the one you've committed your life to? I climbed awkwardly onto the boat, over the rails.

"Where's Duncan?" I asked timidly, not really knowing how to do this.

"He's up near the bow," someone answered.

There he was in the dark, just standing there, his back to me. I walked slowly up to him and touched him on the shoulder. "Duncan," I said softly.

He turned slowly, not surprised. He had heard I was here. He looked at me without speaking, fatigue all over his face.

"I'm sorry. I'm sorry this whole thing happened," I ventured. "I wish I could undo it."

"Do you know . . . Do you know how . . . ?" he tried to say, his face hollow, his voice stretched thin. He gave up, looked away.

"No, I don't know what it must have been like for you. I'm sorry. It wasn't that fun for me, either." He hugged me then, a short, hard hug, and we went back into the cannery, arms around each other, our faces tight. Later, we would hug softly.

THE EVENTS of that single day followed such a stunningly just and ironic plot, I wore a twisted smile every time I thought of it, even years after. The story played like a mini Greek tragedy: the protagonist, impatient, with rising hubris, demands independence, forcing the cosmic machinery to her will. Fate and justice strike: an immediate fall and humiliation, and here the story is christianized—a denouement: not gory, catastrophic death to all, but mercy and rescue. I liked that ending, I was profoundly grateful for that ending, but still, it was a bit off. I am saved by prayer, that is good; dependence upon God is the most rational reliance I know of, but the next part, that I am saved as well by Duncan's patronizing instructions? The irony of it: I am saved by what I am running from. That's not the ending I would have written. I would have made the escape that day entirely successful, made the story a real out-west frontier tale of the hero who saves her own skin and single-handedly conquers the wilderness—white-out, bears, doubting husband, and all.

The incident made the front page of the local paper, as did all Coast Guard activities, so everyone knew. Others who had been lost or stranded sympathized graciously, and others said I shouldn't have been out there in the first place. I listened to it all and made appropriate responses, but inside I was satisfied somehow and felt no shame or embarrassment. Though I needed to be rescued, and was inexpressibly grateful to all who searched and helped, the ending was not the final significance. That I could escape at all, that I could be out there alone in the squall and on that small far beach, that I hadn't panicked, that God followed my journey so attentively, all of that was enough. That beach, that island, the waters of the bay, those cliffs were home to me for that day; I had some kind of claim on them, and they on me.

11

Living in the Kingdom
of Clean-Enough

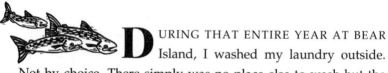 URING THAT ENTIRE YEAR AT BEAR Island, I washed my laundry outside. Not by choice. There simply was no place else to wash but the open porch, and no place to dry but the outside line. On windy days, the sheets and towels would freeze horizontally. I would pry them, crackling, from the line, stack them in my arms and carry them into the cabin. They were pieces of the wind, caught, frozen, made visible. Our clothes, our second skin—jeans, thermal underwear, wool socks, flannel shirts—came into the house with rigor mortis—a sober prophecy for our bodies.

I made no such metaphors the first time I did laundry out there. I came to it open-minded, with no predilection to philosophizing. I know I am blessed that my mother wasn't overly concerned about cleanliness. She did make me take a bath once a week, no matter how strong my protests. I remember bars of

Fels Naphtha soap in the laundry room, and boxes of laundry soap about, but I never heard them called by brand. Mother never discussed the virtues of one detergent over another, nor did I ever see her bending over stains on our clothes, worrying them out with specially concocted stain removers. Such cleaning agents cost too much, and our clothes were not worthy of such attention. Most of my clothes, until I started buying my own with baby-sitting money at twelve, were handmade and twice worn. Mother would make two new cotton dresses a year for each of us girls. The several other dresses I wore had once been Laurie's, then were passed to Jan, and then they were mine, the cotton flowers usually faded and blanched then into a vague pattern faintly reminiscent of some kind of garden. Our laundry lives, most of the time, were not terribly different from most people's. We had an automatic washer and dryer, but then for seven summers our well was so dry we hiked to a stream in the woods with buckets, doubled under their weight the whole long way back, and poured them into the washing machine one bucket at a time, first for washing, then for rinsing.

Despite this history and relaxed attitude, I was unprepared for washing on Bear Island. The first time I did laundry here, I cried. Secretly. And only after, after putting eight loads of grimy clothes and fish-fouled jeans through the same marinade of mud sloshing in a wringer washer that only partially worked. After feeding it all through the rollers and hanging it all out, I went down to my loft and cried into my pillow. I knew only two basic categories then: clean and dirty, black and white. It seemed a horrible perversion of both the symbol and reality of laundering. I did not yet understand this economy, how far we must bend to live on this island where fresh water is so limited. Such an irony, that in a place of such water, we have so little of it for our clothes and our bodies.

Laundry on Bear Island was strictly a communal affair, women's work, performed by three of us—Wanda, Beverly, and myself. On designated laundry days, I stayed ashore to help, though many times I would have preferred the fish over the wash. We washed for everyone—nine of us. Our population had grown by two: Weston and Bev's children, Tamie and DeWitt.

IN SPITE OF DESIRE, education, aesthetics, and decent upbringings on the part of each of us, standards slid every which way. The work began in the banya, where the washing machine was parked. From there we wandered purposely about the island from building to shed to house, gathering any and all dirty clothes, regardless of the owner. As we returned from each building, box in arms, heaped with the castings, our determined optimism would be strained with each new addition. Finally, as we upended the boxes on the concrete floor and began sorting, we were resigned to another four-hour session to get them through the machine and out on the lines. Getting them dry and folded and distributed was another task altogether and not part of the day's concern.

The labor intensity of the whole business trapped us in a strange conundrum. We asked everyone to wear their clothes as long as possible before tossing them in the dirty box. There was always complete compliance, which cut down on an otherwise unmanageable amount, but the downside was that by the time we got them, they were almost irredeemable. The jeans in particular gained a life of their own, most of the borrowings from fish gurry and decomposing kelp. The machine hadn't much of a chance. It was already crippled by its hard years servicing clothes of that ilk: it agitated lethargically, and no longer drained. We filled it first by hauling water from the well in five-gallon buckets, load after load, then hoisting them high to tip the water in. It took six to eight trips to fill the machine and the rinse tub beside it. With the weight of the buckets, the carrying distance, and the limited water supply for the island, we could only fill the machines once, then we nursed and strategized our way from the cleanest clothes to the dirtiest, from towels at the clean end to socks at the other, running ten to fourteen loads through those same two drums of water. After the first load, the wash water turned a light gray, the rinse water had a skim of suds. By the time we finished with the socks, roiling now in a murky soup, we were watching and hoping, even, for rain.

We were pleased with whatever wet fell upon our wash as it hung. We called it the second rinse, more than a simple euphemism for rain. We meant the term quite literally as the clothes hung and swayed between various states of wet, damp, cool, nearly dry, then wet all over again, through three, four, even five days, which is the current record. But this was where the real cleaning came, the purification.

When we were done with the machines, the water came out the same way—by hand. A pitcher was the largest scoop that fit inside the drum, so pitcher at a time we filled the buckets, then carried them out beyond the well to dump. Scoop by scoop by bucket we emptied the machine of its accumulation of grime. We were too tired, all of us, to empty the water halfway through the loads and start again with fresh. We all wanted to, but the rest of the day's work was before us as well, and somewhere along the way we tried to stop caring.

EARLY THAT NEXT SUMMER, after the year on Bear Island, we got a new washing machine, giving us two, one to wash and one to rinse. The new one was a wringer like the other, but ran on gas, so we started it with a pull cord, and adjusted the choke, like a lawn mower or an outboard: it represented the ongoing and somewhat delayed mechanization of our lives. We now felt as though we had entered the Industrial Revolution, with the increased efficiency of a production line, but we could no longer talk to pass the hours; the exhaust from the gas washer and the din of two machines on a concrete floor was hard to transcend. We either shouted at each other, or smiled patiently and signaled, "later!" Still, the clothes were a bit cleaner, the water drained by itself, and our laundering lives felt more manageable. We nearly lost those gains that next season.

IT WAS A FISHING DAY. I was ashore that afternoon, catching up on in-house tasks and enjoying my status as now part-time fisherman. I had fought hard for that, and knew my very survival depended upon finding some kind of balance between the sheer muscular fatigue of that work, and my spirit and mind.

After washing the floor, a week overdue, and cooking dinner for later, when the men came in from the water, I noticed the sun had come out, and decided to take a run across the spit to the lagoon. It was a good run. Though windy, the sun warmed my bare arms and, with a timed pace, I put in a good six miles back and forth on the lagoon beach. I started back, jogging slowly to cool down, and noticed smoke coming from the banya. Great timing, I thought. A banya will feel good later tonight. But there was a lot of smoke. No, too much smoke. I sprinted the last two hundred yards, then, breathless, ran straight for the door of the small red building we had built out of local spruce and driftwood. I yanked the door wide; balls of smoke rolled out. I fell to the floor next to the washing machines and looked up at fire on the ceiling of the bathing room. Flames were roaring through the dry plywood that planed out from the stovepipe. It was half gone already. I backed out, coughing, and ran wildly, shouting "FIRE! FIRE!" to Beverly and Wanda, the only others ashore. They met me, running, on the path, looking as panicked as I felt. What could we do with a tinderbox building, a brisk 20-knot wind, everyone else out on the water, and no hose or pump to put it out? Our fire extinguishers were much too small. Then we remembered—the washing machines! We had to save them. Not one of us urged caution at that point. We collectively ran to the burning banya, pulled the smoldering door open, took a deep breath, charged in, grabbed the first machine, and with the strength and timing of the desperate and heroic, we lifted it out in five seconds flat, then dashed in for the second.

That evening, we gathered around what was left of our wash house: the concrete floor, and on it, unruffled and oblivious, the clawfoot tub which itself had been salvaged from an old banya on Harvester Island, then off in the grass behind it, the two machines, standing askew, looking like the survivors they were. We were all grateful the fire hadn't spread to the rest of the buildings. We had done what we could to prevent it, forming a bucket brigade and throwing pails of ocean water on the adjacent buildings. A ridiculously paltry effort, we knew, but doing that felt better than standing in consuming worry helplessly watching the trajectory of the sparks. The men called us foolish for running into a burning building just for washing machines, but we knew we would have risked much more.

AT THE END of the fishing season, in a speedily rebuilt replacement banya, the whole cleaning enterprise was threatened once again. We had just begun what was to be a day of washing— fourteen loads heaped in the room waiting for their own brand of redemption, when smoke began coiling delicately from the cord of the old Maytag. The room soon filled with the smell of electricity gone bad, and sure enough, she was gone. There was no time to mourn, however. We were out of clothes, all of us, and the washing had to go on. Within minutes, as we rearranged the washroom, we were back to our recent, more primitive days, to the one-machine system where the wringer washed and we took turns rinsing in a large aluminum tub below it. It was hard to relinquish our advances so quickly. I took over Maytag's job and acted as agitator and de-soaper. After I fed the washed clothes through the wringer, they peeled through, sliding into the laundry tub where I lifted them up and down in the water as though making smoke signals—in, out, plunge, slop, dousing my own front as I rinsed as much of the soap out as energy and patience allowed, then back through the wringer and into the basket for the hang on the line while Wanda began filling the machine for the next load. It took much longer; by the fifth load, though I had often seen froth on the fabric the last time through, I pronounced them done in successively shorter times. Two hours later, with still a few loads to go, I desperately wanted to take Bev's two children, two and four, aside, and sternly whisper an edict, looking around furtively lest their mother hear me: "You must wear your clothes two or three days now. The second machine has broken and it is much harder to do the wash, so we'll wear our clothes longer, okay?" They would have had no problem with that, despite the fact that it would have summarily reversed an earlier edict I heard Bev issue a few days ago: "You cannot wear your clothes three days in a row—they're too dirty."

Duncan had no need to alter his fishcamp dressing habits, however. A child of a mother who washed on a scrub board with a hand-crank wringer for a dozen years, he had full appreciation for the labor of washing, had internalized its implications long ago. He could jury-rig a T-shirt along for a week, a sweatshirt for four days, jeans for five, and still look reasonable. I seldom complained, nor did I compliment, because what do you say, exactly—"Thank you, dear, for not putting on clean clothes this morning"?

Eventually, out of curiosity, I began to ask around about other people's laundry systems. Some used wringer washers, as we did. A man down the beach from us told me his routine. Every year he brought out a barrel of T-shirts and pants from the Salvation Army, wore a set until they were either rank or ripped, and then threw them in a pile on the beach and burned them. He didn't own a washing machine of any kind. In a similar "no-bother" spirit, others take their wash to the nearby cannery where workers would wash, dry, and neatly fold for a dollar a pound. And, most bizarre to me at the time, two women I knew with running water and an ample supply, confessed to actually using automatic washers. I was astounded.

I didn't dwell on their good fortune much, though, beyond the first astonishment. For whatever reason, I seldom thought beyond present circumstances. Some visitors no sooner landed on our beach than they began listing all we should do to simplify and modernize our lives. It took all I had to fit myself to the task at hand. Deliverance and happy endings came mostly through perseverance, I had learned, both from my childhood and from my years here.

THOUGH EVENTUALLY Bear Island's water would run, it walked for thirty years, and for all the years I was there. With a pulley, an aluminum bucket, and a line leftover from fishing, stiffened with salt water, I filled my five-gallon buckets and carried them up a hill, then up the steep stairs to the second story of our apartment and on into the kitchen. I could not hang the buckets from my arms, use my shoulders as a yoke and simply swing them on my own hinges—the pails would hit the knobby ground in its uphill slope, slosh and waste, and throw me off balance. I needed to lift my arms, just crook the elbow enough to clear the vagaries of the turf, and like that, I would walk like a steam engine, head down, chugging. The tendons from my wrist pulled like taut wire; my biceps and ligaments grimaced. I felt their complaint—water weighing seven pounds per gallon, the two nearly full buckets a hoist of 60 pounds, more than half of my own weight. I made a rule: no resting until the top of the hill, until I got to the house. Then I would stop, set the buckets down, stand up straight for a moment getting a final blast of oxygen, then up, buckets in holsters again, and the final lift and ascent of the stairs, stairs too steep, built to fit the limited space, with an entire foot between steps. Here my arms crooked yet sharper, the buckets lifted higher to clear the treads, and by the time the breath wore out, I would be up and the buckets on their final swing and release to the bench next to the sink, the sink with the faucet.

The water all went into the kitchen, on a bench near the stove. We had a bathroom, but like the kitchen faucet, it was mostly a symbol, a promise. With neither toilet nor sink nor water of any sort, just a mirror for whatever can be primped dry, the bathroom was a room with the hope-of-a-bath attached. Duncan advanced these conditions ironically when he unpacked and ceremoniously placed on a stand next to the mirror a fifty-year-old antique ceramic pitcher and basin he had bought at a flea market in Oregon. Now there was pouring and pooling water in the bathroom. Still, because of the distance from the water source, we did all our nightly and morning washing, together with our crew, at the kitchen sink. For years, before the sink was plumbed, we all stood outside, on the top porch step, and swished our toothbrushes in cups of water and competed to see who could spit the farthest past the front steps. When we finally got the chance, more than five years later, to install a drainpipe and dig a drainage system, we moved indoors with our tooth-brushes, and all stood about the kitchen sink, crew and all, scrubbing, frothing, and spitting.

This arrangement, this erosion between the public and private, became so habitual, I only happened to notice its possible oddity when company came. They were my first guests of the summer, though the season was more than half over. The husband and wife had flown in from the town of Kodiak, where they were well known as successful entrepreneurs, and were respected for their integrity, wit, and graciousness. I did not know them, only knew of them and looked forward to meeting them. After a dinner of teriyaki-grilled halibut and stir-fry, we settled down to more conversation over coffee and chocolate cheesecake. The meal had gone well. While fixing another pot of coffee, I suddenly remembered I hadn't brushed my teeth that morning. Without thinking, I reached for my brush on the shelf, the toothpaste, and stood there calmly brushing my teeth, continuing the conversation with our guests. Suddenly, as I bent over to spit, I realized what I was doing and held my spume. Slowly returning upright and with more dignity than I had a right to possess in that circumstance, I calmly strolled out to the front step to finish the job in private. I stood there for a few extra minutes, feeling embarrassed and pondering my place in society. My only consolation was that I hadn't suddenly realized my hair was dirty. I could just as easily have dunked my head in a basin of water while carrying on the conversation as brushed my teeth.

THE WATER WAS BEAUTIFUL, sweet, always cold from the ground, and all the more precious because of the weight of its carriage. We used it sparingly, drop squeezed from drop, water used first for dishes, then for the floor, the water from cooking noodles reused for the vegetables . . . a simple economy. The two of us used about six buckets a day; three trips would do us. But our 30 gallon per diem consumption was not just a tribute to frugality. No other ministrations were performed with this water than dishes, general cleaning, and drinking. All other water needs were accomplished elsewhere, in their own buildings, with their own private rituals, transportation, and statistics.

The outhouse, of course, in its distant location at the edge of a cliff—a place of honor or banishment depending on perspective—required no water at all, which was its chief asset. This was a two-holer. Not that it was frequently used in tandem; modesty still prevailed for some activities, but it allowed for twice the usage before the unpleasant task of digging out the contents to start again.

The banya, which refers to both the building and the bath, is a wet sauna, where steam generated from water thrown on hot rocks is an integral part of the cleansing. Wood had to be split and packed first, though. A barrel stove stoked with driftwood— the only source of wood on a treeless island—supplied the heat. For the thick-skinned and iron-lunged, a banya wasn't worthy of its name unless it hit 200 degrees. The water came, as always, via shoulders and arms, but the banya, mercifully, was close to the well. We packed water up the short hill until we filled the metal tub on top of the barrel stove, the source of the hot, and the buckets on the floor for the cold. To be reasonably clean, it took, we figured, two buckets per person.

We did not take banyas spontaneously or frequently. Twice a week was luxurious. Every six or seven days was typical. The clawfoot bathtub sat in the corner, but it was mostly symbolic. It took too much water—and no one needed to be that clean. Instead, we washed in small plastic basins, the same size as our dishwashing basins, and moved through a ritual of steam and sweat, soap, scrub, rinse, perhaps several times through, if there was time. Even then, should we so lounge and wash twice, we used little more than six gallons apiece.

We watched the water carefully, not just because we ourselves carried it, and the well was low, but because others were depending upon it. During the summers, the making and taking of a banya was a communal act, shared by everyone on the island, up to as many as fifteen people. Shared not in a polygamous everyone-bathing-at-once affair, but a serial one-group-at-a-time community: husbands and wives together, family units together, male crew in whatever grouping they chose. If we were first in the lineup, we were especially conscious of how much we used, how much was left, whether we had used more than our share of both wood and water, and if so, after dressing, we would pack more buckets up the hill, stoke the fire with another load of wood. I would do it carefully, though, trying not to work up a sweat after I had just laved off the last layer; and if the fire should need more wood, I would crane my head away from the door of the barrel stove, avoiding any spurt of smoke that would cling to my finally-clean hair. And when we eventually emerged, faces broiled, hair steaming, we were glad at that moment to be clean. We would be dirty again in a day or two, but we knew the process was cyclical and dialectical, not just a constant progression away from clean, but always the swing back, the banya coming in three more days.

OUR ECONOMY only began with the water, and extended from there to every resource we managed. On my first visit to neighboring fishcamps, I was most impressed with Kay's cabin and her method of garbage disposal: she threw her garbage out of a sliding window onto the bank, where the highest tides would pull it out twice monthly. Around her cabins, she boasted an impressive assortment of junk: old generators, overturned skiffs without a prayer of seeing water, rotting mounds of nets. Still, Kay's site was nothing compared to Eddie's, which boasted dozens of disassembled motors and engines sitting about in shredded blue tarp, coils of lines, deflated orange buoys, the frames of old crab pots, two broken wringer washing machines.

I faced the same kind of detritus here; in fact, I had added significantly to it. We kept and kept using cardboard boxes, holey raingear, leaky hip boots. Hip boots that sprang a leak in the knee were cut down to knee boots. When they sprang a leak on the calf, they became ankle boots. When they sprang a leak in the toe, they became mud boots. The porch was lined with boots in these reverse evolutionary stages. We still had raingear worn twenty years ago—one pair a deep green Helly Hansen rain pants with split seams that I duct-taped back together and then stitched through meticulously to make them last another season. Out by the warehouse there was a growing display of coils of lines, buoys, gas tanks, stacks of wire racks whose original purpose eludes me; blue plastic Japanese egg crates that originally held red clusters of salmon roe; a rusted refrigerator and beside it a chest freezer, both leaning against the warehouse and tied together as if to prevent escape. A thirty-five-year-old truck with a smashed windshield, once used for pulling skiffs before we got the tractor, stood in a pool of rust beside two overturned wooden skiffs. Beside both, stacks of rotting lumber, and this just began the list. Much to my chagrin, I have found myself part of the backwoods junkyard clan.

My mother and the six of us fought this desperately growing up. Though we had little money, little enough to forego such luxuries as shampoo, shaving cream, toothpaste, butter or margarine, jelly, paper towels, Kleenex, still, it was clear who we did not want to be like. It is likely that we were poorer than the houses on certain dirt roads, houses that were unpainted, doors hanging off their hinges, with numbers of dirty children and rusted, smashed cars and trucks about, fleets of snowmobiles to be fixed, tires thrown beside the porch. On summer days, tired of our loneliness, my brother and I would walk an hour through the woods down to some of these houses to play and visit, though always after a few hours we would flee, disgusted with the boys' fighting, their drinking, their dirty jokes and propositions. We returned feeling soiled—this poverty was ugly. My mother budgeted one dollar a week for gas, and drove and grocery-shopped only once a week; we could not turn on the oven unless we had three or more dishes to bake; we were each bought one pair of shoes a year, but our yard was clean and neat, the house on the outside was painted; we did not curse: we would not be like them.

But here I was, part of my island looking something like their island of debris, and looking like Kay's and Eddie's places and all of their bush and island predecessors. I had not expected any of this. I would want to say that I trod my Alaskan island lightly, left little mark of my presence in this wilderness, that I had not disturbed the land, but it would not be true. There were reasons for this.

ONE SUMMER, in early June, Duncan asked me thoughtfully, "How would you like another refrigerator?" "Sure!" I responded enthusiastically. I loved my new gas refrigerator out on the porch, but it was very small, and I often ran out of room. Another refrigerator would allow me to store and reuse more leftovers. What arrived at my doorstep was not what I envisioned. It was a large appliance, painted a green that located it somewhere in the sixties or seventies, with an interior lacquered with gummed blood which had seeped into the inside lining through a huge split in the plastic. The reek gagged me from arm's length. And while the freezer worked, the refrigerator didn't, and hadn't for several years. I found out then its vitae: Duncan's father had extricated it from a house in town that had been torn down and then brought it the whole tortuous journey out—from truck to boat to skiff to the beach to a tractor to the backs of the five guys it took to carry it up to my porch. And here it was, this avocado-green albatross. I smiled politely at this offering, thanked the five men who had ferried it up as heartily as I could muster, then stood, arms folded, with a frown until Duncan suggested, somewhat defensively, "What about storage? Use it for a root cellar!" Eureka. I scoured it as clean as I could, sealed the crack that leached the rank odor, and have used it since to store produce on my porch. Like most everything else here, I expect it to live a long life, since it already died once. Whatever comes out here—broken or new—achieves a certain state of immortality. This is the bush way, to husband our resources. Our frugality and commitment to reduce, reuse, and recycle everything, the best and the useless, rags and new, is not just an environmentally correct response. It originates in simpler realities: though useless at the moment, we may actually need these items in the future— there is no big box store around the corner waiting to supply our every need. And there is no easy way to dispose of these goods, so we may as well fix them.

We painted the refrigerator a flat brown, with some leftover marine paint. It matches my porch better than the green, but it is a far cry from anyone's vision of a shiny refrigerator. Each time I came raiding for potatoes, or, if we were lucky, lettuce from town, I would wince at the wave of sour air that met my nose. And then, sometimes, I would smile, a crooked smile as I walked back to the kitchen: It fit our lives out here so perfectly. Since there is no garbage disposal but our own, what else can we do with our junk but keep using it?

Occasionally in my mental driftings during laundry days, or during group toothbrushing and washing, I would locate my friends and peers, now with more college degrees, promotions, advancing, adopting computers and other technologies to simplify their lives. Duncan and I would still be invisible—planning to travel through Asia for the year, and eventually to head to graduate school—he to law school, me to a master's program in journalism at the University of Oregon, yet here, now I was a laundrywoman hand-washing kettles of other people's dirty clothes, a worker in a grimy concrete-floor factory, sharing one small basin of wash water with three other people, burning garbage on the beach, pulling potatoes from a foul refrigerator. Is it possible that I am now more like those families in the New Hampshire hollows than I was when growing up?

12

Gaining Ground
and Losing

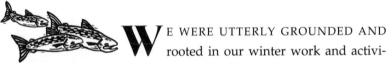WE WERE UTTERLY GROUNDED AND rooted in our winter work and activities, but in the evenings, when the washing was done, when the last coat of paint had been applied, when the wood bin was full, we pulled out the box of brochures, books, catalogues, and traveled to China, Korea, Malaysia, Russia, Japan. We lay in our bed in an eight-foot-wide room, or sat in the front room around the wood stove, usually in the winter dark, wind tearing at the windows, thumbing through maps of tropical islands, photographs of ruins in Turkey, books recounting treks in Nepal and Bhutan, a South American motorcycle trip. Where should we go? How to decide? A train across Siberia? The Great Wall of China? I wanted to cross the Sahara; Duncan wanted to cross Russia. The world was before us, waiting. We had only a few months to go now to finalize our plans, to get through another fishing season,

and then we would be off in September of 1980 for ten months of travel. By living out this year, we were saving nearly our entire incomes from two fishing seasons. There was something poetic about it, too, that satisfied me. The two years, paired together, were almost perfectly antithetical—we would spend one year immobilized on a sixty-acre mound of rock so the next we could circle the globe.

I HAD NOT TRAVELED MUCH, but it would not be my first time out of the country. On our honeymoon, we had taken a Caribbean cruise, given to us at cost from a travel agent friend. It was 1977—pre–*Love Boat,* when cruises were the primary domain of the elderly rich, and the elderly pretend-rich. I had just turned twenty; Duncan was twenty-one. Our college-student status must have been obvious. I had no clothes for the cruise, except a pair of cut-off jeans and a red-and-white striped shirt, so my "trousseau" was a small suitcase of shorts, tops, and dresses borrowed from my best friend from college. Duncan didn't have much either, being generally oblivious about clothes and appearances. We looked so young, and in our thrown-together wardrobe, so unlike a honeymooning couple that our tablemate and lounge chair neighbors thought us brother and sister. After attending a cheesy Wayne Newtonesque nightclub show, greeted by a full audience with applause and cheers, and after our dinner companions at our assigned table told the sixth "Didjaheartheoneabout?"—it became clear that in our inexperience we had made a mistake: Cruises were not at all about travel; they were all about on-board entertainment. We spent our at-sea days lounging on the sundeck with books, waiting excitedly for the days we came into port. While the rest of the bejeweled, emerald-on-every-finger sixty- and seventy-something crowd soaked up the booze and gambling, Duncan and I ran ashore in

every port, feeling morally superior, dashing about on motorcycles, rented cars, feeding our hunger to see, to see, to taste, to
touch. It was only that—a taste and a touch, but we knew we
wanted more. The next year, we took a two-week tour of Israel,
confirming our desire. We both wanted to see as much of the
world as possible.

OUR PLANS coalesced gradually. Our honeymoon served as the
perfect foil for early decisions: What method of travel would
separate us from the kind of people who staged a revolt because
the stack of shrimp at the buffet table wasn't as high as the photo
in the brochure? What kind of travel would help us to see and
experience other cultures and countries as they were, unadorned,
not dressed and suited in bellboy uniforms, not waiting on us
as consumers? How do you travel authentically, if such a thing
is possible? The answer—adventure travel, a form of touring that
was still relatively young. It meant on-the-street, down and
cheap, off-the-beaten-track, group backpack travel. Where do we
sign?

We found a dozen or so companies advertising themselves as
adventure travel groups, all of them British or European owned
and run. By spring of 1980, we had made our decision and
mapped our entire route for the year. We would go with Top
Deck, a British company, chosen because they were the cheapest,
and they went where we wanted to go. This trip, in a double-
decker bus retired from service in London, would take us from
London to Kathmandu, Nepal, in ten weeks, for $800 each. We'd
sleep in the bus or in a tent; shop the local markets and cook
our own food on the bus, and no other expenses. We'd move
quickly through Western Europe, slow down a bit in Eastern
Europe, on through Greece, Yugoslavia, Turkey, then into the
Middle East, Jordan, Syria, Israel, then cross the desert through

Iran, over into Pakistan, India, and then into Nepal. We'd be on our own in Nepal for a month, then we signed on for a leg from Nepal to Australia, taking us through Burma, Thailand, Malaysia, Singapore, and Indonesia. From there we would fly to Australia for six weeks, buy a used van, drive the perimeter of Australia, sell the van when done, then on to New Zealand for a month and then back home. We figured we could do the whole thing for $15,000, which was much cheaper than living at home.

We were serious about this, as serious as we were about living out, as serious as we were about college. This was an extension of college, we felt, necessary as a start to filling the huge gaps in our understanding of the world. We didn't know what the future held for us apart from the one fixed mark in our lives—that we would always return to Bear Island and fish. Some day we would set down year-round roots in Alaska, presumably; some day we hoped to have a family; but we couldn't do either one until we knew what the rest of the world was made of.

AS MY THIRD fishing season loomed, I suppressed my worries and fears, thought only about this trip ahead of us, and how blessed we were to have this means of earning the money to go. I didn't care about the money itself, only that it meant we could go to college, we could travel. Fishing was a necessary means to a greater end.

This season, in a pattern now that seemed unbreakable, was a replay of the first two. Plentiful salmon runs; too few people to pick the fish that found our nets. Halfway through, when we were already so strung out we knew we wouldn't make it through the next six weeks, we did something we had never done before—we hired help.

Fields and Sons' first crewman was not a young buck from

Kodiak with fish scales under his nails; he was a Ph.D. in English literature with particular expertise in Shakespeare. Ron Grosh, my professor/advisor/mentor from Cedarville College, had come up from Ohio to work at the Zachar Bay cannery that summer, both for the experience and to supplement his earnings. With one desperate radio call, we were able to lure him away from his cannery job of sorting fish to become Bear Island's first crewman. Now, after being both Duncan's and my prof, and our friend as well, he had to move hands and legs and shoulders at his former students' bidding. The irony was lost on no one.

"Ron! Go get the gas cans and meet me down by the running-line rock!"

"Ron! Your running-line knot isn't tight enough. The skiff could work that knot free and we'd lose it."

"Ron! Pull the yellow line over the bow—fast!"

I always felt empathy for Ron, knowing how it was to jump into this world from the realm of words and pages. Back in Ohio, he was regarded by all as gentle and refined. He wore a suit most of the time. His favorite hat was a beret, which he wore successfully. Though he was young, thirty-five, he was one of the first real gentlemen I had known. No one from his other life would recognize him now. We would laugh at this sometimes, both of us in our torn raingear, wearing whatever gurried hats on the shelf met our groping hands first. But how would he handle this place, the realm of body only? Could our friendship, forged in the classroom over novels, Shakespeare's plays, then extended by my work as his secretary—me typing letters to the Conference on College Composition and the Modern Language Association—survive even half a fishing season? And what of Duncan and Ron's friendship, which had deepened our last year of college? That seemed threatened most of all. But as the summer progressed, I began to relax. Ron was always gracious, even under duress, and, as a master of language and meaning, he seemed to know that words here were for work, that they must accomplish specific tasks. Just as our beaches were working beaches, not vacation beaches, so, too, language here, aided by volume, must tie a skiff to an arcing line, loop a buoy, hitch a pitching skiff to a tender, pick a sinking net in an hour. Ron worked at these tasks with his whole heart and self, becoming proficient by the end of the summer. Somehow I understood this as an affirmation that the work his prize but now errant English student was engaged in was work worth doing.

IT WAS an enormous help to have another set of hands that summer, but it wasn't enough. We lived on the nets. When not throwing fish behind us, we slogged ashore with the forward lean of the battle-worn, falling into bed whatever the hour. But there was more to complicate the season. By the end of the first month, I discovered I was pregnant. Because of our inconsistent schedule, I was consistently lax with the pink plastic round of pills that represented each day of the month. Sometimes I would miss two days, then pop three at a time. It shouldn't have been such a surprise, but there it was one morning—nausea—and the next and the next. I had not prepared for this contingency, and didn't even have a pregnancy test in my store of goods for the summer. I didn't, but Beverly did. The suspect became confirmed; our whole world shook and rattled. A baby? But what about our year of travel? What about graduate school after that? I'm only twenty-three—the end of freedom. I'm not ready to be a mother! Duncan, are you ready to be father? No. No. We weren't doing that great just managing the two of us. It wasn't time. But it was. Among the moil of emotions came another, a quiet, secret thrill, the wonder of a human being created from as good as nothing; and most of all the knowledge that beneath our lives ran the strong, sure thread of God's presence. We could discuss levels of causality in our best philosophy textbook voices: primary cause, secondary cause, sufficient cause. Theology, too, had its whole vocabulary of terms for causality that included as well the various wills of God: His sovereign will, His decretive will, His permissive will. When we decoded the fancy language, and understood it on a human level, it came to this: Because I had forgotten to take my pills, and since God, though capable of preventing pregnancy, did not, we were now pregnant. It was not, then, and ultimately could not be a mistake. Our plans, then, for the next five years, ten, were flung out the door, not carelessly, but with hands that still knew the span and weight of what they once held.

Fishing became more complicated. Aside from Bev, we did not tell anyone our news; we did not feel very celebratory, and we still had a fishing season to get through. I tried to act as if nothing had changed: the alarm rings at 7:00 A.M., up, make breakfast for the both of us, try to eat knowing the nausea would pass sometime during the pick leaving me running on the left of empty; apply all the layers of rubber and vinyl, and clump down to the beach, pivot into the skiff and labor off into the wind to pluck the nets clean. I made some discoveries those weeks—that morning sickness was inaptly named. Its range was much further than mornings. Afternoons, evenings, it didn't matter, as long as I was out on the water and the skiff was moving in any direction, it all spelled "heave." 7-Up became my constant companion. I wanted to stay in, and at times I did, but it was another frenzied season. I was called, again and again, out to the skiff, by Duncan, by my conscience, by the exhaustion in their faces. Without me, the number was uneven, which meant instead of having three manned skiffs to pick the eight nets, they had only two. I went, reluctantly, sometimes bitter, remembering movies like *Life with Father* that featured people, usually men, who doted on the "new, little mother" with a laughably clumsy energy as they circled around her stationary form, plumped against thick pillows, lounging in a deep armchair. How ridiculous that she should be treated so, as if she were an invalid, but I longed for it all the same, and could not help wondering at this state of affairs, that though everything in my world had changed, nothing had changed: that here I was, pregnant now, still bending over the net, miles from a bed, retching as I pulled in salmon as long as my arm, my back cracking toward a break, it felt like, by the sixth net, and the second skiff load of eight hundred fish. Was there no escape?

ONE MORNING we woke to wind, hardly a new sound, but this an easterly, whining straight down the channel, hitting our house front on the face. The whole building, propped on pilings, quivered.

"What do you think it's blowing, Duncan?" I asked, my eyes fixed on the water now gone white over the nets.

Duncan had the binoculars out and was looking at the seventh set, a mile away. "It's probably fifty, at least."

"You're not going out in this, right?" It was a question because I had seen him and his brothers out on the water when by my judgment no one should be there. And I had been there myself.

He was glassing the third and the sixth set now, his jaw tight. Then, without hearing my question, he was out the door and down to his parents' house—the tribunal. The three brothers would decide between them. I knew the scene without being there: DeWitt, sixty-four, would argue to stay in; Weston and

Duncan would push for going out and trying, at least; Wallace would say wait until low tide, when storms often abated at least a bit. I was hoping Wallace and Dewitt would win out.

"So, what's the story?" I asked as Duncan returned, his face relaxed now.

"We decided to go out around two, low tide. Maybe it'll come down a bit by then."

"Good! I'm so glad!" I gushed. "It's not worth it, Duncan! It's just fish!"

"It might be worth it." He looked over at me, suddenly serious. My lesser level of commitment was a sore spot between us. Then, "Can you come out later with us?"

"Umm, I'll try," I hesitated. "If it's not too bad. I'm not feeling that great, you know," I said weakly.

AT TWO, it had lessened somewhat, down to 40 mph, probably, not less, but because the nets hadn't been picked since the night before, the men could not stay off of them any longer. I was going too. My nausea was gone, and after a four-course lunch, I was ready to do some work. Though blows brought a measure of fear with them, the prevailing mood was a head-down, straight-on determination to go out, get the work done, and return in one piece. The men's entrance into the mouth of most storms was never about pride, or some Hemingwayesque man-against-sea test that served as bait and filler for a later bragfest. Their feats, and often they were incredible feats, went untold. I was glad. Their motives were, if not pure, at least singular—to go out and do their job.

On the beach, the easterly still blasting us straight from the channel, the huddle. They were going over to the seventh set first, where there was likely some damage from the rollers. Then they'd head over to Maxwell's set. Duncan turned to me. "Leslie!

Can you take a skiff down to Maxwell's and just tie on and wait for us there?" he shouted above the wind. A second, then "Okay!" I shouted back, as if this were nothing. Of course I could run a puny little boat not much bigger than a peapod dead on into 40-mph winds and their snotty, thrashing seas, then land the skiff by myself onto a noodle-thin line—no problem! my voice registered. I did not think of saying no. In the heat of the storm, we were leveled to equal need, and as one of them, I would do whatever needed to be done.

I headed out down the channel, the brim of my hat pulled low over my eyes against the salting pelt of rain and airborne ocean. I started off standing in the stern, as we usually do, one hand on the kicker handle, but the direct shot into both the wind and waves lifted the bow in great gusts, and I knew it could flip, it could flip over anytime. Unnerved, I sat on the seat, throttled down, and clenched my teeth as if that were somehow the answer. What was I doing here? I looked around wildly, not able to see any other skiff, any other sign of life or human movement in all the world of the storm. And now here, it was almost time. The net was coming up. I could see the corkline awash in the green waves. What would I do? How would I land and grab the net against this wind? Back then, it would have been enough of a challenge in calm waters, but this? As I neared, I throttled down as low as I dared go without stalling the engine. As the bow crossed the corks, I threw the kicker in neutral, and threw myself over the side of the skiff as the corkline passed under, my arms thrashing for a cork, but no, too fast. Then the prop was caught on the corkline, and as the skiff pitched and rolled, I tilted the 120-pound engine up out of the water until the net cleared. I circled around again, tried another approach, my face streaming, my eyes stinging sore from the salt. I came at it slower this next time, but too slow—the wind kept me at bay until, disgusted, I gassed the engine with a quick wrist-twist, then into neutral, but not fast enough. I tried again and again until it took: the skiff at just the right speed, the right momentum, the flash swoop over the side and bicep curl up into the skiff. But getting the line in hand was only the beginning. The wind immediately flung the skiff behind me, my arms now hyperextended as I struggled to keep the lower half of my body in the skiff. The wind's single purpose was to blast the skiff down the channel behind me; the one obstacle my body pressed against the rail. The full force of the 50-knot winds and the wooden skiff was concentrated in a single crushing line across my abdomen—the baby! What about the baby! I wanted to let go, but knew if I did, and were drifting powerless in this wind, and then could not start the engine, I could die. I could not hang there forever, though, nor could I count on a quick deliverance from the men— they were on another net around the corner and would only come when done. I resolved with a now-or-never shot of adrenaline to simply do it, to muscle the skiff closer to the corkline and get a line through it. Somehow it happened. After tying on with a clove hitch and two half-hitches, I lay waiting on the plank seat as well as I could in the turbulence, panting, arms locked over my belly.

WEEKS LATER, the run was on. The pink salmon had been slowly building, and then one day in late July, they were here. All of them. We knew from the Fish and Game forecast for the year that the pink salmon return would be strong that year—20 million.

Duncan and I were picking together that day. We saw our neighbor's skiffs moving at an idle under near-sinking loads. And we too were filling our skiffs again and again. We worked from 8:00 A.M., not stopping until 3, when we trudged in to shore for a quick lunch, then out again. I went through all the motions, pulling the four-pound pinks through the net, leaning over the side and arms into the water to save my back, ripping each one clear of its mesh, a fresh fish flung behind me every few seconds. I had done this so many times before, but it was different now. Everything was different. I remembered Rose of Sharon in *The Grapes of Wrath,* with her secret smiles and languorous ways, her life wholly and maddeningly interior as she quietly grew her baby in the midst of hunger and uprootedness. How silly her behavior had seemed to me when I had written a freshman paper for college just a few years before. But now I understood. I worked in a haze, my body corporeal as ever, heavy in raingear and hip boots, my boots and rain pants streaked with fish blood, the sleeves of my two layers of sweatshirts wet nearly to my shoulders; every movement weighted with fatigue, but there was a lightness somehow, the presence of another who had thrown a cloak over my shoulders and whisked me away to a place I had never been. I had no body there; it was bright and still; and though I could not perceive it, it felt more real to me than the fish I stood in, than the wooden skiff that bruised my knees.

IT WAS CALM, the water sleeping except for the three roaring skiffs and the frantic conferences between the brothers, skiff to skiff as we tried to follow the tide of salmon from one net to the next. Between us, we did not talk much this day, saving our strength. I was invigorated, in part, as we all were, because clearly this was going to be our biggest day ever. So far we had picked more than six thousand fish, just six of us, and the day was far from gone. We would break the record today, more than twenty years of numbers would fall this day—and pregnant or not, I was in the middle of it. It was not a good day for me, though. By late afternoon, I could not get comfortable. I was warm, then cold, peeling off layers, adding them back, Duncan impatient with my fiddling. A malaise separate from the usual complaints of my body settled in. Then cramps, like my period, mild at first, then stronger. I kept working, but slowly now, wondering what was happening, what would happen. Not long after, something broke, it felt like, and a warm gush, so warm against my cold legs. This was not a period—it was too much, like my insides were spilling out. "I've got to go in, Duncan!"

"What's wrong?"

"I don't know, something's happening. I may be having a miscarriage. Take me to shore!"

Duncan saw my face, and let go of the net and took me in to the beach without a word. I stumbled up the rocks and then the long path out to the outhouse, feeling as though this were not over yet. The cramps were still strong, and I felt full, weighted with something that didn't belong. I pulled off my raingear, the thick rain pants, and was scared to see my jeans soaked to my feet with my own blood, and then, minutes later, the rest of it came in a sudden, full flood. I was watching a movie of myself, and wondered what I would do next. What should I do? How long do I wait? Will I keep bleeding? Was this important, or was this nothing, a routine miscarriage? It occurred to a distant part of me that we could now go on our Asia trip, but I did not feel glad. I had to go change and clean up, that much I knew. I was grateful the men were all out on the water. Only Bev and Wanda were ashore. Perhaps they wouldn't notice if I just slid up to my house and changed quickly. I wasn't quick, I felt tired, so tired; I began to tremble. But Duncan was waiting for me. I had to get back out—all those fish, the biggest day. I chose my baggiest pair of jeans, with room for pads for the bleeding, and twenty minutes later I was back on the beach, Duncan idling into shore now to get me, yelling "Hurry up!" the narrow skiff an arrow point aiming straight for me, my hands shaking as I pulled on my wet gloves, once white but now mud-colored, and there, veining the palm, a delicate string of blood.

IT WAS A RECORD DAY that lasted until midnight. And I was there in all but twenty minutes of it, in those twenty minutes losing more than I thought I possessed. We were free to travel now, free for graduate school, and I was relieved, but a hard knot lodged in my stomach. Why had I gone back out in the skiff? Why didn't Duncan say, "Leslie, you need to go in and just take care of yourself. Don't worry about the fish." Why didn't I insist that I go in? Why didn't I fight for it? Why did I *have* to fight for it? And what about the time I was out in the storm, the net crushing my belly—had that caused the miscarriage? No matter how fast I ran, bitterness seeped in from all sides. How providential, I mused, with a sour smile, that I spent my childhood practicing for this. I am so good at it: the escape to an interior life, the stony face, the twelve-year-old girl sitting impassively between her mother and father, serving as referee, making sure they use only words against each other.

This fishing life was a temporary trade, of course. But the cost was too high; I had lost too much. I wanted children, but even my imagination wouldn't admit them through the door. I could sacrifice my life and the life of my child on the altar of the wooden skiff, throwing both of us piecemeal to the fish, and no one would yell "stop!"

13

Looking for Language

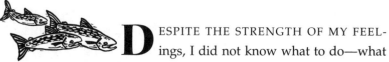ESPITE THE STRENGTH OF MY FEEL-ings, I did not know what to do—what remedies were possible other than to hoist my shoulder against the calendar's wheel and push my way through the rest of the summer. I did not want to think about what might have been, could have been. . . .

After fifteen months on Bear Island, I felt I had wings now that the fishing season was over—I would fly away from everything there. Our new house was good. We were both satisfied with it, and saw it as a tangible monument to our winter. Now— let the next life begin.

We left Kodiak almost immediately, early in September, with our goods for the year stuffed into enormous backpacks, mine weighing forty pounds, Duncan's more. We flew to the East Coast, saw my family, caught a plane to London, met our group

there—twenty others from Australia, New Zealand, England, Ireland, Germany, and Yugoslavia. We met at Victoria Station at ten in the morning, a slow-gathering crowd, coming in singles, pairs: "Are you with Top Deck?" we ask each other, tentative, then five came together, laughing, looking the best of friends, as though they had shared some conspiracy together. A man approached us all afterward, young like us, in sandals and jeans, eyes squinting, walking as though it took enormous effort, as though he might either lift off from the earth, or crumple any second.

"You all heah with Top Deck?' he asked, looking around at us quickly, his New Zealand accent thick.

Assents all around.

"Hi, I'm Richard, your courier," he said, his voice shaky.

"Yeah, we already know who you are!" the group of five teased. "Man, can you put down the pints!"

"Ya gotta drink up all you can, man, while the drinkin's good. Once we get to those Muslim countries, they're dry as a witch's tit." He winked.

Everyone guffawed. He grinned knowingly at the group, then turned to the rest of us, trying now to assume a businesslike air.

"You all have your paperwork for me?" He held out his hand for the sheaves of papers, but it was shaking so badly he could hardly hold them. Duncan and I glanced at each other, eyes lifting.

THE DRIVER of our bus came next, a bearded, paunchy guy whose walk was a cross between a waddle and a swagger.

" 'Ey, good day, mates!" he said with a leer, as he came behind one of the girls, a pretty blonde whose name I didn't know yet. He put his arms up around her and hugged her breasts. She squirmed away, laughing. His T-shirt read "Love comes in spurts" with the appropriate body part emblazoned on his chest.

At that moment, we had a far-from-brilliant premonition that Top Deck and our bus mates were perhaps traveling with a different agenda than we were.

One of my agendas was to write. In some ways I didn't care what happened—as long as I got to write about it. All along the way I wrote lengthy letters home. I kept a detailed journal, as most of us did, and before I left, I had arranged with the local newspaper to send back articles on an as-the-spirit-moves basis. The spirit moved in London; in an underground city in Turkey; from 14,000 feet in the Himalaya, a half day's hike from the Everest base camp; from a three-day trek in the Golden Triangle in the north of Thailand; from an ancient, abandoned city in Burma; from a train that steamed down the length of Java. It was easy to write. As the landscapes of continents, countries, regions, villages unrolled before my eyes like a giant scroll, as we passed from temperate climates to deserts to rain forests, to coastal deserts, through the highest mountains on earth, and down again, we ate astonishment for breakfast. Everything was new every day—nouns collected on trees; verbs conjugated and performed, adjectives coiled like the charmed snakes on Calcutta's street corners. Write about being trapped for hours in a broken-down train in Indonesia in 110-degree heat and the windows don't open. Tell about the gunfire in the Golden Triangle, about the kids who ran around the mountainous poppy fields making their hands into guns and saying the only two English phrases they knew: "CIA!" "USA numbah one!" Write about the desserts in Kathmandu's restaurants—the chocolate pies and pastries that looked straight from New York, how our eyes drooled behind the windows after skinny months of Indian curry and curds—but we spit them out at first bite—they were made without sugar. Describe push-starting our decrepit double-decker bus all the way across Europe and the Middle East, sleeping every night on the floor of the bus three inches away from the next person. . . . Though at times we were overwhelmed with weariness and ennui, fueled by our pace, the sleep-on-a-floor-wherever-we-can accommodations, and a six-month battle with amoebic dysentery, still, the year was everything we hoped for: the pages of my journals wrote themselves full.

BY SPRING, the last arc of the circle was closing. We rounded Australia in a 1964 Morris mini-van, then bused around New Zealand for a month. Three days of planes brought us back to Alaska, Kodiak, then finally out to Bear Island. By early June 1981, I stood on Bear Island's graveled beach chest-high in wet, pungent nets, feeling returned to myself. I did not expect this, but I found myself as happy to be there as I had been to leave nine months before. Salmon fishing in this, my fourth season, was looking good to me. For one thing, there was the very practical matter of money. We watched our pockets empty month by month, with nothing to replenish. And after months of chasing every bend, peering over the top of every hill, I was ready for the routine of fishing and the fixity of island life, to wake up in the same bed in the same place for the next four months, to know my exact location at any given moment. And this would be our first summer in our new house. Best of all, we had hired two crewmen, and I no longer had to be in the skiff full-time. I felt emancipated.

THE SEASON'S PREPARATIONS often began on the beach, mending last year's holes in last year's nets. No one wanted to start the new season finishing the old, but it had been impossible the last three years to find time to mend them before they were stored for the winter. I never minded this particularly. Of all the work to be done, I preferred mending net to anything else. I had always hated sewing growing up—that was something old ladies did. I avoided it with a passion bordering on truculence, including a visit to the principal's office for snidely refusing to learn to crochet in an eighth-grade sewing class. But now, I wore a pair of delicate sewing scissors hung from mending twine around my neck, held a white plastic needle in my hand, and mended as fast as anyone and was happy to do it.

WESTON HAD BEEN the first to show me how to mend. He was the acknowledged expert, who had even written a book on setnetting that was kept in the University of Alaska library. He stood next to me this one day my first summer, demonstrating on what was called a three-holer—a hole that had broken three meshes, necessitating three new knots. It was a quick lesson— his hands flew through the strange motions, leaving me confused by both his handiwork and his running narration: *Cut these hanging pieces from the broken meshes, then start over here in this corner; make new meshes with your fingers, measuring to keep them the right length; for the knot, circle around twice; third time through come back through the middle then pull it as taut as you can and cut it not too close,* and in fifteen seconds he was done. The hole was gone. New meshes held the place of the old. I was impressed, but still had no idea how to do it. The net hanging this way— crooked, twisted, didn't make sense to me. I couldn't see the visual logic of it yet. In the next few minutes, Weston showed me two more: a larger hole, a five-holer, and then a ragged hole that needed a patch, a piece cut from old webbing that is literally sewn into the new. My lesson was over in about ten minutes— I was on my own. I stood at the net pulling slowly through the webbing as it hung on the racks, knowing I could find the holes, but what then? Twice around, then third time around the middle or through it? And how do you start a patch? It was Beverly who came to my aid. She patiently led me through the steps again, and by the end of the day, I was beginning to see it, how the net hung, how the meshes formed a diamond shape, how to count the knots, how to cut out a patch square and sew it in. I began to enjoy it, then, and eventually picked up enough speed by the next summer to volunteer for the biggest tears: the shark holes, the gashes torn on rocks, the fathoms-long kicker rips. For these, I stood in the center of the hole, and with hands spinning I laced up the meshes surrounding me, sewing myself into the net, until the last few stitches, leaving a hole just big enough to squeeze back through and out.

Though there was always pressure to get the nets done for the next opening, still, there was a relaxing rhythm to it, and the ground was solid under my feet. If I worked on the lead line or the corkline, I could kneel in the sand, maybe even sit if I found a bucket. The scenery was magnificent, as always. I hadn't tired of the swoop of ocean around our little island, of the mountains and volcanic spires off to the south and west that trailed off into their own horizon, of the tides that flooded and drained with such constant drama. On rainy wind days, there was little pleasure in it; we endured the wet and cold that stiffened our hands and slowed our work to a numbed proficiency. Sunny days, though, when they came, were inspiring, filling us with air charged with the warmth of light, heating the chill from us, the moist that lingered always in our clothes, our bones. We tanned, burned, even, from our wrists to our fingertips, from our necks to our hairlines, if we weren't wearing hats.

Best of all, beyond and above the weather and scenery, though, was the conversation. Starved for communication other than that forged by the necessity of labor, this was mind time, spirit time, communion. We all craved it. Weston would talk about his latest journal article, this one on the Sodom and Go-morrah motif in the Old Testament; Wanda, who had just fin-ished her master's in music, might talk about contemporary Christian rock versus the hymnody in the old hymn books; I would ask Wallace about his term papers in his economics class.

This day, our first on the nets since my arrival, I stood next to Bev.

"So, tell me about your year, everywhere you've been," Bev began, knowing that was all she needed to say to get us started.

"Well, we started in London . . ." and then I was off. When I had said all I needed to for the first installment—there were many days of mending ahead of us—it was my turn to ask. "So, Bev, what was your year like? How did it go for Israel?"

And she began telling of her preparations for their next year, when they would live in Jerusalem while Weston studied Hebrew.

This was where we unraveled the rest of our lives, it seemed, even as we sewed up the holes in the nets. There was something about this space, about standing out there on the beach under the open sky—the clouds or sun, mountains on every horizon, though it was ocean all the way to the edge. The walls were gone, how could there be a larger space to stand in, and yet, it became a sort of confessional. This was where we could speak the deepest truths to one another. Under all that sky, with noth-ing here to remind us of our other lives, whatever other roles and jobs we worked at during the year, wherever we had been, it was worlds away, and only conjured up by language. We knew the rest of each others' lives only through those words.

As the season progressed, our talk at the net changed. In a world of seven or eight men now and only three women, we

longed most for women-talk, poet-talk. Beverly and I would maneuver ourselves inconspicuously to the same net, working the
net toward each other. We waited days for this.

"Bev, I brought a poem I finished last night." I was cutting
out web from a huge hole and kept my eyes on my fingers.

"Really?" Bev answered with interest and a spark in her eyes.
"How'd you have time to do that? Can you remember any of
it?" She was finishing off a three-holer, with a deft snip from her
scissor necklace, and she was done, now pulling through the web
toward me, searching for other holes. She was wearing her parka
with the fur around the hood. It wasn't that cold, about 48 degrees, but there was a sharp, cold wind from the north that
pulled the heat right out of us as we stood.

"I've got it here in my pocket. It's a poem for Duncan. Wait."
I looked around, saw everyone on the other nets intent on their
own work. We had until tomorrow to finish all eight nets, and
we were only on the third one. This was no time for poetry.
Stealthily I pulled out the index card I had copied the poem on.
"Okay. The title is 'Vocabulary of Love.' " I looked around again
quickly; no one was looking. I read quietly, but aimed my words
above the wind:

> There are words for everything,
> the plastic tips of shoelaces: aglets.
> Chimb: the rim of a barrel.
> Gamophobia: the fear of marriage.
> The curved end of a knife handle: neb.
> We learn the universe by detail,
> precision. Even metaphors, like machines,
> gear word to word exactly where you need them.
> How is it, then, in love we stutter so,

give over thesaurus, lexicon
for what is called the language of the body?

Don't assume fluency in mute touches.
(A hug, or hand on arm,
guess the pressure, gauge the warmth
and length of stroke—)
how can the dumb tongue interpret,
these hands speak back without ambiguities,
ambivalence, the two ways, no three
maybe this could mean?

Listen while I show you:
This thick part of your thumb, the tragus.
Here, the outer edge where your eyelids meet: canthus.
the furrow in your lip, philtrum.

This is how we must love,
specifically and out loud,
naming the spaces of our bodies
as though speaking into being
a universe.

We were silent. I put the poem back in my pocket. We didn't stop our work. Now I was back to my patch and Bev had found a sea-lion hole. Then Bev looked up at me. Our eyes met.

"I like it." She smiled. "I love those words—aglet, neb. . . ."

"Have you written anything this week?" I asked, though now I was counting the number of knots in the hole I'd just cut out for the patch. "Hold it, don't answer, I've got to count—sixteen, seventeen. . . ." Under my breath as I fingered each knot, then,

"Okay, twenty-three by sixteen. Just a minute. Don't say anything until I get my patch web."

"Okay." Bev laughed as she moved to another section of the net. This net, unimaginatively named the Seventh, was a mess, torn up by rocks and sea lions.

I came back, my patch web hung off my shoulder. "What have you written?" I asked, guessing she had written something. With her two toddlers, one of whom seldom slept, living in a half-built house, hauling her water the farthest of anyone and a husband always out fishing, Bev suffered more than the usual island claustrophobia, and I knew finding time to write was even harder for her than it was for me. Yet she had to write, just as I did. It was therapy and catharsis, both badly needed. Like me, she loved books, poetry, Scripture, and best, she resisted any easy answer.

"I've started a poem I think I'll call *God's Whirlwind,*" Bev said quietly. She started in on another small hole. "Remember Elijah, how he stood waiting for God to speak—"

"And the wind storm came," I interrupted, remembering, "and God wasn't in the wind, and then what happens?"

"After the wind came, then came an earthquake—

"And then a fire, or something?"

"Yes, but God wasn't in any of those. God came after, and spoke in the quiet in a very small voice. Elijah expected God to speak through some great display of power and drama—of course, he's God!—but He didn't that time. Just when we think we know God," Bev stopped mending and looked up, "He surprises us, again."

We glanced at each other, then looked down at our hands, still mending.

We were quiet for awhile, satisfied with what had filled the silence. Then Bev began again.

"So, Leslie, have you written anything about fishing yet?"

"No. No. I haven't any idea. I've tried, but nothing will come." I frowned, wondering why my pen was mute, why I was struck dumb over this work that had changed my life—over this life that had changed my life! Even as I stood in this thought, my needle—plastic pen–shaped, the ink the green twine that filled it, worked the webbing of the net, looping, circling, cinching, and here it was, this metaphor I was living out, this white pen spooling out green ink in graceful cursive around me. What was I writing? What did it say? No—I saw only a dirty net, my own efficient meshes that closed up the sea-lion holes. Was this my poem, then, this slimy net hung with kelp, pieces of rotting flounder and jellyfish hanging from its center?

"I don't know, Bev. Maybe I can't write about fishing while I'm here. Maybe I can't write about it at all. Maybe it's knowledge only the body knows—and it can't be translated."

"Don't worry about it, Leslie. The words will come when they need to. At least you're still writing out here. That's a feat in itself!"

"Yeah, no kidding! And this year, who knows? Since I don't have to go out all the time, maybe I'll have more time to write!"

"Good luck with that. As if there's nothing to do on shore!" Bev laughed sardonically.

THERE WAS a lot to do on shore, more than I fully appreciated when out on the water most of the time. I now had a house to keep up. It was only three rooms, but it added cleaning to my daily tasks, something I didn't have to do when staying in the loft. There were meals to cook—full multicourse meals from scratch three times a day; laundry—which took a full day out of every five or six; water to haul several times a day; wood to chop; garbage to haul out and burn; fish to fillet and freeze—we would often go out on Wanda's front porch and find a hundred-pound halibut to take care of. On closures we mended net for days, all day until dark. Still, the on-shore schedule was intense, but it offered far more variety than working the nets all day. I was grateful for the relief.

Duncan and his brothers were as busy as ever. Though we had hired two crewmen this year, one to replace me and another to make the number even for three skiffs, we were still grossly undermanned. I watched guiltily as the men marched off to the salt mines every morning, as we called them, while I stayed behind washing dishes or chopping wood. When the weather came up at all, I couldn't stay in, despite my body's resistance. When the nets were sinking with pinks, when a crewman was sick, when the weather blew up, when everyone was exhausted and needed a fresh pair of hands—I jumped into anyone's skiff willingly, ready to help, glad I could ease the load in some way. I would see Duncan coming up the hill from the water, or he would come to the door, his heavy boots clumping up the stairs. My heart would trip. "Leslie, it's blowing on the outside. I need your help." Or, "Leslie, we've got lots of fish on Seven-Mile. Can you come out and help us?" Or, "Ricky is really beat. Could you come out and give us a hand?" He almost always asked; I almost always said yes. I felt as though I were the one rescuing now. This I could do.

There was a cost to this new, more balanced life, though. Since we weren't fishing together regularly, our only face-to-face conversation time was at the meal table. But we were no longer alone. Duncan's crewman, this year a seventeen-year-old from Southern California, Ricky, ate with us at every meal. The essential adhesive to our relationship, what had drawn us together in the first place, thinned to near silence.

This night, though, promised more. Mid-August, we had just

taken up all the nets, and now it was banya time. Sometime back in Bear Island's history the two events had been wisely paired: the night of the most muscular, rigorous work followed with a body-melt in the hottest, steamiest banya. This take-up, though as arduous as ever, had gone well. I had taken up two nets with Duncan, then worked with Weston part of the time down on Seven-Mile, then had finished up around Bear Island back with Duncan again.

We were just finishing dinner, chili and cornbread, at Wanda and DeWitt's. Since I had gone out, she made enough dinner for Duncan, Ricky, and me. Weston came to the door, red-faced, a towel around his neck. I saw Bev walk by the window with Tamie and little DeWitt, everyone in pajamas.

"We're done. Man, it's a hot one!" Weston wiped his still sweaty brow.

They had gone first this time. Usually they were last, and by then it was so late and Weston was so tired they would skip it.

"Okay, who's next?" Duncan asked, looking up from his chili to view the other possible combinations. There was Ricky and Al still to go; there was us, and DeWitt and Wanda. It was already 10:30—if we had to wait another hour, I would skip it myself. Sleep was more important than being clean.

"Why don't you two go on ahead," Wanda suggested, as if reading our minds. 'I've got these dishes to do, and DeWitt'll stay up late reading anyway. You go on ahead. We'll be last."

"Okay. We won't take too long. We'll let you know when we're done," Duncan says to Ricky as we scrape our chairs back and head out.

"I'll get our stuff if you want to go ahead, Duncan. See if the fire needs stoking."

By the time I got back, Duncan was already in the banya. I undressed quickly in the outer room, which was shared by the two wringer washing machines. The floor was bare cement, the walls unpainted plywood. Aesthetics did not extend beyond the benefits of simply getting clean.

'How is it?' I called, as I peeled off my three layers of sweat-shirts in one sodden mass.

"It's good!" Then I heard deep, long breaths sucked in noisily, ritually. That was a sign that it was really warm. I opened the door quickly, slid in, and stood for a minute, gauging the impact. Duncan was up on the high bench, perched contentedly, breathing in and out like an engine. I checked the thermometer—it was right at 210 degrees, about 20 degrees past my version of perfect, but better too hot than cold.

"How's the hot water?"

"Almost boiling, so be careful." Duncan's eyes were closed. He was melting into the corner, I think. It was good to see him so relaxed. I decided to sit on the lower bench, near the bathtub, where it was a little cooler. The aesthetics in here were no better than the outer room, but no one cared, myself included. I suddenly realized that we were alone together, and there was nothing between us but steam. It felt suddenly too intimate for the spaces we had been inhabiting lately.

I sighed, wondering, out of all I wanted to talk about, what to say.

Duncan heard me. "What's that sigh for?'

"I was just realizing that we haven't really talked for awhile. I miss it. I miss you," I said, looking at him straight.

Duncan lifted his eyes. "Wow! What a nice thing to say!" He wiped the sweat from his face, and then looked at me as though he had just rubbed scales from his eyes. "I've missed you, too. Of course, if you would come back out and fish with me every pick, I'm sure we could . . ."

"Yeah, but now with this counting, we can't talk anyway!" I

retorted, half joking. But I was serious, too. Our new system that year was to count every fish we pick out of every net, to keep track of what each net was producing. Later, after the season, the men would decide which nets to change—lengthen or shorten or get rid of altogether.

'It's the only way we can have accurate records." Duncan said, in a we've-gone-through-this-before tone of voice.

"I know, Duncan, and I think that's good. But I don't have to like it. We can hardly talk anymore—just numbers."

"You don't like it because it shows how much faster I pick than you," Duncan needled.

I snorted derisively, as he expected, and he joined me, both of us knowing this wasn't true.

When we were done, Duncan nodded, conciliatory. "I know, Leslie. But—" and then I saw the same realization hit him—"we can talk *now*! What do you want to talk about?" he asked, now suspicious that I had an agenda involving complaint or change.

I let out a deep breath. We bantered so much, it had become a bad habit. These exchanges relieved our need to talk, but they just lightly chipped at whatever we were not saying. "I just want to talk, Duncan. You know, you and me, alone, just the two of us. It's great having Ricky here, but I wish we could eat alone sometimes."

'Yeah, I do, too. But what are you going to do, say, 'Sorry, Ricky, you have to go eat peanut butter and jelly sandwiches in your room today. Leslie and I need to talk.' "

"No, of course not." I sighed. "But he needs distance from you, too. The both of you come in and I can tell what kind of day it's been on the nets by how quiet it is."

"Well, what's your solution?"

Do I say it? This was so far out I'd mentioned it only to Bev, who had a crewman eating with her family every meal, too.

Somehow it felt like proclaiming the earth was flat—or was it more like the earth was round? I decided to risk it. "Okay, this is way out there, and don't laugh, but someday—"

"—over the rainbow—"

"Exactly—we could hire a cook and the crew could eat by themselves and we could eat by ourselves and they all lived happily ever after."

Duncan began to laugh spasmodically, or was it a cough? Then, "Leslie, we could never afford that. Do you know how much it costs to even have crew in the first place?"

"Yes, I know exactly how much it costs. Listen, this is just a dream. I can have them, you know." I was getting defensive, I realized, and our time together was fast approaching a quarrel.

"Okay, well, dream on, then."

We were silent again. I got up and began to scoop water from the hot water tub over the stove into my basin. Then cold water from the buckets to cool it down. I began to scrub with a loofah. We needed to start this conversation over. "Ahhh, this feels so good! What was the longest we went without bathing on our trip, do you remember?"

"I'd say it was, maybe, two weeks?"

"Remember when I got caught washing my hair in the ladies' room of that five-star hotel?"

"I still can't believe they let us hang out there when we all had dysentery."

We laughed with relief that still felt fresh. It had only been a few months since we had finally gotten well.

"Hey, come on up here." Duncan patted the space next to him, his voice now soft.

"Too hot for me. You come on down here!" I patted the space next to me, smiling.

He slowly unbent his body, stepped down and sat beside me,

thigh to thigh, as we did so often out in the skiff, but now just a layer of sweat between us rather than vinyl. "All right, how's that? How you doin', Leslie?" he asked gently, looking directly into my face. "You really did good on take-up."

"Did *well*," I corrected automatically.

"Who cares?" Duncan shrugged, irritated. "Anyway, you did."

"Thanks. You did, too."

"Did you notice I didn't yell at Ricky once? Not even when he missed the sway the second time?" Duncan said, prodding me for praise.

"I did notice. I was really proud of you. Thanks for reminding me." I smiled.

"Well, I'm trying to do better."

"That's all I ask."

We both leaned our heads against the wall behind us, quiet for a moment.

"How long's the closure?' I asked, finally.

"Four days."

"Good. That'll be long enough to get the nets mended."

Duncan got up and threw a dipper of water on the rocks. Steam erupted. The air pressed into my lungs. We both breathed in loudly and slowly.

"Let's not talk about fishing anymore."

"Okaaaaay," Duncan drawled out. "So, what's on your mind?"

"Did you find out yet how to get on the sub list?

"I think you just submit an application. Did you send off for your prep books yet?" And then it began, the gates opened and we were off, planning our lives again, this year in Kodiak to prepare for graduate school: I would study for them and then take my GRE's; Duncan had already taken his LSAT and scored high enough to get into most any law school he wanted. I wanted some kind of writing program: a master's in English or journalism or creative writing—for what profession I didn't know and didn't yet care. We would live in a travel trailer his father rented out, and substitute teach and do whatever else we could to earn money for the next year.

We were so good at this—planning our lives together. We didn't always do so well living them out, but we wanted the same things. By the time we emerged from the banya, our faces red and sweaty, towels wrapped around us, we were holding hands, talking—

". . . do you think he was really listening?"

". . . we should apply to the University of Oregon, too."

". . . I don't really want to live in LA . . ."

". . . and then I finally got a chance to tell him . . ."

14

An Island of Our Own

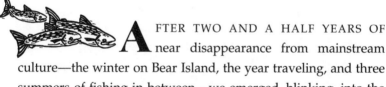A FTER TWO AND A HALF YEARS OF near disappearance from mainstream culture—the winter on Bear Island, the year traveling, and three summers of fishing in between—we emerged, blinking, into the thick of university life. We had settled on the University of Oregon in Eugene, where I had been accepted into the master's journalism program, Duncan in the law school. In 1982, the new air we breathed from our apartment windows throbbed with anti-apartheid protests and marches, gay/lesbian demonstrations, antimilitary skirmishes. We listened and watched with the eyes of outsiders, using our energy elsewhere.

Duncan spent most of his first year of law school shut in a tiny carrel in the law library, a space just big enough so that he could lie on the floor and prop his legs on the desk for a facsimile of sleep. I studied in the other library, keeping similar hours.

Both our programs were rigorous, demanding our utmost attention and energy, yet we found time to play. The only way we could balance ten hours of study a day was to then throw our bodies at any moving object just to keep the blood flowing. We took up racquetball, tennis, skiing, none of which we had ever done before. We threw baseballs and footballs at each other at the park. I took up running and ran five to eight miles every day on sawdust trails beside rivers.

We found a church, friends; I finally got braces; we were thriving in our studies. Eugene became our second home and a model of a balanced life.

I graduated from the MA program and immediately applied for an English MA. The first semester, now 1984, as the professor began lecturing on contemporary American poetry—I sank into my hard wooden seat as though it were a recliner—this was where I belonged.

In the next year and a half, I cut my hair to my shoulders; I began to teach. First as a teaching assistant, occasionally lecturing to a class of 170, then for three quarters, I taught Freshman Composition as a GTF, as we were called, a graduate teaching fellow. I had no particular ambition to teach, especially after the year in Kodiak substituting primarily in the junior high. But if I taught, my tuition would be paid for and I would receive a stipend besides. It was too good to pass up. After a year's apprenticeship, I was on my own.

On my way to the first day of class, my texts and notes clutched to my chest, I heard my heels echoing on the wooden floors of the old brick building, the hallowed halls of education. What was I doing there, I wondered, a quick moment of panic racing through my heart. I was twenty-six, though I looked much younger. I was a great fish picker and web-puller; I had survived a lot of storms—surely I could do this. But the other world was too far away to lend its courage. It was the sound of my clicking heels that gave me confidence. I heard authority in them. I knew the students would all be wearing Birkenstocks and jeans, but as I passed by a glass door and saw a glimpse of my reflection—skirt and blouse, heeled sandals—I knew I had chosen right. It was the uniform that had worked so well in high school and then college. It would work here as well.

By the end of the second week, I was astonished by the passion I felt for this new job, how committed I was to these students. Why hadn't I thought of teaching before? I knew the answer: I was never able to dream that far. And even if I never taught beyond the walls of that university, it felt like an enormous gift.

For those three years in Eugene, the growth we experienced academically and personally was offset by the summers. Bear Island was growing, too, and the changes there made our lives more schizophrenic than ever. We were hiring five crewmen now and fishing five more nets down at Seven-Mile Beach. We hadn't planned on expanding; it came to us unasked through the terrible hands of tragedy.

In the fall of 1977, the cannery superintendent had persuaded Bill Wood to take the *Icy Cape*, a thirty-eight-foot seiner, down to Seattle for the winter for repairs. He hadn't wanted to go, Kay told us. It took two weeks just to get the boat ready for the trip. He and his one crewman made it across the Gulf of Alaska, but in the southeast, near Yakutat, a ferocious blow descended, overwhelming the little boat. Somehow the engine died. The crewman, panicked, ran below and found Bill already in the engine room, trying to revive power to keep the boat jogging into the waves. Just then, an enormous wave threw the boat to its side;

the engine broke free of its mounts, pinning Bill to the hull. The boat broke up almost instantly, the crewman somehow getting out, washing ashore on a nearby island.

Bill had survived so many sinkings, so many accidents in his life, out of sheer toughness and strength, that Kay could not believe he had died. She hired a helicopter to search the area for two weeks, knowing he was somewhere, just waiting to be found. The helicopter landed for good one day, and Kay decided then that she would not give up the work she and Bill had done together on Seven-Mile Beach for twenty years; she knew what to do; she could hire people and run the fishing operation herself.

For the next three years, she hired various relatives for crew, but no one was happy. We visited Kay often during those hard summers. She would invite us in at the driftwood rubber-hinged door with such delight and relief, we were always glad we had come. Kay would bustle to get us chairs, serve us stiff coffee, offer food. In what would be her last summer there, though we did not know it yet, she let down her brave front on one of our visits. We were talking about Bill. Then suddenly Kay broke in—

"I don't know what I'm going to do. Nobody cares about this place. Nobody wants to work it like Bill and I did. I sure miss 'im," Kay began, faltering. She blinked hard, but kept moving, getting a pan from under the sink.

"We all miss him, Kay. He was a good man," DeWitt comforted, his voice soothing, sincere. I saw Duncan wiping his eyes, his head down. My own heart melted at his grief. He had loved him, I think, as a boy, idolizing Bill's strength, his utter manliness.

Kay stopped at the sink, her eyes wet, looked directly at DeWitt and Wanda. "I can't do it anymore, DeWitt. I wanna sell.

And I don't wanna sell to anyone but you. You're the only one I want to have this place, 'cause you know what it means."

DeWitt kept his eyes down, nodding his head slowly, taking this in. His brimmed hat was pushed to the side, as it often was when he and Wanda came to call on their many friends. It seemed to communicate that he was off duty, that he was here not for business, but for friendship. He did not speak for a full minute, knowing what had been offered, knowing intuitively the value of silence.

"Well, Kay," he finally spoke, gently, "I thank you for your offer. We can talk about this later, when the season's over. We'll help you git through the season anyway we can."

Kay nodded now, embarrassed that she needed help, but she was calmer. Then, in her growly voice, with visible effort, "I don't have anything good to offer you, but how 'bout some pancakes? I got some bacon here, too."

"That sounds great," Wanda encouraged, all of us relieved for some kind of activity.

THAT NEXT SEASON, we began fishing that long stretch of beach, each of the sets named in some way in honor of Bill and Kay. Back on Bear Island, we needed to expand as well. We built a new cabin for the crew, who still shared the banya, the outhouse, and our meal tables with us. There were other changes. Wallace was married now, and he and Beth were living at Old Uyak, an old cannery site two miles from Bear Island. *How wise,* I thought, *to start your marriage there.*

Duncan and I were happy with the house we had built, but Bear Island had become too small. After seven seasons there, I knew firsthand about the strange paradoxical space of the Alaskan wilderness, that though we are surrounded by a vastness we cannot even enumerate, we hunch together in small cabins, on tiny plots of ground, living communally. This is because the land that looms so magnificently around us is not ours. Only five percent of the land in Alaska is privately owned, so out in the bush and even in the larger communities we huddle together on tiny lots we can afford, or if anyone buys a larger lot, a half acre, if he could be so lucky, he often subdivides to pay for his own. We compress tighter and tighter while the surrounding mountains stand unmoved.

The expansion of fishing did indeed compress us tighter into Bear Island's already small space, encroaching further upon our lives, our marriage. Having our own house did help us forge an identity as a couple, as we had hoped, and we were sleeping in sheets, but it did nothing to slow the salmon. The fish and fishing still held absolute sway over Duncan's life and the life of the island.

Halfway through my seventh season, I got a cold. We didn't get sick often out on the island, unless visitors came, bringing with them germs from the outside world. The pink run was beginning to build, so I kept fishing and working, as was expected. By the second week, the cold invaded my throat and chest; once I started coughing I couldn't stop, and every swallow nearly brought tears to my eyes. I had stayed in the day before, and this day as well, trying to rest. Duncan and Bob, a young crewman, had come in at two thirty—out since 8:00 A.M. They were both more than tired. They inhaled lunch wordlessly, hoping to squeeze in an hour's nap before heading out again. I sat at the table with them, for moral support, though my head drooped in my hand, and I couldn't eat because of my throat. After eating, just as Duncan dropped onto the bed, he called to me through the open door as I gathered the dishes and began cleaning up.

"Leslie, are you sure you can't go out with us after a nap?

We really need your help. Everyone's done in—we can't keep up with the pinks."

I stood there weakly with dishes in my hand, feeling like a walking den of disease. What part of my body language did he not understand?

I stood in the doorway. "Duncan, I feel really lousy. If I stay in, I can get better faster, and then I can actually help."

"Why don't you go out tonight—being out on the water will make you feel better, I'm sure. Just come, pick some fish, see how you feel. If you feel that bad I'll take you back in."

This was like arguing with a rock. I shook my head, decided it was going to take more energy to fight this than to give in.

"Okay, I'll go," I said, between my teeth.

I managed to pick some pinks at the third set, where they were thickest, but the motion of the skiff added a blinding head-ache to my list of woes. One net led to another, though, as often happened this time of year, and soon I was making the rounds of all the nets. *I knew this would happen*, I thought. I felt so help-less. I had made it through the journalism degree the year before, and I was soon to finish the English masters. Both programs had gone well. Teaching had been judged a success by my faculty advisor. When I spoke, my students listened. But here, no one heard my voice.

It wasn't until nearly dark that I was dropped off, as the rest of the skiffs rounded up and headed off to the tender for the last delivery of the night. I climbed the stairs slowly, ignored the dirty dishes on the table, downed some cold medicine, rolled over once against the wall and fell asleep, mouth open, breathing heavily.

At 6:45 the alarm buzzed faintly, set on its lowest volume. Without thinking or feeling, I peeled back the covers carefully, slid down to the end of the bed so as not to wake Duncan. He could still get in thirty more minutes of sleep. As I dressed in yesterday's clothes, thrown on the floor beside the bed, I took stock. My throat was worse, if that was possible. I probably wouldn't be able to eat again today. My chest still ached and the headache that had started in the skiff the previous night was fully resident now. The great consolation was that after fixing breakfast I could go back to bed.

When it was done—blueberry muffins, oatmeal, and scrambled eggs—I went down to the crew shed and called Bob, then roused Duncan.

"Time to get up," I croaked from the doorway, my throat tightening like a vice. I wasn't feeling sorry for him, though surely he hadn't gotten much sleep again. I was still angry over last night.

"What? What time is it?" In one movement, Duncan rolled around and sat upright, looking confused and panicked. With his hair sticking up like feathers and his eyes wide open in a sleep-dazed look, I could have laughed, had I felt better.

"It's time for breakfast."

"What's wrong with your voice?"

I sighed. "I'm sick, remember?"

He swung his feet over and began to dress, as I had, in yesterday's clothes, though he had hung his on the bedpost. "Can you come out with us this morning, Leslie? Just for a little while . . ."

Then he stopped, when he saw the expression on my face. I did not sit down with them through breakfast, but cleaned up the kitchen in stony silence as they ate. I couldn't wait for them to walk through that door.

I lay in bed nearly helpless the rest of that week, forcing myself up to cook and wash dishes, but otherwise alone. Duncan seemed to not see me as he rushed ashore for food and sleep. We had barely talked for more than ten days. How much longer could I do this? Not just now, but how many more years? I longed to return to Eugene. I could teach, support myself. I had friends there, people who would help me if I was sick. So much was given up to live here—it felt to me that we had relinquished our lives to the lives of the salmon, who were themselves swimming to their own deaths.

Had anyone asked me before we were married if we could do this—put our marriage on hold for four months every year to devote ourselves to fishing to earn our income, I would have said *yes, of course. True love can survive,* I would have said, remembering the words I had embroidered and framed for our first anniversary: "Love hopes, Love believes, Love endures all things." This kind of love would see us through. There it is: *hopes, believes, endures.* This is an entirely reasonable proposition: twine your lives together, growing closer, progressing in warmth, trust, and interdependence for most of the year, then, come fishing, simply shift into cool neutral, glide in a state of suspended emotion. In the fall, pick up again where we left off and move forward again.

Seven years into this I knew unequivocally that marriage was not a vehicle, nor could human hearts be put on ice without freezing. And what of our future? How would children fit into this life? Was there any room for them here? I could hardly imagine having children at all, let alone imagine them here, and when I did, I envisioned them as little herring, like the ones we catch in our nets sometimes, packed among the burly salmon in the skiff, lost, and then finally, when rediscovered, flung overboard because they were worthless to us. I felt as though this had already happened four years before. I could not forget.

ONE AUGUST NIGHT, a week later, I was done. I would not be imprisoned any longer on this island. I found the backpack and began silently packing: extra jeans, some food, a book, my journal, a gun for bears. We were in the minus tides then. Shaking, I waited for the spit to go dry, at 9:00 P.M., and then, without looking back or saying good-bye to anyone, I walked off the island. I didn't have a plan, except that I was leaving and maybe would not come back. There was nowhere to go except the four miles down the beach to the little cabin still standing on Seven-Mile Beach. And then? I didn't know. I only knew I was leaving.

15

A House from Africa

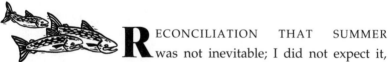ECONCILIATION THAT SUMMER was not inevitable; I did not expect it, but slowly it came. Duncan listened to me; he heard me: *We have to move, Duncan. We have to start over somewhere else, make our own place, a place for children, a place for us. We cannot go on living like this.* He heard the passion and misery in my voice and he knew what I said was true: *Yes, yes, Leslie, you are right. I am so sorry about what happened that summer—the miscarriage. I didn't know, I didn't understand how you felt. We will move and start a new life. I don't want to lose you. We'll make it work.* There were more words, and tears and hugging and declarations of recommitment, and slowly, life began again.

THE FIRST QUESTION as we picked each other up from the ground was—where? Where would we go? There really was no choice but Harvester Island, two miles from Bear Island, where we kept our cattle and stored our skiffs each winter. It was the same island where we had worked on my first visit, where we had jumped from the dock into the frigid water. Now, in a move I could never have foreseen, we planned to live in the shed off that very dock while we built a new house. All the other questions remained: could we indeed do this, resettle an uninhabited island, build another house from scratch? More important, was it really possible to start again? Even with willing, changeable hearts, if fishing did not change, could our hearts move far enough to cover the distance? A house of our own had not been enough before. Would an island of our own be enough? There was no way to know but in the trying of it.

Though the idea and the necessity for it had been mine, Duncan embraced the move and the settling of another island with all his energy. The timing wasn't exactly right, yet, though. Duncan still had the bar exam to take, and we both wanted one more trip before we settled down. In the year before us, from fall of 1986 through to the next fishing season in June 1987, we decided we could do both. We would move to Anchorage where Duncan would study for and then take the bar exam. Then, rather than sit around chewing our fingers waiting for the results, we would travel again, this time for four months through Africa. That would bring us to fishing. We would stay out that next winter and make the move and build our house. And, we would begin to start our family. I was twenty-eight, Duncan twenty-nine.

As we planned, so it went. Immediately after the bar exam in January, we were off once again under heavy packs to ride the back of an expedition truck with twenty-one others, driving from Cairo into Sudan, the Central African Republic, Zaire, Rwanda, Uganda, and Kenya. This trip would be different, we vowed, from the other. We selected our adventure travel company carefully, choosing not the bargain basement variety, as we had done before, but one that cost more, hoping it would attract another kind of traveler. Our hunch paid off. Our companions, from Europe, Australia, and New Zealand, were older, many were professionals: one woman was a doctor; another a lawyer; one man, a Canadian-Bulgarian, was a retired physicist; two teachers; a nurse; a speech therapist; a fifty-something Australian furniture maker. . . . Duncan and I had no label yet, except commercial fishermen from Alaska with a few degrees on the side. Just as in fishing, we boarded the truck in Cairo, leaving our other lives and identities and countries of origin behind for a common pursuit—to experience what we could of this exotic, troubled continent.

Though we had no title or profession when we arrived, we soon gained one: Duncan and I became the designated garbage collectors. The first night, we all sat cross-legged in a circle around a dim fire in a small grassed enclosure euphemistically called a campground in Cairo. The camp chores were divvied up for the rest of the trip. Cooking and dishes would rotate, but other jobs were fixed and daily: packing and unpacking the tents from the top of the truck, water detail, cleaning the truck, taking inventory of food supplies, and other necessary duties of life aboard the vehicle that was our home that season. The jobs were listed slowly, amid joking and bargaining. Some were chosen with delight, as though that person had been waiting all his life to perform this task. Duncan and I sat quietly until near the last, when we heard "garbage disposal."

We knew something about creative organic garbage disposal from our years on the island. We shot up our hands and for the next four months, from Egypt to Kenya, through thousands of miles of desert and rain forest, the garbage was ours.

Our job was simple. After every meal stop, we were to spade

a hole in whatever kind of ground presented itself to us, and bury whatever we had to leave behind. It wasn't much. We ate sparsely those four months, and bought food from local markets whenever possible, food always wrapped in itself. But when crossing the eastern Sahara, and fording whole expanses of sand through Egypt and Sudan, on into the Central African Republic, we often went days without seeing a single habitation or another person. We raided our own stores then, canned goods stocked in England for these weeks.

Before then, along the Nile Valley the first week, we dispatched with the few cans easily. The ground was soft and easily dug. When the earth turned solid as we moved west, and south, toward Sudan, our job became harder. In western Sudan, the ground became tiled in fractal patterns of dried mud that lifted off in our hands. Between the tiles was nothing, as though the ground had shrunk and congealed, suddenly becoming too small for the earth beneath. The cracks were deep, fissures that made you want to pour water down, like an open throat. You could see and hear the thirst, but we had nothing to give but our garbage, a collection of a dozen cans that had held beans, peas, peaches. We tried the spade, but the earth was impenetrable. All we could do was find the largest fissure, and drop them in. It didn't feel right, though we knew there was no alternative. Our truck had not a spare square foot not already claimed by twenty-two bodies already leg-to-leg on the two bench-seats we sat on. There was barely room for us, let alone our garbage. When I dropped the cans, heard them rattle into that space, it felt like feeding someone who was hungry a stone instead of bread.

It was easier and more gratifying to dispense with our garbage in Zaire. The empty spaces, all horizon and unpeopled, closed in with the rain forest, and days now we drove on a narrow earthen track through village after village, the children always running out of their grassed huts with screams of *"tou-riste!" "touriste!"*—French for tourists. Whenever we stopped for the night beside the road, in any sort of clearing we could find, or even for a midday meal, crowds gathered, hundreds at a time, silently ringing our truck, watching our strange activities of building a campfire, cooking dinner. They watched, seldom spoke; they waited. After we ate, we would give to the most authoritative-looking person there the extra food when we had it. But it was not our food they were waiting for.

Our first night with such an audience, Duncan and I gathered the cans and few glass bottles from the day's use, took them to a spot of soft ground, dug a deep hole, tamped it, returned to the truck. The next morning, as we drove away, we saw two local people we had seen the night before run to the site, then dig energetically. After that, we offered our empty cans, glasses, boxes, to the people who gathered. They accepted them graciously, thankfully, and I felt ashamed and began to realize the depth of their poverty. They needed our food, yes, but they needed our garbage even more.

IN THE FIRST PART of the journey, I learned something about clouds and rain—the weather that typifies Kodiak Island, and something about language as well. For the four weeks it took us to plunge and grind our way across the eastern Sahara, we never saw a cloud, not a wisp of fog, not a spit of rain. My journal descriptions of the desert crossing were simply a catalog of dearth. No roads, only telegraph lines. No villages or people, no vegetation, no animals, no food, almost no water, no landscape, and, no weather. It is easier to list what we did see— sun   sand   sky: the sun like a great fire breathing on our heads, the ground, a copper coin, and everything else a neutral blue expanse. Never did the formula vary: sun   sand   sky.

Each night we pitched our tents in the cool dark and woke the next morning knowing the texture of the day to follow— sun   sand . . . It should have been heaven, and all the more so because it was January. Back on Bear Island, I knew, a maelstrom of gales, squalls, snowstorms, hail, and winter rain attacked. In Kodiak, snow tires had to be mounted, windows taped. It was the season of black ice, frozen pipes, nights that bled too far into day . . . but here, just the steady bake of sun into bones.

We took some minor precautions that first week, wearing sunblock, hats, sitting under the roof of the truck. But the sunblock tubes were soon squished empty; we lost our hats and then sat carelessly on the roof of the truck as we drove. No shade either for our canteens; the water boiled. We were constantly thirsty; the wells marked on our maps were mostly dry. Ten days in we were on rationing. We never ran out of drinking water, but our evening dole of bath water evaporated to a liter, then half a liter, then a single cup for all our washings: teeth, clothes, hair, bodies, faces, all lacquered in dirt from twelve hours of dust and sand, merely got swiped at with a damp rag each night in the privacy of our tents. And we were thankful for it.

Duncan and I already had a sense of the value of water from our own island rations from a bucket, so it wasn't this privation that felt new. It was the blankness of it all. Without the dozen different kinds of damp and rain, without fog, without clouds or wind, it felt a kind of blindness. There was nothing to quantify or measure, and worse yet, nothing to name, nothing to which language could be assigned. In my journal, I wrote, *I never thought I could miss clouds, but I do. I see now that clouds map the sky, give us words, perspective, dimensions. They are both the script and the passion that fills it. Without them, the book has no text, the universe is inscrutable. Without them, without a sense of weather, time counts for nothing, the sky is dead.*

IT WAS SOMEWHERE along those expanses that Duncan dreamed our house up and drew it down in the ground of Africa. The first diagram came in Zaire. After crossing the Sahara Desert, I was still drawing on reserves of exhilaration, that I was now able to do what I had dreamed of as a child—to cross this infinite expanse with all its excesses and deprivations. By the time we got to the Central African Republic, the emptiness of the desert gave way gradually to a sparse tangle of bushes, grasses, and vines. On into Zaire then, where the rain forest exploded around us. It was one of many such days, driving the usual pace of 15 mph on unmarked earthen tracks that passed for roads. It was lunch break.

"Leslie, I've got it." Duncan nudged me eagerly as we sat on canvas stools finishing our lunch of canned corned beef and fruit cocktail.

"You've got what?" I asked, surprised at his sudden energy. I was slowly fading into lethargy now, eight weeks into the trip. We drove an average of twelve hours a day, usually traveling no faster than 20 mph because of road conditions. Some days we drove fourteen to sixteen hours, propelled by the coming rainy season, which would instantly render the earthen roads impassable. We had thousands of miles to travel still. Surprisingly, the rain forest became oppressive. For three weeks, we could see no more than thirty feet above to the canopy closing over us, and one hundred feet ahead to the earthen road that thinned again into the forest. It felt as though I were watching a looped film of the same scene over, over. A prolonged fever worsened the blurring, smothering landscape. But there was more. I knew that this would be our last major expedition. Duncan was talking about South America next, but I had no interest. As we wormed our way into the heart of Africa, I felt I saw into my own, and it felt empty. I was tired of travel, and realized that no matter how authentically or inauthentically we traveled, no matter how foreign and exotic the destination, it could not fill our own lives. Seeing other cultures and how others lived their lives was not the same as living our own. I knew when I returned that I would be enormously grateful for having done this, and the Asia trip as well. My sense of the world had changed utterly. But I longed to invest myself in others, to begin that other long, slow journey of family. I felt instinctively that that journey would take more courage, that journey would take me further, deeper than an expedition truck rumbling through greenest, darkest Africa. Thankfully, we were already moving in that direction. Every mile traveled brought us closer. Now, what was Duncan so energetic about?

"The house, for Harvester Island! I can see what it will look like!" He set his plastic plate on the ground and began to draw in the dirt an upside-down V. "Look, it'll have a prow and then eight picture windows. Like this." He tried putting little squares under the V.

"That sounds nice," I said wearily, poking at my corned beef. "Where are you thinking of putting the house?"

"Up in the saddle, you know, just up the hill from the beach, where the raspberries used to be. Here, remember?" And he scratched some lines in the dirt. "We can tuck the house right in there and it'll be protected from all directions."

"Oh. Yeah. That sounds good, Duncan." I brightened a little. I was genuinely glad for his enthusiasm, and so grateful that this project was no longer mine.

That started a series of conversations, maps, and blueprints

scratched out in the dirt between Zaire and Kenya, supple-
mented and nearly finalized on folded squares of my journal
tucked into Duncan's pockets. He worked eagerly on it as we
rumbled through the rain forest, then out into the clearings and
sun of Uganda and Rwanda. I took interest in it, but I did not
have the energy to contribute much at that point. I would later,
when we got back home.

16

Building

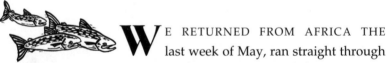WE RETURNED FROM AFRICA THE last week of May, ran straight through that fishing season, and once again said our good-byes to everyone in September as group by group they pushed off from Bear Island. This time we were leaving Bear Island, too. It was 1987, seven years since our first winter out. We loaded the skiff with our few belongings one evening shortly after the mass desertion and made our way to Harvester. The island, its nine-hundred-foot rounded peak and series of graduated shoulders, stood in rosy profile, the blush of evening light like a halo over its cliffs and grass slopes. I had watched this light settle on Harvester Island nearly every night for nine summers from the skiff or from the window of my cabin at Bear Island. I had not seen this kind of light anywhere I had been around the world. I wouldn't watch it anymore, I realized sadly as we drove down the channel

toward the beach. Now that light would be the light I washed dishes by, folded clothes, carried wood. Would I even see it? Perhaps I wouldn't need to, I told myself.

WE LANDED, the skiff growling onto the rough beach, the only real beach on the entire island, the beach that would be our driveway, our on ramp to the open blue road. There were three of us then. Dennis, a good friend of Duncan's from law school, came up to help us dig the foundation.

"Let's start unloading, Leslie," Duncan called to me as I tied up the skiff and then began to wander up onto the grass.

I took a quick assay—the pushki and stands of devil's club, a grove of weedy birches whose leaves were already yellowing, and, just in front of me, two thick spruce, planted in 1916, Duncan's father told me. Underneath them were two derelict houses, one fifty years old with just the wood skeleton remaining, and the other about thirty years old, set on pilings that had all but blown over. Both houses would need to be torn down and burned. They gave some assurance, though. Other people had lived here before.

I returned to the skiff, taking two sleeping bags and a garbage bag of clothes as Dennis handed them to me. "Where are we going with this stuff?"

"To the little shed there," Duncan motioned with his head, his arms full of boxes.

We dropped our gear just outside the fourteen-by-twenty-foot rusted tin shed that would be our home for the winter. Duncan pushed open the creaky door. My stomach dropped. I had forgotten this, that it was still floor-to-ceiling junk: wooden barrels, crates of old beer bottles, piles of crumbling bricks, grayed lumber of various lengths. The enormity of our year's project struck me full in the face—and knees and back and most of all my stomach. What were we doing here? We'd have to fight even for a place to set our mattress for the night.

I looked at Duncan. He looked at me. This was it, our break from Bear Island, our declaration of independence and interdependence. We both raised our eyebrows meaningfully, said nothing, then got to work.

That night, the shed was sufficiently empty to allow our bed in the alcove, a tiny room just large enough to step from the threshold up onto the bed, and to fit a small mattress in the main room. That was good enough for the moment. Now, water. Everything else was irrelevant. We knew there was a well on the island, and that it would be somewhere near the old houses. What we found looked nothing like a well—a slight depression in the lumpy ground. Not a hint of damp—it had completely filled with silt and soil, and as final ornamentation, an old 7-Up can and a boot lay disconsolately on top. Whatever had been there for casing had rotted out completely. Duncan and I stood there looking down at the can, the boot, the dirt. What if this spot yielded no water? Could we find it elsewhere, and how? And how long would it take, and what about all our building supplies already ordered and on their way over from Kodiak—30,000 board feet of local spruce? What kind of shelter would that shack provide against the winter? How readily would the soil give way to a shovel for the foundation? Could we really do this in nine months? And then we just started digging.

It took three days to clean it out, three days of shovel, heave into a bucket on a pulley, let fall all your weight on the rope and hoist it up to ground level, dump it, down again, and by the second day we hit water. Just moisture at first, then the seepage, then it was mud we hoisted and dumped, agonizingly heavy but gloriously wet. By the fourth day the water was several feet deep, clear and clean. We tasted it that morning, looked at each other over the shared cup, and to both of us it tasted like a house and kids someday and a lot of years ahead here on this island.

Next in priorities, we needed to make the dock house, as we christened our shed, livable. It had no insulation or any protection to offer from the coming winter other than its single-layer tin walls. For another three days, Dennis, Duncan, and I insulated, nailed up plywood, built a shelf for basins to wash dishes, and then, upon my insistence, we stopped.

"This is good enough, Duncan," I said that night as we lay in bed. It was cold now, the beginning of September. "Let's start on the foundation tomorrow."

"We should paint the plywood, Leslie. It would look much brighter in here if we painted it all white."

"It doesn't matter how it looks. We're only going to be here this year. We need to get going on the foundation!" I urged. Whatever time we put into the dock house was time away from our own. The goal was to be in the house by the beginning of the next fishing season, eight months away.

"I was going to put trim around the windows. That would make them much tighter. And what about an outhouse? We have to have that," Duncan replied, warming to the topic.

"Oh, c'mon. We don't need trim! That's gingerbread! We've got exactly three weeks left to get the foundation in. And if you build an outhouse, that's a week right there. We'll do fine without one!"

"You want to keep using the beach for a bathroom? Duncan looked at me as if this were a rhetorical question.

"Why not?"

"Wait until winter. See how you like it then!"

Suddenly I laughed. Our first fight on Harvester Island—over an outhouse. "Duncan, I'm not trying to be argumentative. Let's do the foundation, since we have a deadline for that, and then if there's extra time, we can build an outhouse and do whatever you want to do in the dock house."

"Okay, Leslie," Duncan relented with a giving-up smile. "In the middle of the first blizzard you'll be out there on the beach wishing for an outhouse. But okay. We'll start measuring and digging tomorrow." Then we turned to the wall together, twining our sets of navy thermals, arms and legs curled for warmth. We lay there in our cold little shed, the tide rising underneath us until it surged directly beneath our bed, the Pacific Ocean just a few floorboards away.

That morning it was raining, a misty kind of rain, a harbinger of all that was to follow. For the next three weeks as we created a foundation, the rain followed our every movement. The work was fairly straightforward and completely muscular: we had no tractor, no hydraulics, no power of any kind. After measuring, we dug post holes for the foundation pilings, digging the four feet down until we hit the inevitable clay hardpan, impenetrable to our shovels. Sometimes we'd hit a rock, and after an hour of no-budge, we'd measure and start another hole. When the hole was done, we took turns running the wheelbarrow down to the beach for a load of sand, then head-down pushing it back uphill for the mix with water. Another would carry water from the well in seven-gallon buckets over to the wheelbarrow and pour, then mix the cement. Duncan, of the three of us the obvious power lifter, handled the creosote logs we had scouted all summer from various beaches, cutting them in lengths and balancing them on his shoulder from the beach up to their new home. We did this thirty-eight times over: dig the hole down to the clay, wheel to the beach and shovel a load, grunt it back up the hill, carry the water and add it, hoe it all into cement, then measure and cut the piling, hold it in place, pour the concrete. And between every step, long distances, and most of it done in the rain and what the rain left behind—a slick, clayey mud that tricked us to the ground when we needed traction the most. The ground swelled with the rain until it could take no more and so it pooled around us, even on the hillside. The well rose and overran its own square bank until the water turned brown with runoff and because of the cows and their manure; we were sick from our water, running all day to the outhouse beach, but we were mostly sick of the rain. We had to finish, though. The framer was coming September 30. We would join him and his crew of three in a week-long frenzy of framing our two-story house. The rest of the work would be ours alone. If we weren't done with the foundation, he wouldn't come.

We finished one day ahead of schedule. Dirty, all my muscles tried and weary, I sat down that day on the steps of the dock house looking up at those posts footed in the dirt of the saddle of the hill, and realized, dumbly, that it was actually going to happen.

THANKSGIVING. One evening, the VHF radio mounted next to our bed brought us an unexpected invitation from Larsen Bay.

"Harvester Island, uh, calling Harvester Island. Over," a tentative voice called.

We were reading in bed. "That sounds like Maury, Duncan."

"Harvester Island back to the call. Is that you, Maury?" Duncan answered, always pleased, as I was, whenever anyone thought to call us out there.

"Yes, Duncan, this is Maury speaking. Over," he said, rather stiffly.

We smiled. Maury was about seventy. His wife, Robbie, was the school principal in the village. Clearly he hadn't mastered the art of radio talk yet. Maybe he didn't even know it was another dialect.

"Robbie and I wondered if you had any Thanksgiving plans. Over."

Duncan and I swelled immediately. "Well, let me check my social calendar, Maury." Pause. "Looks like we're all clear." Then Duncan laughed at his joke over the air, as was proper. "Shucks, Maury, we'd love to come down. What can we bring?"

And it was set. We had no John and Julia for company that year. This was the closest thing—occasional visits on mail days when we'd stop by and see what experiment Maury, a retired chemical researcher, was performing that day.

We were wildly excited at this prospect of companionship, a real dinner, a shared table, wide-ranging conversation. The day before, a blow moved in, a northeast at 35 knots, then up to 50, then higher, our curtains now horizontal. The dock house was cold; dark came early, before four. We looked out from our dimly lit shed at the white water around us, wishing the wind calm, pleading the water still, hoping so acutely to go. The next morning raged us awake, the wind still ripping at our tin roof, curtains out, and, though it was hopeless, we could not stop our vigilant post at the window, waiting for the miraculous charge, "Peace, be still," and the obedient response of the wind and waves. We gave it up, finally, and reluctantly radioed back, "We can't make it. We're so sorry." We did our best to give thanks that day, over two guinea hens I had bought months ago and stashed in the freezer, but we felt as though banished, in solitary confinement. Duncan and I had chosen all of this, everything down to the gingham-yellow fly-specked curtains that would not behave at our windows, and we still would not choose otherwise, yet that day we felt powerless and lonely. Later, after dinner, we hiked back up to the house and worked for a few hours, hoping to somehow redeem the day's loss.

IT WAS THE DEAD of winter now, the dark eye of January. We had just gotten word from Larsen Bay that some supplies were in, two bundles of plywood chief among them. That was good news. I had nearly run out, and there were still several rooms to go. This was not a small house, not some little cabin in the woods. It was 2,500 square feet, though some of that was attic space. It must have looked strange and exorbitant to others in the bay, who mostly lived in modest cabins, that we would build such a sizable mansion for just the two of us. But it was not just for two of us, and most of the cost of the house was our own sweat labor.

We needed the plywood immediately, but the weather had to cooperate. Knowing the size and weight of those bundles— more than one hundred sheets strapped together—we needed waters like a mirror to bring them home. Two days later we rose to a morning like a hush. This was the day. This would be more than a plywood run, of course. It was also a mail run, a visiting run, a get-off-the-island run, all of which had tremendous value.

This winter was going better than our first, the year on Bear Island seven years ago. I did not feel nearly as isolated, and Duncan and I had figured out, finally, how to work together. The last house, he was chief builder and planner, I was assistant. At times I wanted to do a Vanna White impersonation while I stood by Duncan's side with the appropriate tool, smiling vacuously, stepping aside graciously and gesturing to where the real work was going on. Other times I felt more like the hunchback assistant, scurrying about in a scoliosed position, scowling at the floor, and grumbling at my state in life. This time, we were our own bosses. As we went along, stage by stage, we apportioned the work neatly. I was in charge of all things plywood, responsible for the subflooring, the plywood on all the walls. Duncan was in charge of all things electrical. Later, I would do all the wallpapering, wainscoting, painting, and staining while Duncan hung all the doors and did all the trimming and doorways. It worked beautifully. He could fuss about his troubles, and I could complain about mine, and we gave each other respectful and sympathetic audience, with fault nowhere to be found. Despite these successes, a certain cabin fever still settled around me, particularly when six or seven days had passed without any language from afar. I would feel it mostly on mail days, still enthroned as chief among days, when for those moments as I devoured, then savored every letter, the silence lifted and I felt whole again. This, then, was not just an errand after plywood, this was reentry into the stream of human consciousness.

Geared up in our usual winter garb, streamlined now from our previous winter's dozens of layers to a yellow survival suit over woolen clothes, we set off in two skiffs, each of us driving, mail to go in a bread bag sealed inside of a garbage bag. Everything went smoothly, the unloading at the cannery dock in Larsen Bay, the stacking on the pallets in the middle of the skiffs, a bundle of mail for us at the post office, then the return, now clouds low and heavy, a bit of wind, and a long, slow trip back in spitting snow. The plywood was stacked so high in both our skiffs, we had to stand up on the seat to see over it, but then couldn't reach the handle of the kicker, so I stood on the seat to gain my bearings, then down again, steering for one or two minutes each time by the peripheral waters around the skiff, slow boat from Asia, to lug our cargo to the island. Our faces and hair were wet, the water dripped through to our clothes underneath. It was low tide then, unfortunately, the worst time for unloading. The tide book came out.

"Okay," Duncan paused, finger on the page, finding the right day of the month, "High tide is at two this morning, almost a twenty-footer."

"That's a good high tide. That'll take it almost up to the running line log. Let's wait and unload it then," I suggested, partly out of laziness. I was ready to be done for the day, ready most to read my mail, and, after all, it was 6:00 P.M.

"You sure you're going to want to get up at two A.M.?" Duncan asked, skeptical, with an emphasis on the "A.M." "It sounds good now, but I don't think you'll be too happy when the alarm goes off."

"That's a lot better than hauling all this all the way up the beach. I'll do it, don't worry! Just set the alarm clock."

Two o'clock came much too much in the middle of a deep, black sleep. The alarm beeped in its nonhuman machine tone, unfeeling. We woke up suddenly, even in our sleep expecting this, and hearing before our feet even touched the floor the sloshing of the ocean underneath us.

"C'mon, Leslie. You ready?" Duncan nudged my leg as I sat on the edge of the bed. We didn't have to dress—we wore sweats to bed to keep warm. All we needed was a coat and a pair of boots.

"In just a minute," I answered, my voice dry and raspy. "Is it blowing at all?" I slid onto the floor and began looking for my boots.

"Let me check the curtains. Nope. Not a stir."

It was something like a joke. When the wind blew, from nearly any direction, we could judge its velocity by the angle of the curtains' levitation. Anything over 50 mph sent them straight up, horizontal. Between 50 and 35 they would hover and poof up and down between gusts. Between 20 and 35 they billowed casually, like a fresh summer day, but much colder. During the most horizontal episodes, when we huddled in our one-room dimly lit house in coats, Duncan would vow to trim the windows and make them tighter. After, knowing it would be a three-day project, I would try to distract him once again and keep us going on the all-important house.

The curtains were calm that morning, but the tidal waters, flushed, were restless, and the night was as dark as any winter's night in Alaska under a heavy, clouded sky. It was not too cold, about 35 degrees I guessed, as I stepped out onto the beach. We had a spotlight rigged up on the corner of the dock house, and I could see out past the dock to where the skiffs were riding, ponderous under their load. It took two of us all our strength to pull them in with the running line. Then it began. One four-by-eight sheet at a time for me, and two at a time for Duncan, slid off the pile, my arms stretching for the width, then on my back, bending low for the right angle, then on up the rest of the beach and then the hill to the house, the spotlight fading into black at the top, too many steps to count. After several trips, I caught the pace, my legs warmed, and now it was two at a time for me, three for Duncan. We did not talk, there was so much else going on: Here, miles from anyone, a hundred miles from any town, on our own island, in the darkest winter night, we were ferrying our house on our backs, a few pieces of wood at a time, until we walked more than a hundred pieces from the ocean to the hill, from one world to another.

It took more than two hours that time. Other times the wood was larger, beams, joists, or windows; other times the wind was blowing—we packed one hundred sheets of plywood in a 25-knot wind one evening, me falling, nearly sailing away behind each gust. This is how it happened, the house on the hill—a few sticks of wood, one sheet of tin, one step up the hill again and again.

Sometimes the loads didn't come in time. Our roofing ran short. For the six weeks it took to get the eight more sheets of corrugated metal up from Seattle on a barge, and because we had used all our tarps elsewhere, we shoveled snow out of the house nearly every morning before we began our work for the day.

The winter passed slowly, the house our literal calendar, marking each day with nails into wood, walls thickening, dressing in color, until the morning, just two weeks before the fishing season officially began, we moved from our diggings in the dock house to our own blue-and-white bedroom. It would take us five more seasons, all summers, to finish the rest. And longer still to get to the attic and the downstairs, and still longer for a sink and a modest form of running water.

One year, a high school girl hired as a babysitter for part of the summer said offhandedly, "You're luckier than other people—you've got such a big house out here." I looked at her and wondered what she thought, that our house just sort of materialized; that it was created ex nihilo, spoken from afar into being; that we found it out here on this island and, lucky us, just moved in; that we sat in town and simply put in our order? What was she thinking? I drew a breath, started to open my mouth to try and tell her what winter was like out here, that we built the house without blueprints, that it was built out of local spruce and nothing was square, that our materials hadn't come in on time, that . . . then I stopped and erased the words I was about to speak with a wave of my hand. She looked at me expectantly. "Never mind," I said quietly.

THROUGH THAT WHOLE YEAR and on into the next fishing season, we were trying to construct and build more than a house.

We kept track of the days of the month, hoping our future would begin each month. "Lord, please give us a baby," and then, feeling that wording too demanding and imperious, we would qualify it: "Lord, in Your time, according to Your will." But we remembered that Abraham and Sarah had waited twenty-five years for Isaac. We would pray, and then, knowing God works through the ordinary, set about in the most comprehensive way to make an answer possible. We felt like scientists carrying out a complex experiment for nearly one week of every month. Through the winter days, through all the building and the work of making Harvester Island a place to live, there was this cyclical drama of the possibility of creating a child salted with scientific accuracy, then followed by the stirring of hope and the waiting, the stifling of anticipation and the odd escape of a flutter of joy— what if?

For the first time in our life together, we felt a protracted helplessness. We had planned our lives carefully year by year for the eight years we had been married by then: college, travel, a year in the bush, graduate school, another year out, more travel, and now it was time to begin a family. Aside from that one unplanned pregnancy, as we planned, so it went. So what was the problem? Despite our utmost efforts, nothing took. After a year, without missing the precise timing of a single month and still nothing, we decided to begin infertility testing.

There is nothing convenient about these tests, but add to them the complications of bush transportation and then our fishing schedule, and strange activities result. It was some time in July, after undergoing a series of other tests, all with normal results, that we came to the most challenging one of all. Duncan knew we were on the docket for this particular one, and knew all that it required, but had forgotten about it in the haze of the peak of the pink salmon run. These were the days of gruel that come every summer, days marked at their end by the fatigued leaning march up our hill, the angle of the body and the tilt of the hill both sharper, the progress slowing to a shuffle. This afternoon, as Duncan paced the climb, weariness written into every movement, I stood on the steps of our new house watching, with an odd smile on my face, wondering how to tell him. He looked up at me and a flicker of a smile crossed his face in response, then his eyes questioned.

"Uh, Duncan, this is it. This is the day for the test. We need to go to bed right now." I attempted a provocative gleam.

"Oh, no, not today," Duncan groaned. "Are you sure?" He was in the entryway now, stiffly pulling off the straps of his bib rain pants. "I have to be back out on the nets in an hour and a half. There's lots of fish out there."

"That's fine," I soothed. "I think we can make it. And you remember the rest?"

"Oh." He stopped. "You've got to be at the doctor's office in an hour, right? Or it won't work?"

"No, we've got two hours. It's eleven thirty now. If we run right up to Larsen Bay *after*." I drawled out, twirling Duncan's sweatshirt string in my finger seductively, trying not to lose the mood in all the details, "I can catch the twelve thirty mail plane and be in by one and then I'll take a taxi straight to the doctor's." Then, "Here, let me help you with that," I said in my lowest boudoir voice, teasing, easing the wet raingear over his hip boots.

Duncan began to laugh as I lifted his hat, odiferous with gurry and fish scales, and hung it on a hook. "I don't know, Leslie, I'm awful tired." But he was smiling, too.

"You want to wait a whole other month?" I unzipped his life jacket and pulled it gently off his shoulders. Just four more layers to go.

Duncan laughed again. "Gee, I kind of like you like this. Don't forget how to do this another time, okay?" He looked at me eye to eye and we smirked knowingly at one another, neither one of us feeling sexy, and knowing this was not about sex but about children and a family and the rest of our lives.

Not too long after, with one eye on my watch, we were both down to the skiff on schedule, running full throttle the twenty-five minutes up to the afternoon plane, grateful the weather was good here, hoping the weather was flyable in town. We got there in record time. Duncan dropped me off on a beach just down the hill from the airstrip. After a kiss on the cheek he was headed back to fishing. I walked up to the airstrip and waited, standing, kicking the gravel, mindful of every minute, knowing this whole thing was worthless if I couldn't get there in time. Two pickups, then a third, then two ATVs, rumbled up in a dusty parade, all wheeling onto the airstrip and then sitting, waiting for the plane. I began to get nervous. How many people here were going in? Since we didn't have a phone, I couldn't make reservations. Which plane would they bring? I hoped for the Caravan, which seats ten.

At twelve forty it landed, not the Caravan but the Navajo, which seats six. The air thickened. As soon as the plane stopped, the trucks and ATVs emptied and the pilot, with his clipboard of names, was ringed with the legitimate, the hopeful, and the desperate. Nine people wanted on. I stood there among them cataloguing the supplicants: two cannery workers, two teen girls I recognized from Larsen Bay, a fisherman, and three other villagers, a man and two women. I didn't have a chance. The pilot, whom I recognized as Bob, began reading the names on his clipboard. Everyone listed was there except one.

"Okay," the pilot announced. "I've got room for one more on this flight." He turned to the two men and me, the leftovers.

"I've gotta get in to meet someone," one man implored.

"I made a reservation last night!" the other shouted. "I should be on that list! I told her my name and spelled it—"

"There's another plane coming in two hours," Bob interrupted, in a consoling tone.

That was too late for me. Mentally I took a deep breath. I had to speak up. "Uh, Bob, I have to get in," I said, breaking into the other man's barrage, and emphasizing the "have to." "It's medical," I said pointedly.

The other men fell silent. He looked at me closely, dubiously. "Is it an emergency?"

"Uh, not exactly, but it's urgent." Please don't ask me any more questions, I begged him silently. Am I going to have to explain the intricate details of this infertility test to everyone here? "I have to get in right away. The next plane is too late," I entreated.

I must have looked the part; the pilot waved me on, and the two left kicked the ground and walked away, chagrined.

"Thank you, Lord," I sighed as I ducked into the plane, immensely relieved. The secret was almost too much for me. I wanted to laugh and thank the pilot and tell him we would name our child, if we ever had one, after him, but then I looked at my watch. We were running behind schedule.

I made it to the clinic on time, after a speeding taxi ride, and hoped that for all this investment of energy, the answer would be here, in this test, and the remedy made clear. After less than an hour, I was back out the door, trying to quell hope. We would have to wait more than a week to hear the results, which would be mailed out to us. I felt empty as I left, and began the scramble to return to the island halfheartedly, trying to think of Duncan's and my life together simply as it was, not as I wished it.

THAT NEXT FALL, after we had moved into the house and gone through our first fishing season on our own island, we planned a trip back East. The season had gone well enough to afford the trip, and it had gone well enough otherwise. Duncan felt cut off from the doings on Bear Island, where he had spent every summer of his life since he was four. He had to commute now from our island to theirs to pick up his crewman several times a day. He wasn't sure about that extra time on the water. I was desperately lonely, missing Beverly and Wanda's company, and began to wonder if this was a mistake. I had wanted isolation, and now I certainly had it. Days would go by without seeing anyone other than Duncan. But we knew deep inside that our future was here, and that some day it would catch up with us.

IT WAS STRANGE to be back in New Hampshire. The little bungalow of a house Mother was living in was not home; she had moved twice in the twelve years since I had left for college. I was worn out from the trip there, thirty-six hours of airplanes and airports. The hardest part of the trip was always just getting off the island and into Kodiak. Such a short distance, one hundred miles, but in this region of violent weather, always an issue. I would fly, we decided, since I was leaving first. Duncan would take a fishing boat to town, to bring back all our goods and valuables. He would join me in New Hampshire in a month or so.

When I got there, though exhausted, I couldn't rest yet; I hadn't seen any of my brothers and sisters for five years. Scott was still working in maintenance at a college; Laurie, divorced, glamorous as ever, was selling advertising for a newspaper; Todd was repairing restaurant equipment; Clark, the youngest, was working in a factory; Jan was working as a receptionist.

Mother, at sixty looking her age but still slender, was working slowly on this ranch house, getting ready to sell. My photo album came out, compiled just for this, to show the island, the house we had just built. Everything looked grimy in the photos, I suddenly saw, as everyone clustered, hands on the photo, shooting questions.

"You didn't have an outhouse?"

"How did you work in all that rain?"

"You had to haul all your water up that hill?"

"Why did you use a metal roof?"

"You lived in that little shack all winter?"

The grubby life in the photos was the most reasonable thing I knew, but I didn't want to explain it to them. I had gone on to college and then graduate school, yet here I was doing the kind of work we dropped behind as we left home one by one. But in other ways the work was profoundly different. Building a new house was clean work, and I had already given all of my strength to it, and was ready to give more. I hadn't done that for my mother. I thought back to all our labor and I did not remember much cheer in the midst of the work. Why weren't we bound together in hardship, solidified and uncomplaining as we worked for our own survival? Mother reminded us often that our work kept our family going. But survival for us wasn't enough. The work did not feed our souls and hearts, and we weren't too happy about the way it fed our bodies, either.

I am sorry now for all of that work done so grudgingly, sorry for the weight it added to Mother's heavy load. The work was good: not only the demolition work, but all of us put up Sheetrock and taped and painted and wallpapered like professionals. When real estate agents trooped their clients through our finished houses, people who were well-to-do, they would exclaim over the features, the original hardwood floors, the gunstock corners, the wainscoting, the wallpaper and finely crafted moldings, the exposed beams, the fireplaces, the charming bedrooms. At least once, my brothers and sisters and I caught each other's eyes and then whispered to each other, "If they only knew that all this was done by a mother and six kids!" It was a joke, a fast one we all managed to pull off time and again, house after house. But it wasn't funny. Our handwork was never for ourselves, only for people we would never know. It was not for our future, only for the present. And if we did a good job, then the house sold and we got to do it all over again.

I wish I could redeem some of that time and work done for Mother, infuse love and understanding into those rooms. Was I doing that now? If not love, then hope at least. If God gave us children, if God gave me that chance, I would love them here in these very rooms, the two bedrooms downstairs, the nursery upstairs next to our bedroom, a playroom, a balcony over the family room. And this house would not be sold.

FINALLY TO BED in the small guest room. I wouldn't sleep much that night, I knew. My life was about to change forever— or it would continue month after month with the same predictable surge and plunge of hope. I was in the stage of hope now. On this trip east, I felt unaccountably fatigued and sick. And my period was late. On the way to my mother's, preparing myself once again for disappointment, I had bought a home pregnancy kit. In six hours I would know. Somehow that time passed—the white strip, this time, went pale, then blushed a faint blue, then blue—dark! Waves of incredulity and relief and ecstasy washed over me chaotically, randomly, and every emotion welcome, despite days of no sleep. I would be a mother, Duncan a father. This time I was ready. I lay awake looking through the ceiling.

17

Migration

I COULD BARELY CONTAIN THE GOOD news, but I would not tell Duncan for another week. I almost didn't tell him at all.

Whenever we leave the island, we have to decide how to go: boat or plane. Do we risk flying or do we risk a boat trip? This time, the choice was made for us. I would fly since I was anxious to get back to New Hampshire to see my family, and Duncan would take a boat since he was bringing back all our valuables from Harvester, all the verifications of our personhood and recent activities: birth certificates, marriage license, ring, passports, photos of our trek through Africa, boxes of tax documentation, and three boxes of my writings.

In the scheme of most migrations, the trip is trivial—from a larger island, Kodiak, to our island on the west side—a mere one hundred miles. How small the distance, the length of an eyelash on a state map. On a national map, a distance that doesn't even exist. How simple—and yet, not.

It all sounds so illogical now, but in the previous eight years, there had been four fatal small plane crashes, all pilots we knew and had flown with. It took no imagination to visualize the cargo of our vital statistics in an ugly gasoline conflagration amid a smoldering wreck. Thankfully and somewhat inexplicably, these visions never included me. I knew if I allowed myself a fear of flying, I, who was prone to seasickness in any vessel but a skiff, would be condemned to the single migratory mode of all-day or all-night boat trips in any kind of weather on other people's boats.

I was relieved, though, that Duncan was going in to Kodiak from Harvester Island on a sizable boat, a friend's fifty-five-foot fishing vessel that had seen a lot of hard seas. We used to make the hundred-mile trip in a much smaller vessel, a twenty-five-foot speedboat with twin 200 engines. My mother's first trip to Alaska, she gamely saddled up along with Wallace, Duncan, and me early one May morning for the run out to Bear Island. The weather came up unexpectedly. We wriggled into our survival suits and lurched and pounded over water so rough and white, my mother could not hold on and fell to the deck repeatedly throughout those four hours.

There were other memorable trips on that boat. The worst was in 1982. It was September, the end of my fifth fishing season. Everyone was gone but three of us—Duncan, my father-in-law, DeWitt, and myself. We were the stay-behinds, the ones to close up camp, to carry out the final details of padlocking the buildings; hanging cloths over the windows of the warehouses; turning water buckets upside down so the bottoms won't buckle and bulge with forgotten water that freezes; pulling up the running line and the last of the anchors; greasing the oil stoves to protect from the salt air, and more. The list always covers two full pages and always takes at least two days. When we were done that year, we made our migratory return to Kodiak in the speedboat, a twenty-five-foot Mako, a V-bottomed hull with twin 140s that takes our breath away when opened up on flat water. The others had gone by plane, the usual mode, but the Mako had to return to town for the winter, and logically, the last ones to go would take it. With a top speed of 40 mph, we could theoretically make it to town in just under three hours. This as opposed to a twelve-hour run or longer on a larger fishing boat.

The route from our island to Kodiak is semicircular, beginning on the west side of Kodiak, heading northeast through the Shelikof Strait, past deep fjordlike bays named Uganik, Viekoda, Kashuyak—then squeezing through Whale Pass, a Scylla and Charybdis passage where the tide muscles through in bulges and whirlpools, then out to the open waters of the Gulf of Alaska and the final curve south into Kodiak.

Early the next morning, at six, the weather report on the marine radio was not favorable, but the water was calm as we looked out toward the Shelikof Strait. We could see some twenty miles, and the going looked good, and after a long summer at fishcamp the rest of our lives awaited us. We would go. All we needed was three hours to sneak around the corner into town.

It was a gray day, as so many are, the water and sky and clouds all different textures of the same color. Maybe it could have been called ominous, in some literary foreshadowing. I felt it, but mostly it was morning, too early.

The run out into the Shelikof for the first ten miles was good. We were prepared for the trip, dressed warmly in layers of thermals and sweatshirts, each with a long-billed cap to shield our eyes from wind and spray and a hood tied tightly to secure it;

then wool socks, rubber hip boots, and last, heavy raingear to break the wind and keep us dry. Duncan was driving, DeWitt and I stood, holding on to the frame of the console. With 280 horsepower, we could move, but seldom smoothly. And there were no seats. We had taken out the one seat in front of the wheel, a leftover anachronism from Florida, where the boat had come from. The idea of lounging on a cushioned seat while driving was as unthinkable to us as throwing out a line and water-skiing in shorts. We held tight, but kept our legs loose to absorb the shock of every impact, and huddled our heads behind the windshield.

Not long after we rounded Cape Kuliak, the weather made good on the forecast. No rain, but the wind began almost as though a starting gun had been fired: from breathless to a stiff 20-knot breeze almost instantly; from level waters to whitecaps in a moment; and once started, momentum balled it all to twelve-foot waves, a 35-knot NW wind, and we were bucking into it, already thinking about heading back.

We began to confer on this idea, which was not as simple as it appeared: we were about halfway between places of shelter. Before a decision, the rumbling engines suddenly gargled and then a loud thwack. We turned, already suspecting the culprit. These engines had broken down before. Yet one of our crew, a fair mechanic, had worked them over thoroughly and guaranteed their trip-worthiness that week. We scuttled to new stations. DeWitt took the helm while Duncan gave a quick inspection and I stood ready with the toolbox. The diagnosis was quick and painful—a rod had been thrown. We still had the other 140 horse, and then a kicker, 35 horsepower, as another backup. But the one engine couldn't lift us onto the steppe, the level at which the boat cruises efficiently. We were heavy in the water, with the three of us and our gear, and could eke out just enough speed to keep the bow into the waves, but we rode the worst of every one.

It was clear by now that we needed to turn around and head back to the island. We had no sooner begun to turn, cautiously, so as not to be caught in the roll of the waves, when the bilge pump gave out. The water that was washing over us and pouring into the bilge now had nowhere to go. Within a few minutes the limp became a crawl. "Put your survival suits on!" Duncan yelled above the wind. It was an acknowledgment of emergency that suddenly sped everything to a fast-forward blur: our awkward clamber into our oversized neoprene suits; the boat nearly dead in the water, rolling in every surge, threatening to turn sideways in the twelve-foot waves; sheets of ocean pummeling us; Duncan bent over the pump; DeWitt trying to control the boat; me clinging to the console to keep from washing overboard. But even then I had hope. Something in me trusted—until Duncan leaned over and shouted in a shrill voice to be heard through the hooded suit, "Leslie, if we don't get out of this, I want you to know how much I love you!"

I think this was meant as reassurance. And despite our steady and rapid progression to this state of affairs, I was not yet truly afraid. But Duncan's message was the final stamp of Emergency with only two outcomes possible: that we would survive or we would not. I realized the full extent of our situation. No one knew where we were. We had a radio, but the mountains blocked any transmissions. We were more than a mile from shore, and the shoreline was nothing but vertical cliffs. Rescuing planes could not fly. . . . I began to pray.

Duncan and DeWitt kept frantically working, tinkering, and, some minutes later, water began sputtering out of the bilge hose again. The pump was functioning, but no one whooped or celebrated. There were still too many if's. The Mako, near lifeless, did not respond immediately to the now-functioning pump. It was a slow pump, and far too much water had filled the hull. Yet slowly, gradually, the boat began to respond to the rudder, and nose back to face the oncoming waves, wounded, unsteady, but capable now of direction, and now safer with the bow pointed into the waves.

The three of us returned to the console, holding on as before, but tighter, and all of us leaning forward, urging ourselves through the Shelikof Strait. We headed for Uganik Bay, just the next bay over from Uyak. On a calm day in a healthy speedboat, the trip there would have taken us just forty minutes. Today, it was three hours. We slogged our way in to Village Island, where a friend lived, an Eskimo homesteader named Daniel Boone Reed. We were exhausted, quiet as we peeled off our survival suits. Only our eyes and noses had been exposed, the suit sealing off any entrance of water, yet through that minuscule space came enough water to saturate our layers of clothing, to drench us down to skin.

After two more harrowing trips on that boat, we hauled it out and parked it in a field.

THOUGH DUNCAN HAD not taken the Mako, still, aboard the fifty-five-foot *Trojan* he was not safe. He left the island the day I arrived at my mother's. He stepped onto the deck of the boat when I was standing in line at the supermarket, buying the pregnancy test kit. The drama began close to midnight, Alaska time. They were several hours into the trip, about halfway down the Shelikof Strait. There were three of them, the couple who owned and fished the boat, and Duncan, and then three dogs. The seas weren't particularly rough, but during one wheel watch, the boat began handling strangely, sluggishly, taking too long to rise from the trough of the waves. A quick run out to the deck confirmed the worst: the stern was so low in the water the deck was awash. The other two were sleeping and awoke to shouts and barking. It was too late for anything but a Mayday, survival suits, and the life raft.

That morning, at about ten, the phone rang. It was Duncan. My mother handed me the phone, and I swallowed hard, wondering whether or not to tell him now, over the phone. How could I not? Yet it would be so much better to wait and tell him face to face.

"Hello!" I greeted in a cheery voice, my resolve evaporating, suddenly deciding I would tell. Silence. Then, "Leslie?" in a small voice that didn't sound like Duncan's. "Yes?" I answered, alarmed. Something was wrong. "What is it, Duncan?"

"The boat sank," he said in a shaky voice.

"What? Are you all right? Where are you calling from?"

"I'm all right. I'm here at my parent's house. We lost everything on the boat, though." And then he stopped, and suddenly I heard him sobbing great, deep sobs.

I sat down, stunned with the news. In those next few moments, as the night's events spilled out, I watched the sinking, the three of them abandoning ship, the final grotesque roll of the hull and the whirl of the waters as it swallowed the boat and all of our belongings whole, yet irrationally fearing that if I recreated it too vividly, it could turn out differently. They didn't get their survival suits on, the life raft wouldn't inflate, they couldn't free themselves from the rigging when the boat went down, no one heard the Mayday, no one picked them up in the life raft . . . I am widowed at age thirty. The night I find out I am pregnant my husband drowns in a shipwreck. He would never have known about the baby.

We were on the phone a long time. Duncan wouldn't stop

apologizing for losing everything—the greatest loss of all, he knew, was the journals and all my writings since childhood. But at that moment, it was I who flung it all in the ocean. It was my conscious, willing choice. In the logic of those moments, it was simple—either my husband or my things. I didn't tell him that morning that we were pregnant. It was enough to feel the sting of almost-death, to cry together, to thank God.

THAT AFTERNOON, just three hours later, my family returned to my mother's house for a meal together. As I stood among them in New Hampshire that day and told them what had happened, so close to near-loss, I felt so keenly how utterly different my life had become from theirs. Somehow, when I left New Hampshire, I left certainty behind. Certainty that I would find someone, marry, buy a little house off on a dirt road somewhere, children, some sort of career maybe, a dog, but all of my images of the future appearing in the dark sepia tones of memory. I could not think of this town, of the whole state, even, apart from growing up there. To stay meant certain failure, I felt. To leave meant possibility. And yes, the possibility of my husband drowning on a sinking boat. Some sort of trade had been made when I left, and I would not trade back.

We stood in a circle around our potluck dinner. Someone asked me to pray, and I prayed aloud, thanks to God for this meal and for everyone who was there, and for saving Duncan, and then I started to cry.

18

More than
a Place of Labor

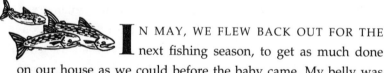I N MAY, WE FLEW BACK OUT FOR THE
next fishing season, to get as much done
on our house as we could before the baby came. My belly was
huge—I had just five weeks to go. I couldn't believe my body
could distend so far and still belong to me. I knew I was fortu-
nate, though; I could still work and get around relatively well.
Most of that time was spent on the front room. We had had an
unexpected setback the year before. When ordering our supplies,
we had ordered a half bundle of pine from Seattle for the trim
pieces. The front room, which had a sixteen-foot cathedral ceiling, was going to be paneled in local spruce. The spruce, however, ordered from a sawmill in Kodiak, never came, and the
half bundle of 1" × 4" pine arrived in Larsen Bay as two entire
bundles. What were we going to do with four times as much
pine as we needed, and what about the spruce? We settled upon

the obvious solution: We used the pine to panel the front room. But every piece had to be fed through the table saw twice for notching, a painfully slow process that gained only 3 inches for every piece put up. By June, I had most of the room done, but the ceiling remained. For the last week, I balanced about on the scaffolding, nailing up the last of the ceiling. For a mistake, it turned out beautifully.

While I was working on the front room, Duncan and some crewmen were installing a piece of technology that would propel us straight into the turn of the century. After twenty-eight years without one, in the summer of 1988, Fields and Sons finally broke down and bought a phone. Not a regular phone, but a radio-phone. It cost $5,000 and took a week to install, the antenna sitting like an extended lightning rod on our house. We had to do most of it ourselves, erect a fifty-foot-high aluminum pole with four guy wires each one hundred feet long tied into creosote pilings we sunk and cemented as deep as we could dig. An official phone person, the kind that makes bush calls, installed the rest of our unit in the attic of "the White House" in Larsen Bay, the cannery superintendent's house, an old, modest building, but the nicest of the cannery buildings.

I didn't really want a phone. We had discussed it off and on for several years. Out of our extended family of fifteen plus seven hired crew, my house was singled out for the then hypothetical installation of this new technology. It was logical, I knew. We built our house on the open south end of our island, which made us two miles closer to the staging unit in the village. No bluffs overhead, no interfering land masses, just a cool straight shot out into the atmosphere in all directions. Not so for either of the other two locations the rest of the family lived at. But here was the catch. The phone would connect the rest of the world to me alone. I would be the message taker and phone slave for twenty-two people, all with varying degrees of relatives and friends, some with lovesick girlfriends, creditors, worried mothers. . . . I did not want this role.

I did not make my protest public. I saw the need for it, occasionally, but, like everyone else, I already had a radio with all its attendant blessings and curses. Voices from the VHF and the CB filled my house, most of them voices I didn't want to hear, many of them people I didn't know: skippers on fishing boats yelling over the radio to their skiff men, "Get away from the rocks!" as apparently he pulled the net too close to a reef; or a float plane flying overhead calling a fishcamp, asking for the best place to land. For five years running, we caught a skip from a trucker somewhere in the Deep South who was using a booster, an amplifying unit so powerful it was illegal. The worst of it came on net-mending days, when we put the radio on an outside speaker so we wouldn't miss any calls while we stood on the beach tending the nets. Then the Mississippi-trucker glossolalia, almost impenetrable to interpretation except for the occasional "10-4," amplified to broadcast, harangued us with an unsettling clash of cultures. He clearly was talking on the radio just to talk, to pass the time. The content of his utterances was not the point. For us, 3,000 air miles away, the radio was only for content— brief, terse bits of information. To be helplessly and continually bathed in this verbal overflow, this abuse of sound waves and airwaves, which we were so dependent upon, irritated us all. When we hit our threshold, the radio went off, and it was quiet again, and no one in the world could reach us no matter what and how they tried.

Yet, as I ducked into the front seat of the plane, two weeks left now before my due date, I was glad to know Duncan and I could now communicate. I was sorry to leave him behind, but I really didn't want to have the baby out there. What did I know about having a baby? The first pregnant belly I had ever seen—popped-out navel and all—was my own. I knew only what I had read and learned from Lamaze classes a few months before, and I sensed that those sessions were sanitized, cauterized versions of what actually happens. The hospital in town—not our new house on the island—was the preferred place for this event. And my preferred companion was Duncan. Our new phone would help ensure his presence.

"Call me tonight!" I said just before the plane door was shut. What a great phrase. We had never said it before out here. Now we could talk every night. The first night, and the second, no call. I kept dialing and getting a strange-sounding busy signal. Worried, I called the Franciscos, our neighbors across the water who had had a radio-phone for several years already. They were able to get hold of Duncan by radio the next day and confirm what I suspected—the phone wasn't working. How would we communicate now? There were actually three choices, which was one more than we had had the two winters we spent out, but it didn't matter to us then that we had neither voice nor ear to the outside world. Now it mattered enormously. Duncan could skiff over to the Franciscos and use their phone, but he could hardly do that every night. Or he could travel the thirty minutes to Larsen Bay, weather permitting, and line up for the three public phones at the cannery. The only way I could get a message through was to call the Franciscos and ask them to pass a message on by radio. If the right person were by the right electronic device at the right time, I could conceivably get a message through in a matter of minutes, but often it took a day or two to pass a message on.

Finally, Duncan called. "How are you doing, Leslie? Sorry about the phone. We don't know what's wrong yet."

"Where are you calling from?" His voice sounded so far

away. He was far away. There was an entire wilderness of mountain ranges and glaciers between us.

"Larsen Bay."

"Too bad you have to go to all that trouble. When do you think the phone can be fixed?"

"Who knows! We need to get the phone man out here again to look at it. But I'm going to fiddle with the antenna and see what happens."

"Well, I guess we need a plan. If I start having contractions, I'll call the Franciscos, how's that?"

"Okay, that sounds good. I'll call you as often as I can."

"That'll do for now, I guess. How's fishing?"

"All right," he said, in just the right way so that I knew they were killing 'em.

"Reds?"

"Yeah, a few," he replied, casual.

Confirmed. That was good. We were still paying off grad school loans. That meant serious competition for the birth, though. "When can you come in?"

"Well, do you feel anything happening? Any contractions yet?"

"No, not yet."

"Let's wait a few more days, then, don't you think? Just call as soon as you feel anything serious."

So our conversations went until my due date arrived and passed. With each passing day I had gotten more irritated. How close would he play it? Three days *after* my due date, the weather shook up and the planes were grounded. I knew Duncan would miss it: I was deeply disappointed. Duncan, though, despite his cool phone calls, had not wanted to miss this event, either. When the weather closed down, he resourcefully caught a boat to town. Eight hours after he arrived, labor started.

JULY 22, 1988, in the front seat of the Beaver: my first flight in a bush plane with my new daughter, who slept in my lap in a Snugli pack, her legs drawn up like a frog's, her lips pursed. This was my favorite plane because it could land right on our beach, and because it flew slowly, almost meditatively, it was safer than the turbo-prop, I reasoned. If you crashed slowly, you had a chance. What other concessions could be made for travel out here? Really, there were none. I checked myself and realized I felt no heightened sense of danger with her tiny presence. Whatever risks there were in flying or taking a boat, we would have to take them—or move, where? Somewhere without cars or highways, boats or planes, somewhere where perpetual safety was guaranteed? No, I would stay.

Dave, the pilot, glanced over at me and smiled as I stroked her head. She was three weeks old now. I would have gone back out to the island sooner, but I was under siege, drowning both in a passionate love for this mewly, red-faced creature, and in helplessness. She cried a jagged scream most of her waking hours, which ranged freely and unpredictably through any segment of the twenty-four. I could do little to console or comfort except nurse her, which worked only when the cry was related to hunger. At her one-week checkup, the catch-all diagnosis— colic. We had named her from the Old Testament—Naphtali— after one of the twelve sons of Jacob. When Jacob gave his final blessing and prophecy to his sons, hands on their heads, he said of Naphtali, "She is a doe set free; she speaks beautiful words." Clearly it would be a long wait to hear any of those words.

Duncan was there for the first week, taking turns walking her through the night. Despite our fatigue, which did not seem to be halved by our doubled efforts, and her refusal to sleep, we marveled continually over this new human being. Of the places we had been, the things we had seen and done in our short, thirty-ish lives—both separately and together—the moment of her birth far surpassed anything we had experienced. I felt as though I had just entered a secret club hitherto unknown to me—not just the club of motherhood, but the club of human-kind. Women had been doing this forever, and I had never paid any attention.

Mothers with babies had always been invisible to me, one of the groups of people that simply did not register, especially during the years in college and grad school. When women gathered in those settings, girl talk centered on the texts and subtexts of the Victorian novel or the Renaissance picaresque novel we were reading; we compared notes on our literary analyses of deconstructionism; we lamented the flabby state of our bibliographies, and hoped to firm up our lines of logical discourse. We had complete academic freedom to discuss any topic, no matter how radical, but the traditional—the subject of babies and children and our own possible futures as mothers—was simply beyond our pale. As academics, walking the narrow ivory halls behind and beside distinguished faculty who had committed themselves to a life of research and teaching, the consideration of any other life or pursuit, including motherhood, was a kind of treason.

Though I still loved much of that world, I had broken free from it. With Naphtali in my arms, I felt as though I were still waking from a blind-but-now-I-see sleep. Our single-minded devotion did not last long, though. After a week, I could see Duncan felt he needed to go. We were sitting on the couch, trying to rest as she nursed. I was still in the gritty phase of feeding. My nipples were cracked and bleeding so that I had to pant and count my breaths as I did through labor to distract me from the pain.

"Are you all right, Leslie? Is it getting any better?" Duncan asks, his face on mine as I close my eyes and count. His hand is on the back of Naphtali's head as she strains at my breast.

"Yeah, I think it's a little better than a few days ago." I want to believe this, though it's not quite true yet. "The books say it takes about two weeks, so I'm halfway there," I smile through my teeth.

"There's no great time to bring this up, but they need me out there, Leslie. They're one skiff short with me in town."

"I know, Duncan."

"Everyone's covering for me, but they're really tired. Do you think you can do this by yourself now?" His voice has tightened.

This was the problem with a summer birth. We wanted to prolong this shared exhaustion/euphoria that was cementing us together, but the other life called.

"It's okay, Duncan," I said, actually meaning it. This was hardly a surprise. It was only a question of when. "I wish you could stay, but I can do it. And as soon as she settles down and I get some rest, I'll be back out there."

"Don't push it. Stay as long as you need to."

"I will."

After two weeks alone with her—alone because I did not know many people in Kodiak—and having paced off many times the tiny square footage of the ranch house I was borrowing, with her little body thrown over my shoulder so the clumps of milk that spewed from her after each feeding would not choke her, I was ready to return.

THE FLIGHT had been perfect—clear skies, no wind, the waters of the bays content within their boundaries. As we neared Bear Island—Duncan had moved back there since I was gone—Dave seemed to sense my mounting excitement. He had three kids of his own.

"Do they know you're coming today?" Dave shouted over the engine.

"Yes, but they didn't know exactly when!" I returned, yelling at equal pitch. The phone was working, but it was at Harvester only, and no one was there to answer it. Since we had never had a phone, many times people came out to visit on the strength of letters alone, with the buzz of a circling plane around Bear Island the equivalent of a doorbell, meaning "Somebody's here; come to Larsen Bay and pick us up." This was a float plane, though— on-site delivery.

"Have they seen the baby yet? They must have come in after the birth, huh?"

"No, just Duncan. They were all fishing. . . . It's been open all this time," I explained loudly. It was all right that no one else came in to see or help with the baby. How could they leave fishing? They would all be anxious now, though, to see her.

"They'll be excited to see you. Yep. A new grandchild. You'll get a real welcoming committee," he said with relish, enjoying the anticipation with me.

Bear Island slid into view now, its rocky profile suddenly just under my feet. The island looked quiet. The skiffs were tethered to the running line out front, meaning everyone was ashore, but not a person was to be seen between the cabins. I checked my watch—4:00 P.M.

"Where is everyone?" he asked, puzzled.

"It's nap time." I sighed. What was I thinking?

"I'll wake 'em up," he said, seeing my disappointment. He banked the Beaver into a sharp curl, diving in a swoop that cleared the cabin roofs by a hand span, it looked. We dove again and again, spinning, my stomach like taffy, my hands cradling the baby against the centrifugal force. Still, no response from the houses. I knew they could not give up their naps. Without that hour or two of sleep every afternoon, they could not survive the eighteen-hour shifts on the nets. Sleep was more important, of course, as were the fish. That is what we're here for, I reminded myself, as though reciting the party line. When will I learn? I thought in a flash of frustration. And I knew then that though my life had changed completely with the baby in my lap, fishing had not changed. It was no more malleable than a block of concrete, and malleability was the virtue I most needed to live here with this baby. I would give up working in the skiff for good, I had decided: I had to, but now I wanted to as well.

Those next weeks of July, it was an enormous relief to let it go, to send Duncan off every morning and afternoon to the nets and the uncertain terrain of water, to stay behind on stable ground. I relished this role at first, using whatever few spare moments I had between feedings and during naps to work on the house, to make it home. The front room was still a tower of scaffolding, waiting for me to find the hours needed to finish the varnish on the new ceiling. The floor was still raw plywood always dusted with sawdust, the porches and downstairs unfinished. But soon I tired of this. By the time I got into a project, Naphtali would be awake again, hungry, and we would begin the next forty-five-minute feeding, just two hours from the feeding before. I gave up trying to get anything done and I began escorting Duncan down to the beach, then staying, walking the shoreline back and forth, eyes out over the water or up at the mountains, then eyes down at the beach itself.

I felt I knew the beach already—after the previous winter using the far beach as a stand-in for an outhouse, and after the hundreds of landings as we ferried our house from water to hill. But I knew little about the sea and rockweed that dressed it, little about the sea life above and below the tide line, little about the birds that flocked it. I had never had time for any of this, but now I would.

On this last return to the island, I had looked out the plane window searching for beaches, a habit since my lost-in-a-skiff episode seven years before, my eyes always tracing both water and land to where they meet. There were long expanses without beaches—just cliffs. I thought of Bear Island, with its single usable beach. When I first came, I had expected long expanses where the land in all its dress and flora crumbled slowly to sand, then leaned down into the continent of water—the proper way for land to meet ocean. There must be a playing field upon which sea and land agree to meet, to mingle, exchanging air, water, soil, inhabitants. Let there be commerce between the two, as it was on the many islands I had been where the sand haloed each shoreline. I was still muffling those expectations.

On Harvester Island it was nearly the same—one usable beach. Though I was entirely dependent on that one beach at Harvester and the single, smaller beach on Bear Island, I would never say they were beautiful, even from the air. I was reminded as I flew that day that most of the shoreline of Kodiak Island is serious, solemn even. In most places the sand is volcanic black. On gray days, the beach is gray; on sunny days, black; when wet, ebony. For sand we count grades of gravel, from fine to coarse to fields of boulders. All beaches are treeless, offering neither shade nor an umbrella. On our two beaches, we hand-over-hand our nets from skiffs to shore, from shore to skiffs. On net-mending days we stretch the webbing from one end of the beach to the other. And though mussels and clams abound, and we want to dig them, we cannot eat them—they contain some of the highest rate of paralytic shellfish poisoning in the state.

Our beach is not a vacation beach; it is a working beach. Perhaps, now that Naphtali and I were onshore, the two of us could make this beach more than a place of labor.

WE SAW WONDROUS THINGS on the beach that summer, sometimes watching from our front windows, often on the beach itself, Naphtali in the front pack in a tight ball as I walked, her head peeking over the top. I don't know how much she saw, but she heard my running narrative that kept us both company the many hours Duncan was gone. A beaver swam over one day. A sea lion carcass washed up another. Deer swam on and off. One morning I woke to see eight deer frantically pacing the beach, their usual graceful stride now jerky and uncertain. They would take turns stepping into the water, then retreating, then in again, their distress apparent. Was there a bear on the island? I couldn't know. I watched that entire hour of agonizing attempts until finally, upon some signal I couldn't recognize, they stepped in to their knees, then their bellies, and were launched, all eight, into the 50-degree water. They were amazingly buoyant, and seemed to know just what to do, how to navigate, for they arrived at what I assumed was their destination, the beach a half mile across, fifteen minutes later.

I noticed the regularity of the black oystercatchers. There was a pair of them, their shrill single note–cry was somehow a perfect match to their midnight black bodies and their startlingly red bills and feet. They were always together in a picture of conjugal bliss. If one was spotted standing alert on the black cliff, a moment more of peering would inexorably bring the other to view, just a few feet away. I was happy to share the beach with them.

One week a Japanese freighter anchored up just a quarter of a mile from my shores. Whenever I took a walk during those ten days, I wended through a garden of bruised onions, soft oranges, browning cabbages that mysteriously sprouted along the tide mark.

Fish in various states of disembowelment were continually washing up, setting the stage for mini-epics of greed and take-over among the shorebirds. One morning, sitting in the chair by the front window, Naphtali nursing, I watched a domestic drama between a pair of eagles and a pair of gulls.

The plot centered around a torn-up pink salmon that had floated to the high-tide mark. The eagles and gulls spotted it the instant it landed and began a furious dogfight—wheeling, dipping, shrieking their way to rights to the carcass. The gulls gave the eagles a good run, being more facile, their turns quicker, but the eagles, out of sheer intimidation, won. The two, both white-headed, signaling their adult, full-grown status, landed and stood proprietorily over the fish. One eagle got to work imme-diately, planting both sets of talons into the flesh, then ripping and tearing the meat with its beak. His appetite was raw, the bloody and pink strings of flesh ripping from the white skin, visible even to me in the house. Strangely, the other eagle did not contest the first eagle's feast, who was eating seemingly with-out regard for its partner. The abstaining eagle seemed intent on something else—the same two gulls, who now stood some thirty feet away, drooling, but convinced of the wisdom of their dis-tance. They stood locked in position, not moving, not even cock-ing their heads, just eyes on the eagle and the dinner they had lost.

It suddenly occurred to me what was happening. "He's the guard!" I called out in delighted surprise, then directed this down to Naphtali as the only other person on the island. The second eagle standing there so unconcerned over the portion be-ing consumed by the other eagle was acting as guard. His belligerent stare alone held the gulls at bay. He stared not only at them, but his head made routine turns around both ways to ensure a clear coast and an unthreatened plate. This eagle, eagle number two, whose patience I admired and who I decided was the wife, held no accounting of how much was being taken by the other. "What kind of agreement do these two have?" I wondered aloud. Or was I fabricating the whole scenario? In a moment the answer came. The eagles, in the blink of an eye, switched positions precisely. The second eagle now tore into what remained, tugging chunks of salmon meat, chugging them whole, while the first stood guard. The new guard, now with his own belly full, was not quite as concerned with his duty, however. After a few minutes, apparently bored with watching the two gulls, he began to amble away, despite the fact that the gulls were gaining courage from his inattention and inching forward. I could almost see the delinquent husband eagle whistling as he went, trying to look as nonchalant as any eagle out strolling on any beach. In fact, he did stroll, down to the water's edge where he began, strangely, to wade in the incoming surges, looking like some old bowlegged beachcomber. I began to laugh out loud and wished Duncan were here to share this with me. Periodically he would dip his head down, and skim his beak sideways in the gravel. All of this not according to agreement, I was sure. Soon even his wanderings began to bore him, and without ado, he lifted off, leaving the other eagle still feeding, the two gulls in rapt attendance, and decidedly closer. A few minutes later the second eagle finished all that was good of the fish and flew off as well.

Since eagles pair for life, they were undoubtedly a husband-and-wife team, and clearly not newlyweds. They had been together long enough to establish a system, and then long enough for one to know just how much to stretch it, nibble at it, yaw it his way without directly breaking the rules: "But honey, I was right there if you needed me. All you had to do was screech. I know I left a few minutes early, but you obviously had those gulls under control. I could see you didn't really need my help. And besides, I just went off to look for more food—for you!"

OUR FAVORITE BEACH ACTIVITY OF all, though, was to listen for the returning skiff, and when I could see its bow nosing into shore, I snatched up Naphtali and we walked down to the beach to greet Duncan as he came in from fishing. I felt a bit like Donna Reed already, welcoming the coming-home husband with baby in arms, lunch simmering on the stove. It was some comfort to me that I was wearing old jeans, usually, or sweats, and could hardly be described as coiffed or manicured in any form. Definitely no pearls. One month into this, I was already finding out that motherhood was not something to dress up for—it was down-on-the-dirty-floor work.

"How's my baby?" Duncan would call, as soon as he saw us.

"She's doing great. Fussed and cried all morning, but that's normal. How's fishing?"

"Fine, good. What's she wearing, Leslie? I haven't seen that outfit before." Then, in a higher voice, "You look like Little Red Riding Hood, Naphtali," and he bent down to kiss her.

"You want to carry her up to the house?"

"I'm all wet, Leslie. Wait until I get all my gear off."

"Well, I'm all wet, too."

"I see that. Are you leaking? Your shoulder's all slobbery, too."

"Thanks for noticing. I don't know why I hung up my rain-gear—I need it more now than I did in the skiff."

We both laugh as we begin the climb up the hill to the house.

WHEN WE TIRED of the beach, and tired of waiting for Duncan to return, I took Naphtali on walks around the island, or up to the top. Sometimes I was gone for as long as two hours, needing the day to pass, needing her to sleep. The rocking motion calmed her when little else could. I needed as many minutes of quiet as I could get from her. Her presence so filled my life, my waking and sleeping moments both, that I no longer felt alone here on Harvester Island, but it was deathly quiet here compared to life on Bear Island.

ONE CALM AUGUST AFTERNOON, after lunch, I decided to go out fishing with Duncan. How would I take Naphtali, though? I practiced in the house, first dressing her in a warm sleeper and a winter suit. Then I stuffed her little form into her life jacket and laid her in the aluminum tub I used for rinsing laundry. It worked—she was thoroughly immobilized, but she began screaming instantly. I could see the life jacket was not made for lying down. I tried the infant carrier next, propping it up in the tub. She quieted for a moment, more comfortable, and she could see over the sides. This looked promising.

"Duncan! I think this'll work!" I called from the front room.

"All right, let's get ready then. I'll take the tub down."

I picked her up in the carrier and set her down on the porch while I got my gear on. She began to cry, the sound and pitch already a part of me. I hurried, pulling on knee boots, sweatshirts, lifting the orange Grunden rain pants from the hook, stepping into them, the straps going over my shoulder, hooks into slots, then the yellow Playtex dishwashing gloves, then the cotton gloves, and the neoprene sleeves over that to hold it all in place. As I dressed in all these layers, despite Naphtali's unhappiness, I felt happy to be going out on the water again, happy to leave the island and its walls of cliffs.

At the skiff, Duncan set the tub on the shelf in the bow and tied it in place. I carefully set her down, still screaming, in the center. Duncan started the kicker, both of us watching to see what our month-old daughter would do with this new noise. She stopped suddenly at the sound of the engine. We glanced at each other, excited. Maybe she would like this! We motored slowly over to Pacquette's, the net closest to us, my hand on the tub until I saw it was secure. The bow rose and rocked up and down in a gentle motion. She was already looking sleepy. Duncan slowed, I picked up the net, and we began the work. The sun was shining this day, and in our bright raingear, with Naphtali quiet in the bow, I felt a kind of glow about us, that Duncan and I were working together, that our daughter could be out with us. Perhaps it would work—being here at Harvester. Maybe there was a way to live here and fish together without it controlling and dividing us. For that afternoon, it all felt in perfect balance.

19

Oil Spill

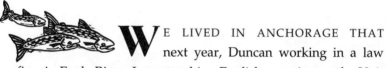WE LIVED IN ANCHORAGE THAT next year, Duncan working in a law firm in Eagle River; I was teaching English part-time at the University of Alaska. While we were both pleased to be using our educations, Duncan was not happy living in Anchorage, and he claimed that, along with the other half of the state that didn't live there, "Anchorage wasn't Alaska." The traffic, the stoplights, his thirty-to-forty-minute commute to work, the high-speed highways boasting one of the highest accident rates in the country—none of which existed in Kodiak—were the black marks of urban living. But jobs for just-graduated law students in 1989 were not easy to find.

At the end of March, as we were beginning to think about packing for Harvester Island, the news broke: "The *Exxon Valdez* has gone aground on Bligh Reef in Prince William Sound, spew-

ing thousands of gallons of crude oil into pristine Alaskan waters." We were stunned, along with the rest of the state, and followed the news closely day by day. Exxon sources came on repeatedly, assuring that the oil wouldn't spread, that it was contained and everything was under control. But it wasn't.

It was horrifying enough that Prince William Sound had been oiled, but the news reports began to voice our own fear: that the oil was drifting, making its way down to Kodiak Island. Rumors and reports told us nothing and everything: the oil had hit and blanketed the whole west side; no, the oil had hardly touched the strait, but it had smothered the east side. We didn't know what to believe. As soon as classes were out and Duncan could leave the law office, we hopped a plane to Kodiak and then to Larsen Bay. As we flew, we were all eyes on the water—was that the oil there, that dark smudge on the surface by Sally Island? The pilot shook his head no. Or that long string of shadow in Uganik—was that oil? No again. I began to feel hopeful. We landed right on our beach—we had taken a float plane—and immediately I ran the shoreline, Naphtali in my arms, still expecting the worst, that this island would produce the same death-and-dying images we had seen from the Sound. I followed the string of open mussel shells, pumice, and dried grasses that marked the last high tide. Where was it? Here was some, a puddle of black goo. And over there, another. Beside that one, a few more small pools. But not the whole shoreline as I had feared. I heaved relief, calmed the mounting panic I had felt as we flew.

Over the next few days as I continued the survey, I realized that the oil we were seeing had traveled some two hundred miles to get here, and arrived in a different form than it left. Over the miles, it had broken up into globules, islands that drifted off on their own, and hit the beaches quietly, often unseen until something living touched it. Some oil arrived on our beach already thickened with bits of feathers, bones, each clump keeping its own grisly record of its victims. Some places it pooled conspicuously in dark puddles, like black blood, but in others it melted into the sand and gravel, so the visible spot fanned out much wider beneath.

My relief was premature. It didn't take much oil to kill, we soon learned. The media posted tragic photos of birds and otters who looked as though they had been hand-dipped in sludge, but just a few drops of oil could kill water birds as efficiently. Just a drop here, there, could violate the integrity of their natural oil-coated feathers. Just a smudge of oil and cold ocean water bleeds into the skin, and the bird dies of hypothermia and cold. Thousands of murres had already died like this. What about the salmon? The runs of salmon in Prince William Sound and around Kodiak Island were some of the healthiest and most abundant natural resources in the world. Would they survive? And even in the midst of contemplating this possibility—that the salmon runs would be wiped out entirely, my mind, self-ishly, flew straight to the season before us: What if we couldn't fish? We had eight crewmen this year, most of them struggling college students who had flown up from all over the country, depending on this income to make it through another year. Our four families had already sunk a large chunk of money into this season as well as hard weeks preparing to cast the first net to retrieve some of it back. What of us?

THE NEXT WEEK, June now, passed slowly. We didn't know if we should keep working on our gear, preparing for the season, or if we should undo the arduous three-week process just finished and shut the fishcamp down, call a plane and fly off, to spend the summer back in our respective places, among roads, cars, people. And what would we do there? Since 1952, Duncan's family had not missed a single salmon season. Already, my history was compiling; I had been there for eleven seasons. We didn't give up hope yet, though. We kept the nets loaded in the skiffs for weeks, expecting any day to hear the good word that the run of oil had ended and we could resume our normal lives and fish. When we listened to Exxon's people, we felt sure we would fish. They had already invested large sums of money toward this, buying new seine nets, new fishing gear for boats all over Kodiak. Their motivation was obvious.

The word, when it finally came to the cannery and then to all its anxious fishermen, was not what anyone wanted to hear.

"The entire season is closed, Leslie," Duncan reported tiredly as he pulled off his Stormy Seas jacket on the porch.

"Did Fish and Game find oil on some fish?"

"Yeah. They were doing those test fisheries around the island—and they found oil on some of the salmon. So they're shutting it all down."

I came out of the bedroom, where I had just laid Naphtali down for a nap. I paused, understanding the emotional impact of those few words. A summer without fishing? Impossible! Would Duncan survive? I had heard him say to others that "fishing was in his blood." I imagined microscopic schools of salmon nosing their way through his arteries, their very movement somehow necessary to his body's life. This news was not unexpected, though. Prince William Sound had lost their season, and we had known we could be next.

"Ah, Exxon couldn't keep it open after all! Well, I trust Fish and Game. They're trying to protect the resource." I could see Duncan wasn't ready for my immediate let's-look-at-the-good-side approach. "It's necessary, Duncan, don't you think? You know, the purity issue."

We had talked about this already. Even apart from the slim possibility of contamination, we didn't want any suggestion or perception that Alaska salmon was tainted. It was better to allay all fears by simply sitting it out. There was always next year.

Duncan nodded. "Yes, it's the right thing to do, from every perspective."

I knew he meant it, but there was a hollow tone to his voice. I sat down, my mind busy with possibilities. For the first time, and maybe the last, I would be free to leave the confines of the island for a summer. I almost couldn't think of it—what would I do? What would Duncan do, and what about income? We depended almost completely on these earnings. I was only teaching part-time, and Duncan's job did not pay well.

"There's more, Leslie," Duncan began again as he sat down heavily at the kitchen table.

Standing, I looked down at him expectantly.

"Exxon is hiring local people to clean up their mess, as compensation of sorts for losing the fishing season. They've already started training and hiring in town—hundreds of people, I guess. Maybe more, a couple thousand. And they finally agreed to hire us, the setnetters, since we're already here. But what a battle just for that small concession!" He shook his head.

"How ridiculous, that we had to fight for that. At least let us clean our own beaches! Of course we're going to do a better job." Then I thought a minute. "Maybe that's why they didn't want us in the first place."

Duncan gave a short, bitter laugh. "Kind of ironic, huh? But you know what else? They won't hire unless we go through training. These Exxon guys from Texas are going to train *us* in boat safety and wilderness survival!"

I laughed with him, incredulous at yet another absurdity in this upside-down world. "So, after this so-called training, how do we clean? Are we going to do bioremediation or the pressure wash here?"

Much was being made of these relatively new techniques. One consisted of applying microscopic oil-consuming organisms to the affected areas, which broke down the toxic wastes into nontoxic by-products. The other was less promising. People in wetsuits manned pressure washers and blasted the beaches with steaming hot water. We knew before hearing the scientific appraisal of this method that it was atomizing and erasing the oil from the surface, yes, but it was simply melting it from the surface into the substrata. It symbolized perfectly Exxon's modus operandi.

"Nope, thank goodness. We're going to clean the old-fashioned way. They're going to supply us with all the cleaning stuff—oil-absorbent rags, bags, and I don't know what else. We'll go out every day—"

"—that's good! It'll give everyone something to do. It's better than just sitting here."

"Right. It'll help us to earn something, anyway. Otherwise we might as well pack up and leave. We'll dump anything with oil on it into the bags—gravel, rocks, driftwood, anything—and they'll come around in boats and pick it all up. We'll keep track of our own hours and then be paid every two weeks." He grimaced knowingly, as if he had somehow foretold this.

"What are they paying?" I almost didn't want to hear.

"Sixteen dollars an hour."

I sat across from Duncan at the kitchen table now, absorbing this. It was an interesting amount. It was almost double the hourly wage jobs in town, and yet it probably wouldn't go far enough to pay off our expenses and compensate for a lost season.

"I'll tell you what else they're doing, Leslie. I just heard at the cannery that in Kodiak, they're hiring the local seiners, lots of them, to go out on cleanup, and they're paying huge amounts, like fifteen hundred dollars a day for two months. Sixteen dollars an hour won't do much for us, but they're trying—"

"—they're trying to buy everyone off!" I was angry again. "That's been their mode all along. They figure that if they throw enough money at us and at the town, that we won't sue for their negligence."

"That's right." Duncan nodded.

There was emotional consensus among everyone we knew in the bay and in Kodiak—all were angry that this had even happened, but the details, as they came out, fueled those emotions to the point of outrage. By now the details of the story had slowly leaked out: the captain, Joseph Hazelwood, had previously lost his driver's licence for DWI; he had been removed from his position as captain on another Exxon tanker for drunkenness; yet Exxon still put him behind the wheel of one of the largest ships in the world. He had been drinking that night; the ship, when it struck Bligh Reef, which was well known and clearly marked, was in the hands of the third mate. The *Valdez*, now aground on the reef, sat and leaked its cargo for more than a day before anyone acted to stop it. The single oil spill response barge in Valdez was in dry dock.

In the beginning, the Exxon publicist in Valdez was immediately on the air, assuring that the oil would be cleaned up in a few days. Then he said the oil wouldn't spread beyond Prince William Sound. Soon after that, they closed the air space around the reef—for safety—but we knew otherwise. Then other Exxon spokesmen were claiming that the oil wasn't toxic. Each new piece of information confirmed that the accident had been entirely preventable, and that Exxon was doing all it could to control the national media's coverage.

The local papers that came to us in the mail told a different story. They ran headlines throughout the summer of businesses shutting down, suicides, depression, higher crime rates. Almost as bad, the fishing fleet was divided as each boat competed for a lucrative cleanup contract. Who got it and who didn't meant that one family paid off their $30,000 boat mortgage policy—the "spillionaires"—while their neighbors went deep into debt. We were glad to be out of town, on our own quiet island, far from what read to us as madness.

But the summer was far from quiet, and the madness seemed intent on finding its way out to us. Boats, helicopters, and planes began arriving, disgorging on our beaches a startling amount of stuff: stacks of square white absorbent pads; industrial-sized boxes of Tide detergent; rolls of large polyvinyl bags; boots, green plastic raingear; rakes, shovels, and pitchforks; fifty boxes of riotously colored bouquets of absorbent strips called pom-poms; Typar, a synthetic oil-absorbant material; anchors, anchor lines, and chain. Seine boats on contract to Exxon plied the shores to collect the vinyl bags; animal rescue workers came in Zodiaks for oiled birds, otters, and eagles; a Uyak Bay fisherman was hired to drop pom-poms anywhere along the bay's waters to impress airborne media with the cleanup efforts. Helicopters landed routinely on Harvester Island, partly because we had a radio-phone. Lawyers flew out from town to meet with the fishermen in our house.

Spliced among these frantic activities was our own daily schedule. Each day, the brothers deployed themselves and the crew, all sporting the Exxon goods and tools, to the beaches, beginning with their own on Bear Island, where the oil had slopped onto the rocks and boulders, making removal difficult. They dropped the movable rocks into the clear vinyl bags; the boulders could only be scrubbed with pads. When done, they moved over to the lagoon, then on the beaches opposite Bear Island, then into skiffs and onto other beaches heading into Larsen Bay. They worked twelve-hour days, regardless of weather, often bending over rocks and gravel, pelted with horizontal rain. They never ran out of work because the oil kept coming.

Seven-Mile Beach was itself a full-time job. My brother Todd was there, living in Kay Wood's old cabin, which now threatened to pitch into the sea in the next big storm. We hadn't planned this. Todd had driven up from New Hampshire to visit us, arriving just days after the oil spill. Since he had left his job back home, we urged him to come out to Bear Island with us and work the cleanup. His duty was to patrol a five-mile stretch of beach with an ATV. With a close eye on the tide book, he ran the beaches at the peak of high tide, no matter the hour, to catch the tar balls as they floated in. If he missed them, they would sit and melt into the sand and rocks, undetectable unless the surface were dug or pried up. He continued cleaning twelve hours a day for fifty days, long after Exxon's claim that the oil had stopped.

One day, near the end of July, Duncan and the crew skiffed over to a beach they had heard was particularly bad. Even before they landed, they could smell the oil, though they couldn't see any. They started cleaning the rocks with the absorbent pads, where they could see a sheen, and discovered, as in so many other places, that the oil had seeped underneath. They began digging trenches and found that the oil would drain into the trenches where it could be soaked up efficiently with the pads. Happy to be so productive, they energetically dug a series of trenches, sucking out many gallons of oil. The vinyl bags, filled with the oiled pads, lined the beach.

Then a sound—a helicopter. It landed at the other end of the beach. Before the blades stopped spinning, two orange survival-suited men jumped out.

"This beach is not designated for cleanup!" one man barked as they marched past the rows of bags toward Duncan and the others.

"It's dirty. It's one of the worst beaches we've found!" Duncan shouted back, gesturing to the bags and the crew still at work.

"You're not supposed to be digging underneath the surface," the taller man spit out in a now-familiar Texas drawl. "This beach is not identified on our map as one that needs cleaning. Go somewhere else!"

THROUGH ALL of this chaos and disruption, I found moments of quiet. While others were digging up beaches near and far, I stayed the summer at my self-designated spot—my own beach at Harvester. I hadn't the energy for travels. Naphtali was a year old this summer; I was still nursing her, and was tired from that physical drain coupled with her continuing resistance to sleep. By June, I discovered another reason for my fatigue: I was pregnant. We were delighted that we would now be four, and that this conception hadn't required anything out of the ordinary. Somehow it provided all the more reason to stay. Of all the summers, this summer I could have left the island. That locked door flung open for one wild, giddy moment, but I could not leave as long as oil continued its silent seepage onto the beach. And the oystercatchers. I stayed for them, and for the bald eagles and gulls, the terns, murres, puffins, and whatever else was at risk on our beach.

One morning, the stakes rose yet higher. In my second week

of tending the shores, I discovered in the gravel a softly rounded hollow, and in it, three perfectly shaped rocks, speckled gray, black, and white. Eggs—my couple was going to be a family. I wondered at the vulnerability of their nest. The eggs were superbly camouflaged, but they lay in the open on a stretch of gravel as inviting to the foot or hoof as any other. It was pure brazenness or utter foolishness. There was neither fault nor credit on their part, but on mine there came an enormous sense of responsibility. It was now my job to protect an entire family. As the mother of a baby myself, I was learning about the fierce devotion of that tie.

The parents-to-be were not happy with my appointment as godmother, though. They were furious with me and every morning greeted me and all my extra appendages—rakes, shovel, pitchfork—with shrieks and dive attacks, beating me away from their nest. I could not reassure them except to widen my berth around their eggs as I worked. I sifted and sorted, shoveled, marched, and tended that ground—all with Naphtali in a backpack, peering over my shoulder as I worked. Just a few drops was all it took. I could not forget.

A few weeks later, while maintaining my regimen, something moved at my feet. I froze, and there by my toes, equally rigid and startled, crouched a chick, gray and white, as speckled and camouflaged as its egg had been. It was paralyzed, as was I, and I knew that with all of its beating heart it was trusting in the force that pinned it to the ground. One chick, at least, had made it this far.

THEY DID, in fact, make it through that poisonous summer, the three of them, as did our family of three. Had I not surrendered to a new life on shore with the arrival of Naphtali, perhaps I would have missed them, these oystercatchers. And while I hated what Exxon had done, I knew I was changed because of it, that I was no longer just a beach walker on this island: I was guard, mother, steward, charged with dressing and keeping this piece of ground given to me.

20

Staying Ashore

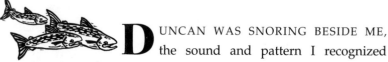DUNCAN WAS SNORING BESIDE ME, the sound and pattern I recognized from the depths of each summer, meaning we were in the middle of the pink run. What about Noah? I listened for baby sounds through the wall, heard none. Maybe tonight he will sleep longer. I gave Duncan a shove to encourage him to roll over; he did. I willed my body to relax, repeating the mantra, "You're resting, at least. You don't have to sleep—just rest." I didn't think I'd slept since Naphtali had been born almost two years ago. Noah, now six months old, was somewhat better than she had been at her age, but I feared my body had forgotten how to sleep.

Noah Shelikof was born in January 1990 at the Kodiak Hospital. We thought he'd be born in Anchorage, but the oil spill changed that. Those 11 million gallons of oil had an unexpected

and ironic effect upon our lives. While it took away one occupation for at least one season, maybe more—salmon fishing—it provided another. Duncan was offered a job with a law firm in Kodiak to work on the litigation against Exxon. It was a job we both believed in, in the town he had grown up in, with a firm he had long admired. We said yes. I wasn't sure what it would mean for the future, but for now, and for this last year, it proved to be a good move.

It was not long before I heard a whimper from the nursery. Noah still awoke for two feedings a night. If I didn't get to him in time, though, he would wake Naphtali, who slept in another crib against the far wall. I had waited too long: he launched from a quiet fuss to full-blown howl within seconds. Naphtali awoke and began crying.

"Leslie! What are you doing! This is the second time tonight!" Duncan rolled suddenly, startled by his own waking. "Go feed him—you know I've got to sleep!" He rolled over again sharply.

I was already launched out of bed and down the hall, angry at myself for my timing. This was the third night in a row. During the winter, Duncan would never have reacted this way. In the months before we had come out, we had reveled in our new son, just as amazed at his birth as we had been at Naphtali's. We followed his every development microscopically, celebrating each new achievement with the same joy we had felt with our daughter's. We were hooked—sunk deep in mother-love, father-love. And Duncan had been every bit as goosey as I was, and just as willing to get up in the night to comfort him or feed him a bottle. But now fishing had reclaimed our lives—our days and our nights were in service to its demands. The two thin sheets of plywood and the bit of insulation that separated us from the two babies in the next room were no longer enough.

"Where's my Dra-dra?" Naphtali wailed, sitting up in the bottom of her crib. With each child, and with every new fishing season, I was still learning how to live on Harvester Island. I was only two years into this—sleeping on a bed of nails every night, guarding over the baby's feedings and Duncan's sleep, and I was not doing such a great job. I tried not to resent this role, tried to remember the years of my own night-and-day fishing, how impossible it becomes to keep working in the skiff without rest. Duncan couldn't tell his brothers and the rest of the crew, "Sorry, guys, can't help you out on the water today. The baby kept me up all night."

The next day, I figured out another system. I moved the playpen downstairs for naps and nighttime, so Noah wouldn't awake anyone up but me when he cried. The playpen looked absurdly, even cruelly out of place among the axes, the wood maul, table saw, rolls of insulation, chainsaws—it was our shop, and was unheated. I felt moments of pity for Noah, his tiny yellow-sleepered form, and wished for some soft little nursery with cotton-candy clouds and unicorn wallpaper borders instead of this, but it worked. I drifted in shallow sleep until he cried, then scudded down in Duncan's old deck slippers, climbed in the playpen, scrunched into a ball, curling into the corners with Noah against me, until he nursed himself back into a milky sleep.

It was not likely, given the nursing schedule and the kids' ages, that I would be able to fish much that summer. We had already tried going out, all four of us, but Naphtali had persisted in hanging over the side, and Noah wouldn't sleep in the tub as Naphtali had the year before. We hadn't picked many fish that morning. I wondered if I would go out at all. More than once, as I lay in the playpen or on the mattress, I envisioned this scene: Wallace, Weston, and DeWitt march up to me in their hip boots and raingear up on the beach where I sit—what else?—

nursing a baby. "So, what are *you* doing for fishing?" they query, eyes ablaze.

"Uh, I make sure Duncan sleeps at night?" I offer, hesitant. Is that enough?

IT WAS A SUNNY DAY. The room outside my windows, the room with the wallpaper mountains and paper sea, was bright—the first break in the rain and clouds for a week. My heart almost choked me as it lifted into my throat, a lump of hope. "Let me be joyful today," I whispered before I got out of bed. Duncan was already out on the nets.

I fed, then changed and dressed Noah and oversaw Naphtali's dressing, though it didn't really matter if her clothes clashed, were on backward, or inside out or all three. After breakfast, I began the laundry. I hadn't planned on laundry, since it was put-out, just in case the men needed more hands for fishing, but I had no choice—we were almost out of clothes. The day before the kids had had diarrhea and vomiting, which had nearly doubled the wash in a single day.

Noah went in the backpack, and I began dumping the last of the water from the plastic Extra-Tough garbage cans that served as our water receptacles into the wringer washer. The cans were empty now. Three of them gave us a supply of 150 gallons, which usually lasted five or six days. Bad timing that morning—I would have to go down and start the pump that pumps from the well up into the back porch and the cans. It took about twenty minutes to fill them and the washer.

"Mommy, I want to help!" Naphtali insisted.

"Great!" I exclaimed, more enthusiastically than I felt. I wanted her to get this very important message—helping makes other people happy! Thankfully, they both appeared to be over the virus.

I settled in for a laundry day, not daunted by the work ahead. It was only three years since we had left Bear Island, and my memories of laundry days there were so sharp and detailed, I was still enjoying my deliverance. The last five years, our piles had grown yet higher as we had hired more crew. By the time I had left, we were washing for fifteen. In lighter moments, we had laughed at what we were doing, when passing the dirty underwear or the sweaty undershirts of men we didn't want to know this way. We preferred to know them on the outside only, while mending net, or at the meal table, and we had wondered, with a smirk, if they had ever blushed when they had gotten their underwear back, knowing where it had been. But lighter moments had been hard to find those days. It seemed like pure luxury, no matter what happened, to wash for my own family only.

As I started down to the well, I was scouring my mental recipe file for a quick fix for lunch. It was too late for a roast—maybe a canned ham and mashed potatoes, and I thought I had one head of lettuce left for a salad; I would make some quick corn pone, a fruit salad—okay, lunch was under control. I would work on it between loads. But first, water.

The little pump at the well was a hand crank, like everything else, it seemed. I remembered the gas wringer washer with a pull cord at Bear Island. The tractor, ATV, and generator at least started with buttons or knobs, but they had their own tricks to play. For my ten years at Bear Island, the generator started with the placement of a handle over the gear shaft, then a slow circular crank, working up to a furious spinning using all my weight. As the spin reached its best speed, one hand was thrown over to turn the compression lever, while the other, with a single jerk, had to pull the crank off the whirling shaft. When the men were out fishing, Bev and Wanda elected me, with my fishing biceps, the generator starter. At times I was surprised to find myself in relationship with so many machines. I felt no kinship with them and yet was forced into intimate knowledge of their workings, and somehow had to breathe the spark of life into each one.

The pump was not responding today. I fiddled with the choke, throttle, pulled the cord again and again—and suddenly it began a slow chug. Yes! It revved promisingly. I choked it down to a purr, then, satisfied it could be left for a moment, I raced back up the hill, Noah bouncing in the backpack, fussing, to check the end of the hose—was the water flowing? Sometimes it didn't, and fearful of burning out the pump, I watched this carefully. No—no water. I ran all the way down the hill full tilt, jumping over the hillocks near the well, and shut the pump down, removed the plywood cover, readjusted the intake hose, tried again.

The pump had broken down before; it had burnt out, caught on fire, leaving us to buckets now and then, but that now and then hadn't included children. My life had come this far—I had carried water for eleven years, but I couldn't go back to that now. I would not give up. An hour later and four more trips sprinting from porch to well, the water was flowing again. Now I went back down the hill and turned on the generator—knobs to turn, switches to throw, and it lurched to noisy life. The last piece now—was the washer working? No, the wringer was jammed. I wrestled with the rubber rollers, banging and adjusting the handle until they finally squeezed into place. Noah began to snuffle—he was hungry. As I pulled him out, I saw the clothes heaped in dirty pyramids on the linoleum exactly where I had sorted them two and a half hours ago. I had just managed to gain back the morning's losses. Relieved at least at that, I settled into the feeding, holding him tenderly against me, letting the chair hold me.

THREE HOURS LATER I was apathetically hanging out the eighth and last load. There were still about four more left, but the water was too dirty to continue and I was too tired. I would do the rest tomorrow. Lunch was only half done, which meant everyone's schedule would be off.

A skiff hummed into sight, coming from Paquette's set. I thought it was Wallace and his crewman. I could tell by the yellow and orange pattern of the driver—Wallace was the only one who wore a working survival suit. They must have had the nets out because the skiff was riding high. I leaned out over the clothesline—the yards of multicolored towels, baby blankets, my daughter's Little Mermaid underwear—toward the fence of beach and open ocean beyond. *Remember that? Remember just being out on the water when the only thing you had to worry about was getting fish from the net—all you had to take care of was yourself? I missed it—the water under the boat, movement, to feel speed combing through my hair. To pursue a single task, to think about one thing only and then just to do it, to follow orders, or just tell the crewman what to do—simple.*

MY LIFE NOW was onshore. I used to dream of this, filling our new house with children, giving myself to something that would last and that really mattered, to make a life here beyond fishing. Indeed, all this is happening. But where was the joy? I had it—sometimes—but I felt inadequate, impatient much of the time. Perhaps I was better at picking fish than I was at mothering. How had my mother done this with six children? She said they were the best years of her life. Back in Kodiak, when I shopped

with the two children, old women and even women my own age stopped me in Safeway and told me, with a nostalgic light on their faces, that "these are the happiest years of your life." What happened to these women that they enthroned these hard years so? Would I do the same? I doubted it, and finally concluded they hadn't raised their children on small, rainy, roadless islands.

What had I done in moving from Bear Island to Harvester? I was cut off from my best friends, Beverly and Beth, whose company eased so much loneliness in summers past. I had exiled myself from the help and support of family, first, my own family in New Hampshire, and now my extended family here. Great. Go ahead and feel sorry for yourself—guess whose idea it was? I grimaced. And guess whose idea it was to step out of fishing, to cut myself off from that brotherhood as well? They don't even know I am missing—no—no—stop. The maze takes about thirty seconds to run—I was tired of the route. St. Paul, remember St. Paul. "I have learned that whatever state I am in, therewith to be content." This was my assignment.

THERE ARE COMPENSATIONS for being here, I told myself. While I lost female companionship, I was no longer part of the crew's lives. That was a loss, too, but a necessary loss. Every summer at Bear Island, I was drawn into these young men's lives. We worked beside each other in the skiff, stood days mending nets together. I knew their life stories; I became their sister. Some came and grew up here under the duress of the salmon season, came as boys and left as men. A few were nearly crushed.

Ricky, one of our first crewmen, stepped off the bush plane onto the gravel strip in Larsen Bay in black suit and tie. I cringed when I saw him for the first time—he looked so young, so very thin. How old was he? I asked. Seventeen. He was a champion high school runner. Yes, but how strong was he? We were new at hiring, and even then would not have hired a teenager, but he was the son of a good friend and needed to earn money for college. Did he know what was before him?

Ricky worked mostly with Duncan. When I saw his pale face and eyes growing hollow, I joined them in the skiff to lighten the load. When we delivered each skiff load of salmon to the tender, sometimes just a few hours between deliveries, and Duncan climbed over the rails and into the galley to sign the delivery ticket, in those five minutes when we were supposed to be cleaning the skiff, Ricky would fall asleep on the stern seat.

One day we were picking down on Seven-Mile Beach. The water was typically querulous, the usual swell and lash to shore, meaning we held the net with a little firmer grip, but not much more. We were on the line. Duncan was in the stern, since he was running the kicker; Ricky was in the middle; I was in the bow, the power spot responsible for pulling the skiff along the line. We had fish in these nets. Duncan was glad and still had energy from somewhere, but Ricky and I didn't really care. We were at the point of the season when salmon no longer meant money and paying bills but more work and less sleep. We knew we had three more nets to do after this. Duncan was not happy with our visible fatigue and nipped at us to keep us going.

"Okay, let's get moving here," Duncan prodded, as he waited for Ricky to finish with a tangled pink salmon.

Rick gave a last twist and the fish fell free. He unhooked the net, then pulled back in a lean with me as we hand-over-hand moved a skiff length to the next section of net. We were at the buoy now that we called the sway keg, which kept the net from billowing out as the tide ripped through.

"Let her down. I'll shoot us around," Duncan called. We

dropped the net back into the water, carefully making sure the corks were floating. The wave action, though, slipped a cork under the net as Duncan backed away.

"C'mon, guys! Watch your corks!" he complained, disgusted, shifting back to the net.

Ricky and I looked at each other, not registering our feelings. We knew the routine. Ricky leaned over, I crouched beside him. He lifted the net and I dunked the cork through.

As we finished the maneuver, the kicker suddenly popped, then made a grinding sound and died.

"Grab the net! Grab the net quick!" Duncan shouted as we began to drift. The two of us, still in the bow, threw ourselves over the railing, arms out our full length, but the net had already slipped out of reach. We swiped at the water anyway, demonstrating our full effort, but too late.

Duncan pounded his fists on the kicker, then ripped off the hood. "Get me the toolbox!" We both dove for the box under the bow. I took it back and placed it warily on the seat beside Duncan. "Watch the waves," Duncan warned. "We'll smash on the beach in five minutes if I don't get this going."

We were indeed drifting close to shore now. The waves were breaking just thirty feet ahead of us. If we went through the surf, that could mean broken bones and a splintered skiff. It had happened numerous times to the couple who had fished down here before us, but I didn't think the surf was that bad that day. Strangely, I was not worried about being dashed to pieces; I just didn't want to be yelled at anymore.

In less than a minute, as Rick and I watched for capsizing waves, Duncan announced, "The lower unit's out. Nothing I can do. Shoot!" He yelled, pounding the kicker again. The two of us stood, dumb. He so controlled the skiff that we felt utterly powerless and offered no help.

"Okay, let's get the oars out and start rowing," he directed suddenly.

"Uh, this skiff doesn't have oar locks, remember?" I offered carefully. "We were going to get another pair . . ."

Duncan raised his fists to his head in frustration.

"The skiff is small—we can still keep it out of the breakers with the oars," I attempted.

"No, we can't," he dismissed me angrily. "Okay, here's the situation," Duncan said finally, his face burning. We were just fifteen feet away from the surf now. He now talked fast and loud, to be heard over the breaking water. "We've got to get down to the next net to tie on. That's the only way we'll keep out of the surf and save ourselves and the skiff. We can wait for help there. The three-wheeler is parked just by that rock there. I've got an extra line. I'll jump out into the waves as the skiff gets close. Then you and Rick use the oars and push yourselves back out. I'll tie the line onto the three-wheeler and it can pull the skiff along down to the next net. Okay? Got it?"

What kind of plan was this? I wondered. How amazing that we were at the one place on the beach where the three-wheeler was parked. I didn't have any time to consider the soundness of this plan, though it struck me as overly dramatic. I had no other plan to offer.

Duncan was poised now on the stern, ready to leap. We were just feet away from the breakers, the water was going white all around us. There was familiarity in this—we had done this before, deer hunting down here, but not without a kicker.

"Get the oars! Get the oars! As soon as I jump, push back out!" he yelled behind him. Then he launched himself off the stern into the water.

We plunged each oar into the surf, leaning back for the landing and the push. This was it. I swallowed hard. If we didn't get the skiff out of the curlers, we would go through them. I instantly remembered Kay's accounts of the skiff flipping over on top of them in this very place. Duncan had made it to the beach now, wet to his waist, the line tied to our skiff slung over his shoulder. He was screaming and waving his arms at us. "Get out! Get out of there!" We were pushing with pure adrenaline, our fatigue forgotten the instant the kicker died.

The bow, thankfully, was turned toward the water, and with a dozen more desperate lunges we were clear, then a few more and we were three skiff lengths from the curls. Ricky turned, looked at me with wide eyes, dropped his oar and hunched over, panting. I hung on to the oar, turned to look at Duncan now. He had the ATV at the water's edge. I could see the line tied to the back bar. He was motioning furiously at us. "Get ready!" he hollered sharply. He climbed on, I could hear him revving the engine, and then he started, the three-wheeler motoring free, the line still slack. I didn't know what would happen, but I had been through enough crises here to know it wouldn't be good and it would be my fault. Ricky looked at me, scared, which meant now I couldn't be. "It's okay, Rick, we can do it," I reassured, my voice falsely confident.

Suddenly the line went taut, the skiff jerked; the bike balked but kept going. The bow swung around and we were moving now, but not parallel to shore; we were being pulled back into the surf.

"Rick, get the oar!" I called, leaping to the skiff sides again, trying to pole us away.

Duncan saw what was happening, slowed, then half-stood from his seat, "Use the oars! Use the oars to keep off the rocks!" Then, "We've got to keep going! Stay off the rocks!"

And he kept moving, maintaining the momentum, glancing at us and gesturing wildly with his one free arm as he went.

Every second pulled us back to the breaking water and the rounded rocks I could see now just under the foam. I stomped the oar in and pushed back with all I had, Rick beside me. We were grunting with our effort and fear, the ocean thundering in our ears, the roar of the three-wheeler, and Duncan's yelling above it all: "Watch out! Get out of there! Push harder!"

Rick jabbed my cheek with the oar handle; I tripped. The skiff hit a rock then and Rick fell too. In those three seconds, we were about to be swept into the breakers. Broken bones? Drowning? What would be next? Duncan was hollering so loud now I thought he would have a heart attack, but even then this didn't stop. Nothing would stop this nightmare. We cleared the skiff from the rock, then jolted on another. A breaker caught the stern and threw us both to the floor again.

"Rick, this is it," I hissed, between clenched teeth. "We gotta get out of here. Let's do it! We're almost to the other net!"

But it was another torturous howling minute before we reached the net. At some point it was quiet. The three-wheeler stopped, a skiff came down to check on us and we were towed back to Bear Island. The skiff was banged up, and it was our fault. We had made it back in one piece, and I knew Duncan had made it happen, but this did not cheer me.

IT WAS 3:00 P.M. when we limped up to our apartment. I dumped some canned chili on the stove, opened some corn, and put out some bread. Rick, Duncan, and I sat around the table, our faces tense and locked, avoiding one another's eyes. No one talked. When Duncan finished and darted out the door, Ricky and I froze for a moment, then went limp, still silent. I had to speak. "Rick, you need to eat. You're losing too much weight."

He turned to me, empty. "I'm not hungry," he mumbled. His eyes filled with tears and he looked at me, shaking his head. I pressed my hands against my mouth to somehow stop what I knew was coming, but I couldn't. He dropped his head to both arms on the table and began to sob in deep shudders. I was weeping, too, head up so I didn't lose it all. I was crying for Ricky. Later, when I was alone, I cried for me.

RICKY LEFT at the end of the season twenty pounds thinner. He walked off the island and into the skiff wearing his torn raingear, a scrappy mustache, with a couple of old buoys he had scrounged off a beach slouched off his shoulders for souvenirs.

Though he survived the season, I could not keep carrying that weight. As long as I was crew, and Duncan was boss, I gained blood brothers in the skiff, but lost my husband. Were there other women out there who felt this way? I couldn't know. I began to suspect that the old story of husbands in boats and wives ashore was not wholly some sexist division of labor. It could, strangely, protect and preserve a marriage. Living here at Harvester, and staying ashore, would restore my allegiances to their rightful place. Had it? Yes, I was sure of it.

21

Nursing Babies,
Killing Fish

MY RESOLUTION TO STAY ASHORE did not extend to every skiff—only skiffs with fish in them. I would still travel about on the water when necessary. Just as in our winter days, "necessary" meant a compelling need to reenter the rest of the world—which meant any place other than our own tiny universe on Harvester Island.

One morning, mid-July 1990, I awoke from a week of rain to a buttery sun. I knew we must go out today. Naphtali felt it, too.

"Can we go to Bear Island today?" she pleaded in her just-turned-two voice. She sounded like one of the Munchkins in *The Wizard of Oz*. "I wanna go see Gramma and Grampa."

The ocean lay before us, warm playground. It was not calm—there was a swell from this week's blow still, but the water was glittering blue. Duncan was out on the nets and would be gone another three or four hours. I wanted to go as badly as she did.

Bev and I, both starved for each other's company, had made tentative, weather-dependent plans the night before.

"Aunt Beverly is coming down to visit this morning. I'll tell you what, after her visit, we'll take her back to Bear Island in our own skiff—if the weather stays good!—and we'll all visit Grandma and Grandpa, okay?"

"Yaaaay!" Naphtali leapt up from the table. Noah, seven months, sitting in his highchair, banged his fist into his Cheerios and echoed the chant. I was cheered.

After the morning visit, the kids' afternoon nap, and our two uninterrupted hours of talk, Bev and I were filled, and set to the work of returning. It took an hour to get ready: first Noah's feeding, then the rummage for boots, coats, life jackets, disputes over ownership; then potty breaks, the search for the aluminum tub that is Noah's waterborne car seat. I crammed him, resistant, into a life jacket that was a bit too small. Then we gathered our own gear and dressed; untied the running line straps, pulled in the skiff, loaded up, pulled out, saw if the 40-horse outboard would start—and we were off.

The water was sedate at Harvester and through the channel. We burned through like a car on a racetrack just for the joy of it. I loved running skiffs. For these moments, I was not a passenger watching the world pass by; I was the one moving the world. Naphtali pulled off her hat and let her hair whip, Noah was all mouth and teeth; even Bev, who had been here just a few weeks, felt the elixir of speed and grinned.

As soon as we hit the open water between Bear Island and Harvester, where the Shelikof blusters in unrestrained, the swells rose suddenly—the remains of that week's blow. The bow, where Bev and Noah were sitting, was now bounding. Spray rained with every landing. I throttled down. "Bev! Bring Noah back here!" She lifted him from the tub and carried him one-

armed, her face tense as she edged her way back, the other hand gripping the skiff side. "Naphtali! Hold on! Hold the rails!" She was not concerned and began to protest. "Just do what I say! Hold on or I'll spank you!" I shouted angrily, tired of decisional democracy and not caring how I sounded. I watched the water anxiously, keeping the bow into the waves, assessing. If I had been out fishing I would have thought nothing of this, just a minor annoyance, but with the children, every action and decision became freighted with an incalculable weight. Should I turn back?

I decided to keep going, since we were exactly halfway, and we were not actually in any danger, I told myself in the voice of logic. My mother's voice was not comforted, though, and whispered heavy doubt.

We were midway between the two islands, with less than a mile to go, when the kicker started choking. Just as I turned to investigate, it died. Almost instantly, we were rolling in the waves. I ran through a quick check while my stomach started cramping—gas hose attached, enough gas in the tank, though a bit low. I detached the hose—hose and filter were working—what else? My chest tightened, we were not beam to the waves yet, but we would be momentarily. I was quite sure the swells were not big enough to break over us and swamp the skiff, but I didn't want to find out. The sudden lull was disquieting. You didn't have to run skiffs very long out here to recognize silence and the sound of suspirating waters not as soothing and restorative, but as ominous, threatening.

I tried to start it up again—it took then died in two seconds. The same again. Water in the gas, I thought.

"Bev, is there gas in that tank under your feet?" I said, trying to sound in control.

"Yeah, about half a tank," Bev answered nervously, with the same edge and attempt to suppress the edge in her voice.

SURVIVING THE ISLAND OF GRACE

"Can you put it up here on the seat?"

I began the operation of switching tanks while the skiff bobbed and dipped in the waves, nearly sideways now, each roller rocking the skiff, nearly dipping the rails in the water each time. Bev had a firm hold on Noah's life jacket.

What if this tank was no better—which was very likely, since the tanks were all filled and mixed at the same time. I went through the routine, praying now under my breath. I would do whatever it took to keep my children safe, but I knew, too, how terrifyingly fast you could come to the end of your own re-sources. Someone on the Bear Island nets might see us, if we were lucky, or I could row us over to the lagoon if I could keep control in the swells. I was on my third crank when I heard a motor—a skiff coming! It bounced slowly toward us and then pulled alongside—Wallace!

He approached, a wry smile on his face as he took us in: a toddler, a baby, and Bev and me. High-powered team here, I could hear him thinking.

"Looks like you got a problem," he said, typically laconic.

I was suffused with gratitude for his appearance. "Won't start! Water in the gas, I'm guessing."

We tied our skiffs together while he jumped in to try his hand. Watch it start right up, I thought. But it didn't, to my relief. Wallace nodded; I clove-hitched my bowline to his rail and he towed us the rest of the way to Bear Island.

As we traveled, I thought of Joe Darling, a young Alutiiq man who had lived in Wallace and Beth's place at Old Uyak before them. He had gone off one day in the skiff and never come back. They never found his body, just the skiff. He left a wife and two little sons about the ages of my children now.

I never answered aloud a question I asked myself that day seven years ago when first pregnant with Naphtali, the day after

Duncan's boat went down: "How will I travel with a baby?" I expected a dramatic answer, a slash across the time line of my life, Before Children/After Children. Before Children I did this, but After Children I did that. I heard a young mother once say that since having a baby her driving style had changed—she was much more cautious. I heard another say she gave up rock climbing. Was I supposed to give up trips in the skiff with the kids— was this the moral from that incident? No, it wasn't possible. I refused to be condemned to total dependence upon Duncan or anyone else simply to step foot off our beach. Years before, my second or third summer, another woman, Cora Reft, and I took a skiff six miles across the bay to go berry picking. The men were very unsure of this—women going alone. The weather came up, making our return slow and sloppy, waves breaking on our sides. We returned late, wet, but with full berry buckets. The men were angry with us. We were glad we went.

NEAR THE END of the month, I lay feeding Noah on the couch. I had just finished six loads of laundry, but since it was take-up, I stopped early to make lunch. Duncan, who usually wrestled and teased with the kids after lunch, was nearly silent through the meal. They had been fishing for almost twenty days without a break. The nets were a mess, and the whole mess came out in a few hours. It was blowing SW 25, gusting higher, the kind of wind that would bring blue sky, but it always carried a price tag. This wasn't terrible weather, but it would make everything harder on everyone. They were already so tired. *I should go out to help*, I thought guiltily. No, I should stay. The kids need me here. This was the higher good, I was certain.

After a thirty-minute nap, Duncan left, clomping down the graveled hill to the beach and skiff. I was on the couch again, nursing Noah, my eyes closed. Suddenly Duncan appeared in full raingear, his face serious but soft: "Leslie, if you can come out for take-up, we can really use your help." My heart fluttered—I was needed in the skiff. My arms suddenly felt Noah's full weight, his body stretched against mine. I cradled his head protectively while my thoughts raced. *Yes, let me get out of here, this box. Let me get out and be that other person, but who is she? I think I know her—raingear, hat pulled low over her face. She zooms the skiff and picks fish as fast as the brothers. But I'm not sure if she's still there.* I felt like a pool of milk, my whole body given to this baby. As with Naphtali, I had learned to melt the hard lines of my own life and will and molded completely to his needs. I was daily aware how literal this giving of life was, this almost hourly transfer of my own best energy and strength from my body to his. It required a passivity so thorough and so contrary to my nature, it threatened to consume me. I must go, then. I cannot lose that other woman.

But I was not sure I wanted to go with Duncan. The last take-up with him had been a replay of earlier days that shouldn't have happened, not after twelve years.

Duncan remembered, too. He saw my hesitancy, then. "You can stay with us—I'm doing the Harvester nets—but I need someone to get ahead of us and pick them. You can take the extra skiff and one of the crewmen. We're going to be in trouble quick unless someone stays on them." I smiled at him quickly, proud of his largesse and consideration. He knew I would choose picking nets over taking them up any day.

As I geared up in the entryway, I was rattling a list of instructions to Sarah, my high school help for this month. I was so thankful to have her. I spent my spare time scheming how to keep her out here longer than the month she had agreed to. "Sarah, feed Noah formula when he gets hungry or fussy, just fix grilled cheese sandwiches and open some soup for supper for when we get in, ah, Naphtali can watch a movie tonight, but she needs to be in bed by ten, no later, be sure and read bedtime stories, try to keep Noah up until I come back—don't let him take a nap past seven or he won't sleep at all tonight, I'll be back sometime between nine and eleven, okay?" and then I was down the path, in the skiff, on the water.

Duncan dropped me off in the empty skiff; John, a college student from Oregon, jumped in with me. He leaned over the bow to pull up to the buoy to untie. I started the 60-horse kicker. This one was a hard starter. It took more than a dozen full-body pulls, but it rumbled to life in a cloud of exhaust and, with a twist of my wrist, we were on our way. As I watched the other skiff with Duncan, Corky, and Glenn hoist and fall in the six-foot waves in front of us, a backhand wave caught me on the chin and neck and washed it away, all of it—children, house, island, diapers, dirty dishes, laundry. I was not a mother, not a woman; I could not feel the nursing pads I had stuffed into my bra in case I leaked: I was one of the people responsible to get eighteen nets up in the next five hours. I felt gloriously free.

OUR ADVERSARIES that night were not just the nets and the winded waters, but the kelp and the fish. Each net hung heavy with enough kelp and fish to necessitate picking the length of each net before pulling them up. We worked as fast as we could, knowing the clock was ticking our movements down to an immovable deadline. We were responsible for at least five nets, two of them full-length nets, at 150 fathoms each. I calculated silently: if all the nets were as dirty as Pacquette's, the first one, it would take forty-five minutes to pick and clean each net. Then, we would need to help pull in whatever nets were left. It would be tight. John and I talked only rarely, just enough to coordinate: "Let's pull across to the other side." "See anything down there?"

"I think you'd better lift the kicker—the net's floating under us."
"Pull out that bull kelp there." Even a single net could sap all
our energy. Each of us out on the water had to figure how to
pace and play out our strength for all the nets we were assigned.
Somehow we each found our own means of making our way
through the work. I wished now that someone else were running
the skiff. I was not sure I could do this that day. My strength
had gone to another.

With a little more than one hundred fish, we were now done
with the first net. As we headed to the next net, the Salmonberry,
I began to get my water legs back. I fell twice in the skiff while
picking, trying to synchronize my labor with keeping upright. I
remembered, to relax and let my body take over, to give itself
up to the flush of liquid beneath the skiff; my whole body, from
the balls of my feet to the clinch of every muscle group, all its
knowledge fitted to this—to keep standing on that single layer
of aluminum skin between me and the hard, gray water when
that water would throw me down. While all my flesh worked at
this, then the rest of the work began.

At the next net, and throughout the evening, there were a
few moments of calm like parentheses inserted into the night's
story as John and I worked. I watched the fish as they came over
the railing. Even now, in my thirteenth season, I saw them much
as I had my first year here. Just as then, I felt thoroughly dis-
connected from these creatures. I pulled them from the nets, often already dead, sometimes still alive. I did not feel their deaths,
though I often studied them, their gaping mouths, their gills
straining in the strangulation of air. They made gurgling sounds,
and often flayed about in a final thrash toward the life of water.
All of this I recognized either as simple muscle reflexes, or as
desperate efforts to live, and yet I was not moved to pity. It only
struck me how entirely dissimilar we were: they so cold, cauled

in gurry, limbless, eyes unblinking, mute, and most of all, I knew they were on their way to die, nearly all of them, the millions that swarmed Alaska's waters, headed kamikaze for the stream-bed and spawn-out and a horrible, leprous, rotting kind of death. And yet now, still so beautiful, I marveled, so obviously and purposefully created, so deliberately fashioned with skin like a suit of mail, the fit on fit of scale to scale. I stood in them, these dying and bloodied creatures, loving the artistry of their bodies, feeling happy to have caught them, that their lives ended here in my boat. An hour ago I had been nursing my infant son; now I was killing fish and liking it.

We were almost done with the set we call the Eagle. The tide was turning, and the net silently swung under the skiff, where the prop was running. I was working on the last fish before I moved forward—it was a big silver, about ten pounds, and he was in a bag of mesh. The silvers are the prettiest of all the sal-mon, I thought. But they weren't worth much. The cannery was paying only 85 cents a pound that year, down from two years before. All the prices were down, though, since the oil spill. Reds were formerly $2.80 a pound; the year previous they had been $1.80, this year $1.50. Pinks were down from 85 cents a pound, now to 45. And there was no end in sight to the slide. Fueling it was more bad news—fish farms. Chile, Norway, Russia, and Scotland were all starting to raise salmon in pens, fast-feeding them growth hormones, animal protein pellets of uncertain ori-gin, and because of the density of fish, they were fed antibiotics as well, to stave off the diseases that flourished in such an en-vironment. Seafood prognosticators said this unnatural mass-produced salmon would flood the world market; our own natural, wild salmon would soon fill nothing but a niche market. We wouldn't be able to give them away, some said. Duncan told me of the days they sold their fish for a quarter apiece. Surely it couldn't happen now, not in the 1990s. We were discouraged, but there was nothing we could do but go out and pick fish.

I spun the silver around counterclockwise and his body was free. As I leaned down to pull him out, a giant wave picked us up and sucked the net under the prop. The kicker suddenly gurgled and stopped with a choking sound.

"Shoot!" I yelled, knowing instantly what had happened.

"You in the net?" John asked, his voice neutral.

"Yeah. Wouldn't you know!" Everyone gets in the net sooner or later, sometimes as often as every few days. But that was no consolation now. I leaned over the kicker and, using all my weight, pulled it back and locked it into position. It was a bad one—the webbing was wound around the prop in a huge knot. "Oh, man! What time is it, John?"

'It's almost eight."

"Just an hour to go." We hadn't even picked the last net. I hung out over the stern and began to pull the net from the prop, first this way then that with hard, short jerks as the waves picked me up and threatened to dunk me headfirst. "Do you see Duncan anywhere?"

"No, I can't see him! You need any help there?"

"Yeah. Come back and give me some slack."

We were both hanging off the stern now, pushing, pulling the web free one mesh at a time. Every minute marked its passing with the sound of water—we knew we would be late. Then we heard a skiff. Behind us, it was Duncan in an empty skiff. They must have already taken up the other three nets and then changed skiffs.

"Great time to get in the net, Leslie!" He was shaking his head, but he was smiling slightly. Then, "Just cut the meshes and get out of there! We're going to run out of time!" His face was serious, but he was not angry.

He turned to the others in his skiff, and to John and me in mine. "Gentlemen, it's eight twenty-five." All eyes are upon him. "We've got thirty-five minutes to take up the last two nets. Leslie!" He turned to me again. "Did you pick the seventh?" He was talking in that machine gun way that didn't waste a second.

"No. We were going there next."

"Last I saw there was lots of fish in it. John! You jump in here with us. We may have to pull these nets up fish and all. Leslie! You go over to the seventh, straight to the hook, and start picking. Just keep going until we pull it up behind you!"

I waved my arm in acknowledgment. He whirled the skiff around to start taking up at the shoreline. I had already cut the meshes free from the prop; I unhooked the net, pointed the bow around the corner, and was gone in a flood of wake and wave.

The next net wasn't far, just a three-minute run, hanging off the end of Harvester. Though I had headed off alone, Duncan's skiff already out of sight, I felt tightly connected to him, and to the others as well, all of us knotted together, strands pulled into a single net. With the spray of my wake framing my eyes, I thought about this, how perfectly Duncan and I had worked together at times, not only our bodies synchronized—pulling the same line, stacking the same net, building the same house—but in almost every endeavor, both of us uniting our wills to focus on a single goal, and accomplishing it. I knew, too, how many times our wills had crossed, how we had arrived at our destinations shambling, limping, bearing the wounds of our collisions. I wanted to be done with that. I wanted to fix this moment and this feeling to last the rest of our lives.

THE HOOK, the farthest end of the net, came into view. I throttled down, sinking slowly into my own momentum, and surprised myself by reaching down and nabbing the net out of the water first try. I saw blotches of silver beneath me—I was guessing 150 maybe, just in the hook, which usually meant at least as many in the rest of the net. Without anyone to help lift, the net was as heavy as the ocean itself. But I had only minutes to go. I forgot how tired I was, that I had just picked four other nets, and went straight into overdrive, a place I hadn't been for awhile. I was doing what Bill Woods used to do that had garnered so much admiration, what the brothers occasionally did in dire situations—picking fish alone. I felt strong and capable. Most of the fish were pinks, which meant I could pick one every few seconds. My hands were flying now, the fish were flying, and there were no sounds in this world except the ocean against my boat, arctic terns crying, the fish plashing; there were no people, only the towering snow-clouded mountains of the horizon, and closer, little Bear Island rising up gracefully to cliff. I was singing—pieces of my favorite hymns and choruses, my voice thrown down to the fish in my hands as I worked, then into the air as I threw the fish behind me. It was so good to be alone there. It was so good that I was not alone—there were five other skiffs out there somewhere with people who were moving and bending between skiff and ocean as I was, whose muscles were contracting and releasing in exactly the same motions as mine, each of us invisible to the other, but all of us shadowing some unseen, ancient rite. I was picking these fish for all of the others. I was picking them for my children. I was picking them for God—they were from Him. I thought of Jacob, old and full of years, who "leaned on his staff and worshipped." Yes, worship. I looked around my skiff—this was worship, all of it. In a few seconds of recognition, I marveled at my life, that out of the few things I thought I could do and be, that I was *this* instead.

BY THE TIME Duncan came around the corner, I had nearly finished the hook. I waved and kept picking, singing softer now, knowing I had ten to fifteen more minutes to work until he was behind me. Every fish I got made it easier for them. I had picked a couple of hundred, I guessed, looking at the bulk of the bodies around me. I heard Duncan calling out instructions as he worked: "Hold the line while I untie the sway!" "Okay gentlemen, off we go!" "Corky, catch up with me—pull more leads!" He sounded better. He knew we would make it. He was so good at this.

They were racing now but the net was so heavy with fish that it came in slowly. They were at the hook. I untied and drifted out of the way. Those last twenty fathoms the net—empty— nearly jumped into the skiff. One final pull and the lead ring clunked over the side—the official end of the net. Corky dropped wearily to the seat, John plunked down on the leads.

Duncan pulled out his watch from his pocket. "It's eight fifty-nine," he announced. They grinned weakly at each other. Duncan looked over at me and smiled—comrades. We had done it again.

Suddenly my breasts tingled and burned—Noah. I had been out six hours; that meant I had missed two feedings. I felt as though I would burst. Under my Grundens and life jacket, my shirt was already soaking. Casually, I crossed my raingeared arms and fish-blooded gloves over my chest, pressing, remembering with relief that the men could not see and did not know. I knew, though: I was a woman and a mother again.

SOON AFTER, I leapt from the bow of the skiff onto Harvester's beach, climbing the long hill to the house. The fatigue of my night's work suddenly pressed upon me, and the hill became a mountain. I remembered the kids now for the first time tonight. We had been talking about having more children, but I couldn't think of that then. I was just hoping that Noah was starving-hungry. And then, all the other concerns from the house descended upon me: Had Sarah kept him up so I could sleep tonight? Are the clothes dry on the line so we would have something to wear tomorrow? When would Duncan get back? I saw the light on in the nursery. What was Naphtali doing up? Sarah met me at the door holding a red-faced Noah who was crying hungrily. Naphtali stood in the doorway crying, "Mommy! Mommy!" Noah reached out his baby arms for my neck; Naphtali cinched her arms around my legs. They were pressing their wet faces and all their hungers against me with such force, I could not move.

22

Between Land
and Water

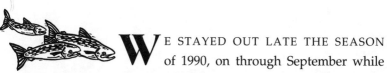 W E STAYED OUT LATE THE SEASON
of 1990, on through September while
we fall fished for the late run of silver salmon. Half the bay
emptied out by then: boats returned to the harbor in Kodiak;
families returned to school and to jobs. Leaving the island was
easier now that we were living in Kodiak. That winter, our second in Kodiak, we rented a little ranch house deep in the spruce
trees down on a lake named Dark Lake, appropriately named
because the sun never found it, no matter the weather. Duncan
returned to the law office and his work on the oil spill; I was
hired at Kodiak College and was teaching English part-time,
writing on the side. I felt incredibly privileged, for those few
hours a week, to stand in the classroom and muck about in et-
ymologies, composition, metaphor, poetry.

I never wanted to live in the town of Kodiak, other than the

winter we stayed to study and substitute teach. Alaska, yes, but I had resisted a permanent move to Kodiak these thirteen years of marriage, glad for travel, graduate school, anything that broadened the world for us. I knew even before we were married that Duncan hoped to return and settle down there. But I was afraid. I was not afraid of slumming around the world, but this represented everything I feared: living in a small town, like the ones I grew up in; knowing everyone, losing privacy and anonymity. I remembered back to one town in particular, the parties at neighbors' houses, how the respected men of the community would come out onto the lawn, drunk, screaming our names and yelling obscenities at us because we wouldn't let them snowmobile on our land. How the kids at school taunted us, calling us Scrooges and other epithets because we didn't give to UNICEF when a group came to the door. Maybe Kodiak would be the same. I feared, more, the boundaries of a life lived within the shores of two islands. I had agreed to a lifetime of summers on the second island—what now about the first? Could I live a life this confined, this small?

WE HAD GOTTEN the call from the law firm in Kodiak out here, at the end of the oil spill summer. After the three beeps signaling the phone had hung up, we sat quietly in the front room for a moment, each with our own thoughts, mine tightly racing around a minuscule track. Then Duncan did something that completely surprised me.

"Leslie," he began, his face solemn as he looked directly at me. "I know how you feel about moving to Kodiak. I'm not going to take this job. I won't take it if you don't want to move to Kodiak."

I looked at him, eyes wide. I knew how much he esteemed this law firm. I knew how he felt about Exxon and how much he wanted to see justice done. I knew that he hated living in Anchorage. On every account, this was a dream job.

"I want to release this decision completely."

"You're putting the whole weight of the decision on me?" I asked, now realizing that this was perhaps not a mercy and kindness after all.

"This is not some manipulative ploy, Leslie. I really mean it. We need to do what's best for all of us, not just me. I don't want the job if you don't want to move to Kodiak."

I sat there blinking, full of wonder that it should happen like this. There were voices, though, that needed to speak. The dark voice of self on my left shoulder said, *Great. Don't take it. Stay in Anchorage. You like teaching at the University.* But the other voice, speaking softly, said *Good. Let it go. You've been carrying this fear for thirteen years. It's too heavy to keep carrying.* Finally I spoke. "I don't know yet, Duncan. I want to be sure about this. Did he give you a deadline?"

"Yeah, he said to let him know in a week."

"Okay, a week." But I knew in my heart already what I would say. I saw the handprints of God all over this. A strange peace settled on me. I looked over at Duncan sitting in the chair by the radio-phone, peaceful, utterly relaxed. He smiled at me, then said softly, across the room, "I love you, Leslie." My heart swelled. He had let go of what he wanted most. I would do the same.

THAT CORNER of my life was settled, for now, but life on the smaller island was not. This whole enterprise of two people joining lives, of creating lives with that union, still felt fragile and threatened each time we landed on the black gravel of our beach. This summer, 1991, was no different.

All summer long I quietly watched the clock and the calendar and the tide books, hoping the purity and singlemindedness of my attention and desire would make it happen: that God would so direct the affairs of weather and hearts and Fish and Game that I could attend my brother Todd's wedding. He was going to have a real wedding—in a church, with bridesmaids, guests, a reception. He and Renee were planning the whole ceremony together. I was proud of Todd, that he had found such a wonderful partner, and that they would truly celebrate, despite our own family history of minimizing holidays and festivities. And even better, he was marrying in Anchorage and planned to live in Alaska. He had stayed on after the oil spill cleanup, landing a job in Anchorage, where he had met Renee.

Of all my siblings, I was closest to Todd growing up. Now he would be just a plane ride away! He called with the news in the spring, just before we left for Harvester Island.

"Leslie, Renee and I have set a date," Todd said, his voice controlled, but excited. He had good reason to be. He was thirty-two, and more than ready for marriage and his own family.

"Oh, please say it isn't in the summer!"

"Sorry, Leslie, but August was the best month for Renee's family. She has a bunch of people coming up from North Carolina. Can't you come?" Todd asked, his voice hopeful.

"I really, really want to come, Todd, but I doubt it. When in August?"

"The eighth. Just come for a few days. Renee and I really want you to be there! I need you to be there," he ended, quietly.

"I want to be there, too, Todd." I sighed. In the last two years, Todd's life had turned around. He had returned to faith, ended a bad relationship, and had come to Alaska to start a new life, as I had. I knew in some small way I was part of that. But this was out of my hands. "I don't think I can," I finally returned, discouraged. "The only chance is if we have a closure and if the weather is good. That's not very likely. But listen, let's pray about it." I heard myself utter this as a cliché, but we both understood the magnitude of the obstacles: they were mountainous. You simply did not leave fishing while the nets were in the water. No one ever did it. If you had a permit in your name, as I did, then you were required by Fish and Game regulations to always be on site while the nets were fishing. If you left for any reason, your nets would have to be pulled up, and everyone would lose income. I would have been happy to sacrifice some of my own finances to go, but it meant everyone sacrificed: our college student crewmen, my brothers- and sisters-in-law, all of whom were as dependent on these monies as we were. In times like these, the common good felt oppressive. But there were two more problems. There was a chance that Fish and Game could announce a closure, which would free me to leave, but then the weather had to be flyable—both here in the bay and in Kodiak, *and* the water between Harvester Island and Larsen Bay, where the runway was, had to be navigable by skiff. There were many windy, clear days when planes could still fly, but the seas were too rough for a skiff. What were the chances of these three events—a closure, clear-enough skies, calm-enough waters—coinciding on the exact three days in August that I needed? I didn't hold out much hope.

ON AUGUST 6, Fish and Game unexpectedly announced a three-day closure. The weather was clear and calm all over Kodiak Island—the mountain had been moved. That afternoon, I joyfully threw my things into a garbage bag, our usual luggage for the skiff, leaped into the boat, and took off.

The caged bird had been released, for three days, singing.

The wedding was everything I had hoped. Still warm from the flash of the photographer's bulbs, the hugs and handshakes,

Todd's and my recountings of childhood events, my new friendship with Renee, I boarded the plane in Anchorage, then the
bush plane in Kodiak slowly, almost meditatively. It was too
soon to leave; I wasn't ready yet to return to the confines of the
island. While flying the four-seater 206 back to Larsen Bay, so-
berly looking down upon the crags of Kodiak's interior mountains, and the stormy waters that often isolated the island's
shores, I realized that in some ways, I was living the life that I
feared the day I saw those New Jersey suburbs, and the day I
marched off Bear Island, gun on my shoulder—a life of dependence and confinement. Twelve years into my Alaska life, the
fears had become more specific, and involved numbers that
seemed to measure the span of my life: two babies who de-
manded everything I possessed; winters on one wilderness island the size of Connecticut with 13,000 people and 94 miles of
road; summers, 80 miles away on a bush plane to a 350-acre
island, population 4, that no one can leave, even for a day, for
as long as the fishing season lasts. And I knew that I would be
there on that island for every summer for the rest of my life. I
had been given a reprieve this summer; for that I was supremely
grateful. Perhaps there would be others; perhaps not.

It seemed I could never fully escape the issues of confinement
and geography. Two weeks later, at the end of the season, we
were all faced with it again—it almost cost a life.

IT WAS ONE of those days when the sun drilled us with heat,
enough heat to send me digging out the one bathing suit top at
the bottom of my jean pile, and the one pair of shorts. It had
rained most of the summer. The thermometer needle had latched
onto 45 and wouldn't let go. This day Naphtali and Noah were
both napping. I was out on the grass feeling like a movie star
because I got to wear sunglasses, stretch out on a towel, and

throw skin to the skies in rare languor. A book and a tall glass of iced tea with actual ice completed the fantasy. These were the days we dreamed of, the narrow string of warm, sunny days we sometimes got in August, sometimes as many as ten in a row— we called these days "summer."

A half mile across the water, my sister-in-law Beth and her two children, Ryan, four, and Rachelle, one and a half, were playing on their beach. Beth, too, craved the sun, lifting her pale skin full face up for as long as she could without losing track of the kids. They were happy today, and it felt so good to be out of her tiny cabin, a cabin that sat recklessly on the bank, speaking its age and status as the only remaining structure from a turn-of-the-century cannery. Rachelle and Ryan were at the water's lip, flirting with its surges. Because of the steep slope of the beach, even a dead-calm day like this still produced some action on the gravelly beach. So much to do, though. A sink full of dirty dishes, a full-course lunch to be fixed.

Beth turned to the two. "Ryan, keep an eye on Rachelle. I'm going to go up to the house for a few minutes. I'll be right back." A quick run up the wooden steps and the thrill of actually getting some work done without Rachelle underfoot. She was at the age when cupboards were prime excavation territory, and sealed food containers were puzzles to be solved, success measured by the height and texture of the mound of oatmeal or sugar on the floor. But now—a moment of peace! Beth began filling the sink, darting every few seconds to the window, checking. They were there, every time, of course. She chided herself for her fears, her overprotectiveness. Of the four Fields women, Beth was the most cautious, the not-so-secret police over seat belts, life preservers, warm mittens, extra blankets. Like me, she had grown up back east, but in the suburbs of Long Island. The ninety-year-old cabin she and Wallace and their children lived in, on a bight of beach known as Old Uyak on the west side of Kodiak Island, was 5,000 miles away from Huntington Station, but Beth had adapted admirably.

The dishes slid through Beth's hands this morning, stacking quickly in the rack. Ryan appeared, standing quietly beside her. "What are you doing here?" Beth asked. "Where's Rachelle?" She stepped to the window—the part of the beach she could see was empty. Throwing down her towel, she ran outside, down the steps to the beach—just gravel, both ways, the eighth of a mile that ended in cliffs on both sides—no Rachelle, no tiny bundle of red coat and Ked sneakers, no curly blond hair. Where? Then, out, under the water, maybe twenty feet from shore—red. Beth exploded into the water—Rachelle face down, nearly touching the bottom, her clothes, her hair with that gentle, flaccid sway of undersea plants. Beth lunged at her, lifting her limp form up to air, then kicking at the water back to the beach. Remembering the first-aid video she had just watched that spring, she turned her upside down, frantic. Foamy liquid drained from Rachelle's mouth. She sputtered and began to breathe, but her chest labored too heavily for each breath. *Was this it*, Beth thought, *what she had always feared? Was this how her life was going to go after all?* Beth screamed as she ran to the house. She drag-lifted Rachelle's nearly still body over to the radio. "Bear Island! Bear Island! Harvester! Harvester! Does anyone read?" She shouted into the mike, with the other hand pushing, urging Rachelle to clear her lungs. No response on either end: the radio quiet; Rachelle, eyes closed, near motionless, her skin gray as she drifted in and out of consciousness. "Mayday! Mayday! Does anyone hear me! Mayday! Mayday! My daughter's been underwater and is unconscious. Bear Island! Anyone!" "Spiridon

Camp! Rocky Beach, Seven-Mile! Does anyone hear me! Please help me! Mayday!" Beth called a hundred times, it seemed. Nothing.

Back at Bear Island, the men were out on the nets behind the island. Because of the weather, they were fishing leisurely and in T-shirts. Wanda and DeWitt were out of the house, sunning and beachcombing on the south side of the island. The skippers and deckhands on the tenders and fishing vessels were out on deck, shirtless, in sunglasses. At every fishcamp it was the same. The world of Uyak Bay, with its usual rules and strict protocol of work first, had shifted to "summer vacation" for the day.

I was reading in the grass beside the warehouse when Christy, the high-school nanny, came charging down the hill. "Leslie! Leslie! You'd better come quick! It's Beth!" She was too breathless to continue. I leaped ahead of her, flew up the hill, and slid to the radio, just beginning to hear sounds, horrible sounds from its speaker—Beth's voice distorted, in sobs, desperate. "Tell me what to do!" I heard her plead. Christy was beside me now.

"What is it?" I shot at her, eyes, hands wanting to reach at something, touch, help this—whatever it was.

"It's Rachelle. Beth found her underwater!" Christy panted, her eyes as wide as mine.

"Pray, Christy! Just pray!" I shouted, then turned to the radio. "Beth, can you hear me?"

I heard the phone dialing then, each push of a number amplified like a siren in my living room. Who was Beth calling? Then—

"Kodiak Island Hospital," a crisp, calm voice announced.

"I need the emergency room!" Beth nearly shouted, still panting.

"ER." A male voice now, equally calm. I took a breath—my

first since entering the house. Someone will know. This icy isolation was finally broken—his voice felt like a hand on my
shoulder.

Then Beth, in short, panicky bursts, relayed what had happened.

"Okay, Beth. . . . Beth, are you there?" he asked as her voice
trailed off. I could hear whooping noises in the background.

"I'm here! What do I do?"

"Is she breathing?"

"Yes, but not very well. She keeps losing consciousness."

"Don't let her fall asleep. Whatever you do, keep her awake.
Do you read?" and then the click and beep of the transmission.

"Yes, I read. Don't let her fall asleep." Then I heard her calling
Rachelle's name loudly before the mike clicked again and was off.

Everything in me screamed to be there with her, but I knew
I had no skiff, no way to get across the half mile of water. The
aluminum skiff that was designated as mine had been moored
out because it was extra work to keep two skiffs on the line
instead of just one. I shook with the chill of helplessness. Then
I thought maybe I could launch the *Holy Roller*, a fiberglass peapod boat the kids played in. It usually took four of us to launch
it, but maybe I could do it. I tore out of the house, ran down the
hill full tilt, scanning the beach as I ran. There it was, beside the
running-line log. I grabbed the rope handles and pulled, fully
expecting it to breeze down the beach into the water. It barely
moved. How could this little boat weigh more than the knowledge that a child you loved could die? And Beth—my dear Beth,
my best friend—how could she survive this loss? I dug my feet
into the gravel and pulled with all my weight and strength,
knowing I could do this, remembering photos of a child lifting
a car to save someone's life—it scraped a few inches. How far
did I have to go? No, it was low tide—two hundred feet to the

water. I tried one more time with the same effect. I could not reach her. I could do nothing here to help. I was furious now, furious that I was so thoroughly stranded, furious at the water that separated our islands, that all of us lived so far away from help. Seething, I ran back up the hill. As I entered the house, I heard another voice, this one from the radio, the radio that had sat silent, dead all these minutes.

"—a plane's on its way, Beth. It should be here soon." It was Jerry Johnson, our neighbor, anchored just a half mile away in his fishing boat, speaking in soothing tones. Beth was crying, her voice as I had never heard it: "She's breathing better now I think—oh! She's vomiting, she's vomiting all over," and then the click of the mike off, the radio dead at her end. "Are you there?" Jerry asking, still calm, knowing that was his role. The ER doctor, too, was still on the phone—"Beth? Can you hear me? Beth, are you there?"

"Yes, I'm here!" she finally answered, her voice thick.

"Take off her wet things. . . ." The doctor's voice was gentle and calmly authoritative as he led Beth through the next steps. Rachelle was beginning to respond, it sounded like. Christy and I alternated between staring at each other as we listened to every word and lifting or bowing our heads to pray.

Within ten minutes, a plane that had just taken off from Larsen Bay heard Jerry's call for an airplane, any airplane. Any airplane would not have helped—it had to be a floatplane. This one was. The pilot, heading to Kodiak, veered to Old Uyak, and suddenly appeared in front of her cabin. The pontoons hit the beach as Beth, cradling Rachelle now in a blanket, spilled down the stairs, still crying, shaking, Rachelle still gray, in and out of consciousness.

As soon as Beth was off the phone, I got on the radio. "Bear

Island! Bear Island! Bear Island! Is anyone there? Come back! Anyone by the radio, come back!" Again. Again. I hated the sun this day. Again. Again. Then the snap of a mike: "Bear Island back to the call," and DeWitt's raspy voice.

"Rachelle's been in the water, she's unconscious, a plane is about to pick her up to take her to Kodiak. Where's Wallace?"

"Oh, no!" Silence, then, "He's out behind Bear Island, I think. We'll try to get him," then off.

DeWitt grabbed his rifle, Wanda an orange rain jacket, and together they climbed the steep hill and rounded the summit until they saw the skiffs on the nets. He shot three times into the sky while Wanda waved the raincoat. Wallace and the others looked up, dropped the net, and sped to shore, knowing there was an emergency but nothing else. From the skiff, and DeWitt's voice shouting across the beach and water, Wallace heard "Rachelle has fallen into the water and Beth can't find her!" All five skiffs about-faced and steamed full bore down the channel to Old Uyak. Just as they appeared, the float plane took off down the channel. Beth, straining at the window, with Rachelle's quiet form in her arms, saw Wallace just feet below her. As they rose above the skiffs, pontoons just clearing the men's heads, she saw Wallace's arms shoot into the air as though trying to catch them. She saw his face, then could read his mouth as he shouted, "What's going on?"

Ten minutes later, another plane rerouted from Uganik Bay landed on Beth and Wallace's beach and picked up Wallace for the thirty-minute flight into Kodiak. For the entire flight, he did not know if his daughter was dead or alive.

Rachelle recovered, with no trace of damage. The two planes that came should not have been there that day and perhaps wouldn't be again.

IT WAS A HARD WAY to end the summer. All of us were shaken. Questions I had asked myself so many times before came at me again. How could I know what the limits were and where to draw that line in the sand that marked out a place of safety and survival for us and our children? What if the skiff had swamped that day in our little outing between the two islands? What if the pump hadn't suddenly started working on the speedboat that trip into town? What if Duncan hadn't gotten into the life raft? I could keep us onshore as much as possible, yes, we would be safer there. But—Rachelle. Even if I anchored all of us to the beach, someone still could fall into the water and drown. Whatever limits I put on us, I realized, would not be enough.

That night, after Naphtali and Noah were asleep in their cribs, Duncan and I lay in bed, exhausted, our arms cinched tightly around each other. We were quiet for a long time. Then I spoke.

"What if we had lost her?"

Duncan sighed, his breath catching. "I don't know."

"What if that had been Naphtali or Noah?"

Silence covered like a blanket. Then, "Leslie, are you ever sorry you married me?"

I thought for a minute, wondering what this question means. "You mean, am I sorry that I'm here at Harvester?"

"I mean just what I said. Do you ever wish you hadn't married me and come to Alaska?

"Of course! Lots of times!" I suddenly laughed, wanting to keep this light. "When we were clapboarding the house in howling rain for three days, when you yell at me in the skiff, that time you knocked me down with an oar—"

"—That was an accident!" Duncan automatically retorted, not sure if I was serious or not.

"I know. Just pushing your buttons." I felt Duncan smile over my shoulder. I became solemn again, knowing I hadn't answered the question. I spoke slowly, knowing that in these moments we were hearing our deepest selves, and that, here, in the place we were making, our words almost became the thing itself—like God creating the body of the world just by saying it. "Duncan, I'm glad I'm here. I'm glad I'm here with you. I look back at my life, how I grew up, everything that's happened here, even. There are lots of things I would never want to return to—except to fix them, to make them better for my mother, for my brothers and sisters, and for me, too. But all of it is important, somehow. It's how I got here—maybe it's why I came in the first place. I don't know. But I do know that you are the one God gave me, and this is where God has brought me."

I felt him nodding his head. "I know, too, Leslie. But sometimes I think back to that summer—I'm afraid I'll lose you again.

"You won't. A lot has changed since then, Duncan. I'm afraid you're stuck with me. I promise."

Silence again for several minutes. I relaxed, my arms loosened. I was beginning to find that corner in my head where sleep resides. Then Duncan spoke again.

"What do you think about another child?"

I was not surprised. This had been an ongoing subject since Noah was born. "Yes, but not for awhile. It's hard to think about having more kids out here, Duncan."

"What do you mean?"

I let out a long breath, deciding how much to say. I decided to plunge ahead, but carefully. "Fishing still rules our lives out here, Duncan. I'm not sure there's room for more children."

"We've made a lot of changes in fishing, Leslie. You don't feel that's enough?"

"You've made incredible changes—changes I only dreamed

of when I first came. I'm so glad we're here on Harvester. I'm not working in the skiff every day—that's great! And I don't have to wash strangers' dirty underwear by hand anymore. . . ."

"Count your blessings!"

"I am! I am!" Then, more serious, "I don't know where I belong, Duncan. I don't seem to be able to surrender myself to this domestic life on shore—I feel suffocated—but I don't want to be fishing all the time either. And I miss you. You're gone on the water, or you're working at Bear Island most of the time. I worry about the kids—how they'll fit into fishing, the danger, all that. It's not a place for children. That's just a few years away. . . ." My voice trails off. I realized how I must have sounded.

"Leslie," Duncan finally responded. "You worry too much. We've been through all this before."

"I know. Never mind." I sigh. I knew these worries were mine to carry. I felt so alone in this. And I knew I would continue to carry each one of these, unless I could lift them up to the hands of Providence. *I will choose to trust*, I told myself finally, in the silence we had now created. *I have to let faith span the chasm between what I fear about the future and what I know about God.*

"Let's sleep, Leslie. I'm really tired. I'm glad we talked."

"Me, too. Good night."

THE DAY BEFORE I left the island, I woke early. The children were still sleeping. I untwined my legs from Duncan's, careful not to wake him, and went out to the front window to look at the day. It was a low minus tide, the ocean's cloak pulled back farther than I could remember. I looked across at Wallace and Beth's place, remembering. I sighed with relief again, for the hundredth time. I put on my boots, walked down near the water's skirt and made my way from rock to rock to a beach seldom accessible. From around the corner I could hear the hum of a boat; two ravens sat on a cliff above me, spatting. I waved them away, and could hear now the water licking its lips, and nothing more. It was so good to sit there alone, quiet. The kids and I would be returning to Kodiak tomorrow—college classes were about to start. Duncan would stay out for another month, finishing the season. It would be a difficult month without him, but I was anxious to teach again, to get in a car and drive about freely, to feel movement.

I thought about our conversation that night in bed. Was I sorry I had chosen Duncan and this place and this very particular life that came with it? No. How could anything be other than it was. But when I chose all of this back in 1977, I did not know what I was choosing. I looked off now and saw a glacier to the east, the mountains hovering over the bay, their ridges sawing the air; I could almost hear distant rivers foaming to the wide gray Straits. It was as wild and clean and vast a place as when I first had come, but I hadn't known how or what to measure then. What if I hadn't come? I try to see who I could have been had I stayed in New Hampshire, but I can't see anything clearly, only the girl that used to be there: She is still not pretty; she is crying—no, she has decided she will no longer cry. Her face is blurred, but I know what she is looking for—wholeness and freedom. I came here with Duncan at twenty, certain I had found it in him and in this clean, cold ocean and green mountain island. I know now that what I was looking for is not something that can be found, not in a place or a person—it must be made, and it is made out of whatever is around you, whatever is given to you.

I sat quiet for some minutes, hoping to hold these moments still, to keep my place on this rock. Then, what was that?—a click, no, a popping. I leaned into my ears, and suddenly—why hadn't I heard it before?—it was all around me, a cricking and snapping as if the beach were waking from sleep, pores opening, tongues unsticking. I could see no movement, could not account for it at all. I waited, my ears tracing the pattern to the largest boulder on this part of the beach, about forty feet away. It was blistered in colonies of barnacles and mussels, blue mussels and thatched barnacles with tall volcano-shaped cones that are yellowed and look like fossilized teeth. I moved closer. Yes, it was here, the patter now inches from my face, yet I could still see no movement, no life beyond shells sealed tight. I waited. There it was again. This time I saw—a barnacle, the beak of the barnacle, like a telescope in rotation, was rounding the perimeter of its own shell, ticking the edges as it went. Then, scattered within my close range, I caught another tip, the orbit of another maw, and another. Now adjusted to these dimensions, the whole rock came alive with the diminutive circuit of these beaks. They were not feeding—the tide had been out for hours. It appeared to be a preening session, or perhaps an early-morning stretch, or the gyrations of digestion after a good breakfast. I didn't know. But I was struck by such vulnerability—no escape from attack. No escape at all. Such obscene limitations! I almost smiled as I understood. Here, halfway between land and water, was the barnacle, a creature that literally grows its own cliffed walls. His own form—given by God Himself—entraps him; it is his prison, his island. But I saw: It is also his mountain fortress, the very grace that sustains his life.